Livestock

ANIMAL VOICES
ANIMAL WORLDS

Robert W. Mitchell, series editor

Livestock

FOOD, FIBER, AND FRIENDS

Erin McKenna

The University of
Georgia Press
ATHENS

This book was made possible in part by the generous
support of the Oregon Humanities Center.

Library of Congress Cataloging-in-Publication Data

Names: McKenna, Erin, 1965– author.
Title: Livestock : food, fiber, and friends / Erin McKenna.
Other titles: Animals voices, animal worlds.
Description: Athens, Georgia : University of Georgia Press, 2018. |
Series: Animals voices, animal worlds |
Includes bibliographical references and index.
Identifiers: LCCN 2017037415 | ISBN 9780820351902 (hardcover : alk. paper) |
ISBN 9780820351919 (pbk. : alk. paper) | ISBN 9780820351896 (ebook)
Subjects: LCSH: Animal welfare. | Livestock. | Human-animal relationships.
Classification: LCC HV4757.M35 2018 | DDC 179/.3—DC23
LC record available at https://lccn.loc.gov/2017037415

CONTENTS

ACKNOWLEDGMENTS

This book has taken a long time and the help of many people. I would like to thank the students who worked with me and all the farmers named (and unnamed) in the text who took time to respond to our questions and show us their farms. Most of the work for this book took place while I was in the philosophy department at Pacific Lutheran University. Special thanks are due to the PLU students who worked with me: Sarah Curtis, Jonathan Stout, Danielle Palmer, Kelli Blechschmidt, McKenzie Williams, and Gregor Uvila. McKenzie and Danielle also contributed photographs to the project. PLU supported this research with a sabbatical leave, Kelmer-Roe grants for student-faculty research, and Wiancko Foundation grants to Environmental Studies. Special thanks are also due to Claire Todd, Rose McKenney, Kevin O'Brien, Bill Teska, Brian Naasz, and Sergia Hay. I would also like to thank Tracy Williamson for helping with all the paperwork. I am now in the philosophy department at the University of Oregon and would like to thank Bonnie Mann for her support in helping me finish this project. That support included invaluable work by three graduate students—Russell Duvernoy, Lauren Eichler, and Margaret Newton—to get the references and index in order.

As with all my work I would like to thank the community of philosophers in the Society for the Advancement of American Philosophy. I rely on the work of many of those philosophers in this book and have benefited from conversations with many more. My special thanks are owed to Doug Anderson, Scott L. Pratt, Mark Johnson, Lisa Heldke, Paul Thompson, Gregory Pappas, Marilyn Fischer, Charlene Haddock Seigfried, Larry Hickman, Lee McBride, Jacoby Carter, Heather Keith, Steven Fesmire, John Kaag, Carol Hay, Tadd Rudnik, Ray Boisvert, Brian Henning, Kim Garcher, Denise James, and Cynthia Willett.

Some ideas contained here have appeared in works published elsewhere. Those works include "Philosophical Farming" (*Journal of Contemporary Pragmatism*, August 2012), "Eating Apes, Eating Cows" (*The Pluralist* 10, no. 2, Summer 2015), and *Pets, People, and Pragmatism* (Fordham UP, 2013). Pieces were also presented at the Food and Agriculture Conference, the Society for the Advancement of American Philosophy, and the Living with Animals conference.

Finally, and most importantly, I would like to thank all the other-than-human beings who made this book possible. Meeting the animals on the farms was often the best part of the research: scratching pigs, holding baby goats, greeting turkeys, being mobbed by sheep, petting bulls, being spit at by clams, playing with cats and dogs. And finally, special thanks also go to my own dogs, Tao, Nemesis, Maeve, and Kira, who traveled with us to visit many of these farms.

Livestock

CHAPTER ONE

Respectful Relationships

A PRAGMATIST ECOFEMINIST TAKE
ON LIVING WITH LIVESTOCK

Cold, wet, a little seasick, and thinking, "I hope we don't die," my students and I were in a boat off the coast of British Columbia, headed toward a vortex that we were told is hazardous to navigate. Apparently there had been a big rock that got in the way of boats, so someone had the idea to blow it up. Problem solved! But while the rock no longer posed a direct danger to boats, the swirl of currents that took its place posed its own challenges. I thought, "Here is an example of the bad version of 'being pragmatic.' Encounter an obstacle—remove said obstacle. Without greater understanding of the context and relationships involved, such an approach is almost guaranteed to create new and more difficult problems." Ironically, we were in the boat as part of this project to study how the history of farming animals has taken just this approach to "problem-solving" and has created a vortex of its own—a system that is bad for humans, other animals, and the environment.

This trip had become our only hope of seeing a fish farm. Few of those connected to fish farms in the United States would talk with us. Given that some philosophers have been at the forefront of the animal rights and environmental movements, I suppose it is not surprising that there was some suspicion about a philosophy professor's motives for contacting them. However, the Canadians were taking a different approach to the growing criticism of fish farms—and of salmon farms in particular. They were running a public relations campaign inviting people "to come see salmon in the wild." It was the "truth." The pens were placed in the "wild" and beautiful coastal waters of British Columbia.

Once we were through the vortex, I relaxed and began to enjoy the beautiful scenery. Wooded islands, beautiful water, and emerging sunshine. Our guide told us the Canadian government was working to preserve "Canadian resources" so that they could be used by future generations. This use included recreational boating and camping, fishing, logging, and farming fish. While fish are not normally thought of as livestock animals, they have been farmed since the fifth century BCE and today humans farm more fish than they do cows. Just as with more traditional livestock, new technology allows for more intensive methods of raising these animal beings for food. However, as with the farming of cattle, pigs, and poultry, fish farming poses risks to the environment, the human consumer, and the animals themselves.

No matter who you are, where you live, what you do and don't eat, your life is entwined with livestock. Human history, as well as our present condition, has been intimately shaped by our relationships with those animal beings now commonly seen as livestock. While there is cultural variation, in the United States those animals include chickens, turkeys, sheep, goats, pigs, and cattle. These beings have been domesticated and have long been used to provide humans with eggs, milk, meat, wool, and leather. Cattle and oxen helped make farming possible (and in some instances more problematic) by providing the power to plow and pull wagons. The bodies of these various animals have also been used to provide humans with resources such as glue and gelatin—things that moved technology and food in different directions. Today cows can be found in a myriad of products, some of which include detergents, fabric softeners, toothpaste, mouthwash, lipstick, soap, shampoo, candles, marshmallows, chewing gum, jelly beans, gummy bears, mayonnaise, Jell-O, crayons, paint, wallpaper, floor wax, cough syrup, lozenges, vaccines, and many medications (Hayes and Hayes 26–28). The list goes on and on. In addition, their manure and composted corpses made the farming of crop foods more possible. Even a vegan today, especially if she or he eats organic produce, is eating food that has benefitted from the contribution of animal by-products. There is no way to extract oneself from the lives and deaths of other animal beings.

Less commonly seen as livestock (not domesticated in the ordinary sense of the term), fish, rabbits, llamas, alpaca, bison, ostrich, and elk are farmed as food and fiber resources. Even insects are now emerging as farmed sources of food. Horses too have long provided power and poop to help increase human productivity. But horses have also been used for their hair, hide, and meat, though it is less common to breed and keep them primarily or only for those purposes. They became an important "tool" of transportation and made it possible to ranch cattle on the open range, as dogs helped humans with sheep and goats. Ranch horses are often seen as livestock. While dogs and cats are used for food and fur, they are not commonly seen or raised as livestock, though this does occur in some places. Similarly rabbits, minks, foxes, and chinchillas are kept for some combination of food and fur. Many other animals were and are hunted for these purposes but are not generally kept by humans.

Humans saw the most commonly used animals as a valuable resource and began to keep them in confinement in order to feed and care for them. As humans took greater control of the lives of formerly free-living animals, much about both those animal beings and the human beings changed. Not only did food and farming change, but the health of human and other animal beings also changed as disease resistance and gut bacteria were altered. Materials from the animals altered the possibilities of production, and their hair and hides (as well as their images) altered the form and content of art. Access to, and control of, these animal "resources" transformed social and political relations. While the animals contributed to science and technology as their bodies were used to study anatomy, disease, and genetics, humans then used science and technology to increase the production of what are perceived as cheap meat, eggs, and dairy through breeding, feeding, and confinement. As a result, chickens now outnumber humans, and there are a billion or more other livestock animals. This explosion has allowed for a never-before-experienced diet that is available in the United States and is spreading worldwide. The new diet has come at the expense of the well-being of land and animals, though, and many U.S. consumers have come to demand alternatives. Although the organic label, in the end, does not mean much for the lives of livestock, most consumers think it does. Given this perception of the label, it is interesting to note the increase in organic livestock production. In 1992 the United States produced just over 1,000 organic hogs, but in 2008 production had increased to more than 10,000; organic production of beef cattle increased from almost 7,000 to almost 64,000; organic production of dairy cows increased from just over 2,000 to almost 250,000; and organic production of broiler chickens increased from just over 17,000 to over nine million (O'Donoghue et al. 63). This increase demonstrates a concern on the part of consumers. Even if the consumers' concern is primarily a concern for human health (and possibly the environment), it acknowledges the connectedness of humans and the other animal beings they consume. This book explores some of the complex and changing relationships among human beings and those other animal beings commonly seen as livestock.

The history of the term *livestock* is complicated. One source suggests that this was the original notion of *stock* that people today connect to the idea of stock in a corporation. The live animal beings were the real capital held by companies that financed colonization. Another suggests that it was in the Americas that the term *stock*, meaning wealth in general (money or goods), transferred to the animals and became *live stock* (Ogle 3). The term *stock* also has the sense of supplying and handling merchandise, as in stocking wares in a store. Before technology allowed for the keeping of meat, the best way to store or stock one's meat was on the hoof. These understandings of the word seem to reduce the animal being in question to monetary or commodity value. These understandings also have the effect of lumping a number of different species together as if there were no real differences among them. I will argue that such a reductionist view of animals is problematic and should change, but I continue to use the term. It is a way to acknowledge and understand the really different situatedness of different animal beings who have come to be enfolded in human communities in particular ways.

There are many animal beings who live in mixed-species communities with humans. Some "wild" and feral animals live around the edges of these communities. Then there are those animal beings who have been domesticated. Those who are considered as pets often live within the homes of humans. If they are not in the home, they are generally at least well sheltered and well fed, whether they are "useful" or not. Others are seen as livestock and are cared for mainly (or only) because they are seen as providing some use to humans. Focusing on these use values, some people no longer use the term *livestock*. They have gone further down the road of commodification and refer to "protein-producing units," or "egg-producing units." Ecofeminist philosopher Carol Adams notes a USDA description of cows, pigs, and chickens as "grain-consuming animal units" (28). I do not want to follow this path. While I prefer to talk about cow beings, chicken beings, pig beings, and so on, the term *livestock* does serve as a historical reminder of how certain animal beings have been, and are, seen and used. It also serves as a reminder that there is an economic aspect to any relationship with animals raised for the purposes of food and fiber. While I agree with Adams that it is problematic to understand other animal beings solely in terms of humans' desire to use them—in her words, to "ontologize them as edible or consumable"—I also think it is problematic to try to cover up the fact that we have used and do use them in these ways. Since such use is not going to stop any time soon (and I don't argue that ending the use of livestock animals is a viable or good goal), the question here is how to find more respectful relationships that include a use component but are not reduced to that alone.

In *Pets, People, and Pragmatism* I examined human relationships with animal beings commonly seen as pets. There I focused mainly on horses, dogs, and cats in order to develop an ethic of respect rooted in the tradition of American pragmatism and feminist theory. I sketched an approach of living with horses, dogs, and cats that entails respecting the evolutionary history of these animals, their species-specific behaviors, breed tendencies, and individual variation. I have advocated an experimental approach that accounts for plu-ralistic and changing circumstances. Rather than seek absolute moral stands on issues pertaining to the relations between human and other animal beings, humans should seek to make actual relations better and seek to create dia-logue and cooperation among currently opposed groups (e.g., People for the Ethical Treatment of Animals [PETA] and the American Kennel Club [AKC]).

One place where such dialogue rarely occurs is around the issue of live-stock. Philosopher Mary Midgley notes, "Although both for people and ani-mals a steady movement to eating less meat is needed, and although what the animals need most urgently is probably a campaign for treating them better before they are eaten, a tribal division into total eaters and total ab-stainers still tends strongly to capture our imagination" (27). But such a di-vide is not accurate. People who live with pets are involved in the livestock in-dustry, whether they themselves eat meat or not. Those who live with horses are buying feed from the same system that provides feed for cattle, pigs, and poultry. Those who live with dogs and cats usually feed some amount of meat and other animal by-products (e.g., bones, hooves, rawhide) to these pets. One estimate notes that if every cat in the United States ate just two ounces of meat a day this would come to about twelve million pounds of meat each day. To put it more visually, this would equal three million chickens a day (Herzog 6). People with pets often buy this food without much thought for the lives of the livestock animals. While pets are loved and pampered, most livestock cur-rently living in the United States have few stable social relationships (either with humans or with others of their species), live in cramped and unhealthy confinement, and are transported and killed under stressful conditions. I ended *Pets, People, and Pragmatism* by pointing out the irony of sacrificing one group of animal beings who are now generally kept at a distance from most humans in order to feed (and often overfeed) another group of animal beings who live in close contact with humans.

According to Hal Herzog, such an irony is not surprising since most people don't think that deeply about other animal beings. Even those who do think about how humans relate to other animal beings often have a host of contra-dictory beliefs, and usually their actions contradict one or more of the beliefs they hold. For instance, in *Some We Love, Some We Hate, Some We Eat*, Herzog shows that while many in the United States protest the killing of baby seals for fur, object to the use of primates in lab research, and promote the adop-tions of dogs and cats to prevent them from being euthanized, U.S. consumers still eat seventy-two billion pounds of meat a year. Herzog writes, "It is true that an increasing number of people believe that animals are entitled to basic rights, including, one presumes, the right not to be killed because you happen to be made out of meat. But, despite our stated love for animals, ... [we] kill

200 food animals for every animal used in a scientific experiment, 2,000 for each unwanted dog euthanized in an animal shelter, and 40,000 for every baby harp seal bludgeoned to death on a Canadian ice floe. And, in spite of what you sometimes hear, over the past thirty years, the animal rights movement has not made much of a dent in our desire to dine on other species" (176). Herzog argues that this is unlikely to change, since eating the meat of other animals is "'in our genes' just as it is in chimpanzee genes" (202). Although he notes that human beings have the capacity to ask questions about what is right and wrong when it comes to whom we eat and how we treat those we eat, he concludes that, in general, "other than our personal pets, the treatment of animals is not particularly high on most people's list of priorities" (240).

I think there is some evidence, though, that many people are rethinking human relationships with a wide variety of animal beings—including livestock. In January 2015 the *New York Times* ran a story about the abuse of animals used in government funded experiments at the U.S. Meat Animal Research Center in Nebraska: "US Research Lab Lets Livestock Suffer in Quest for Profit." Since livestock are exempt from the Animal Welfare Act, which protects some laboratory animals, there has been less oversight of such work. Experiments done with the intent of supporting the large and powerful meat industry have gotten a pass. But, as Michael Moss noted in his article, some of the ranchers themselves objected to the work at this center. The work was supposed to help the shrinking beef, pork, and lamb industries remain profitable in the face of chicken becoming the most consumed meat in the United States in 2014. The research focused on production, often at the expense of welfare, and resulted in a great deal of animal suffering. As the *Times* article notes, "the center's drive to make livestock bigger, leaner, more prolific and more profitable can be punishing, creating harmful complications that require more intensive experiments to solve. The leaner pigs that the center helped develop, for example, are so low in fat that one in five females cannot reproduce; center scientists have been operating on pigs' ovaries and brains in an attempt to make the sows more fertile" (Moss). Here again is the approach of "blowing up the rock" and creating an equally or more dangerous vortex. Failing to take the overall welfare of the animals into account, treating them like machines with discrete parts, scientists create new problems for both human and other animal beings. It also led to less respect and care for those livestock animals at the center. Many died of starvation and preventable (and painful) illnesses.

This kind of treatment is now getting more attention. There is bipartisan support in Congress to extend the Animal Welfare Act to include livestock animals, and less than a month after his article appeared Moss wrote another: "Lawmakers Aim to Protect Farm Animals in Research." In that piece Moss quoted representatives who found the level of cruelty unacceptable. In addition, Moss continued, "Tom Vilsack, the secretary of agriculture, has ordered increased protections for farm animals used in research at the center and other agency facilities. The department named an ombudsman to hear internal concerns about animal welfare, and started a review of its research." The fact that such events are now seen as newsworthy and get the attention of many U.S. readers is a sign of change. This is a change that has slowly been entering the world of "livestock production" itself, though not yet the research arm of the industry. Moss noted that the center's work ignores the increasing demands from consumers (individuals as well as restaurants and stores) for meat products that come from humanely raised animals.

This change in demand, while still small in the overall scheme of things, is indicative of a change in thinking that is starting to move into a change in habits. In this book, I will show that the animal beings we commonly see as livestock have evolutionary histories that are as rich and varied as those of pets. Their species-specific behaviors, breed tendencies, and individual variation need to be respected. And I will also argue that if one *does* respect those aspects of the animal beings commonly seen as pets, *one should also love and respect those animal beings commonly seen as livestock.* This entails working to change some aspects of the current condition of most livestock in the United States. At the same time, however, I will examine ways we can balance the needs of the animals with the environmental and social impacts of raising and consuming them. There is no clear solution to all concerns, but the pragmatist ecofeminist approach offered here entails working to ameliorate (improve) the situation in as many ways as possible.

This approach often lands one in "the troubled middle." Herzog says,

> Those of us in the troubled middle live in a complex moral universe. I eat meat—but not as much as I used to, and not veal. I oppose testing the toxicity of oven cleaner and eye shadow on animals, but I would sacrifice a lot of mice to find a cure for cancer. And while I find some of the logic of animal liberation philosophers convincing, I also believe that our vastly greater capacity for symbolic language, culture, and ethical judgment puts humans on a different moral plane from that of other animals. We middlers see the world in shades of gray rather than in the clear blacks and whites of committed animal activists and their equally vociferous opponents. Some argue that we are fence-sitters, moral wimps. I believe, however, that the troubled middle makes perfect sense because moral quagmires are inevitable in a species with a huge brain and big heart. (11–12)

Pragmatist philosophers also wrestle with this troubled middle and share Herzog's concerns about moral absolutism. Moral absolutists tend to have an overly simplistic view of an issue or theory that allows them to be certain they are right. Usually, the more one knows, the more complex and less clear an issue becomes. Pragmatism deals with the ambiguities without falling into the arbitrary. Herzog asks, "What are the implications of living in a world that is morally convoluted, in which consistency is elusive, and often impossible? Do we throw up our hands in despair? Does moral complexity mean moral paralysis?" (264). Herzog says no, and I agree. Bringing the perspectives of pragmatism and ecofeminism to the discussion of these issues can help us sort through the myriad of choices we face individually and as a society. What's more, I do not think all of our inconsistencies are as inevitable as Herzog suggests, nor are they harmless. Pragmatism and ecofeminism provide often overlooked ways of thinking about the issues surrounding how humans relate to other animal beings. The two approaches have the added benefit of addressing how one can move belief into action; philosophy can help change thinking and behavior.

My book on pets and this one on livestock are both representative rather than exhaustive. Here I will focus mostly on human relationships with fish, cattle, sheep, goats, pigs, and poultry. There is some discussion of horses, rabbits, and the emergence of insect farming. Toward the end I move to farmed bison and elk as I prepare to trace how the ethic of respect I have developed can also move to those animal beings we usually call free-living or wild. Obviously, this work builds on what I wrote in *Pets, People, and Pragmatism,* so I will briefly sketch some of the central points of that work. There is a great deal of overlap in the explorations, but here the focus is on our relationships with animals who serve what many see as more utilitarian purposes than the companionship that shapes many of our relationships with "pets." However, as the title of this book suggests, there can (and should) be an element of friendship in these use relationships as the line between pets and livestock is a fairly recent one. Ecofeminist philosopher Val Plumwood noted that such a line emerged with the advent of intensive fishing and industrialized animal agriculture; animals have become primarily of value to humans in terms of affective or utilitarian relationships. This means that "non-privileged animals assigned to the 'meat' side of this dualistic hierarchy die to make meat for the pets of people who think of themselves unproblematically as animal lovers—kangaroos, dolphins, penguins, anonymous and rare marine animals in yearly billions are slaughtered at some remove to feed the cats and dogs whose own deaths as meat would be unthinkable to their owners" (Plumwood, *Ecological Crisis of Reason* 163). Chicken, beef, pork, and lamb are regularly used in dog and cat foods as well. With the rise in food-related sensitivities in pets, duck, elk, deer, bison, and salmon are also used but most consumers don't realize that these "wild" animals are also now commonly farmed.

In the last sixty or so years this divide has come to entail a *very* different kind of care and life for those animal beings not seen as pets. Living in what Midgley calls mixed-species communities enriches our lives, but it also entangles us in a complex set of relationships with a variety of other animal beings. With regard to livestock in particular, the irony of confining and killing one set of animal beings in order to pamper others (including ourselves) is something about which we should think more carefully. Plumwood points out that our current system of "rational agriculture" leaves much to be desired. We find "chickens and calves held in conditions so cramped that in a comparable human case they would clearly be considered torture. Its logic of the One and the Other tends through incorporation and instrumentalism to represent the Other of nature entirely in monological terms of human needs, as involving replaceable and interchangeable units answering to these needs, and hence to treat nature as an infinitely manipulable and inexhaustible resource" (119). Plumwood suggests that this way of viewing the animals that people and pets eat needs to change. We need to respect the lives that sustain life and "respect animals as both individuals and as community members, in terms of respect or reverence for species life, and . . . aim to rethink farming as a non-commodity and species-egalitarian form, rather than to completely reject farming" (156). In this book I share her hope for a "non-oppressive form of the mixed-community and a liveable future respectfully shared with animals" (166).

To get to such a future, though, I begin with past and present experience. How did various animal beings come to be domesticated? What has this meant for their experience of the world? Should some aspects of these experiences change? Humans have been involved in the domestication of other animal beings for over ten thousand years, but not all animal beings can be domesticated. If an animal being is too prone to flight, too limited in feeding habits, too difficult to breed, unable to get used to some level of confinement, or unable to get comfortable around humans, domestication is difficult. While dogs may have been the first to become domesticated—over ten thousand years ago—livestock species were not far behind. Clutton-Brock argues that humans started keeping rather than just following animal beings they wanted for meat and skins around nine thousand years ago and that by 7000 BCE there were changes in the morphology of goats, sheep, cattle, and pigs (19, 66).

While many stories of this process like to focus on human intentionality and control of the other animal beings, this is among the least likely of the possibilities. Humans had neither the technology nor the experience to keep strong, flighty animals in confinement by force. There is a growing consensus that the animal beings themselves found enough of an advantage in life near humans to cooperate in forming mixed-species communities. Richard Bulliet, in *Hunters, Herders, and Hamburgers*, suggests that the social nature of human and some other animal beings made the forming of relationships possible. He says, for instance, that the domestication of pigs should be understood "as a naturally arising symbiotic relationship, rather than an extraordinary discovery," that occurred in multiple places at different times. "The wild porcine species *sus scrofa*, from which all domestic pigs are believed to descend, is widely spread geographically in Eurasia and North Africa. . . . Some societies grazed pigs in forests where they could eat acorns and hazelnuts and root for tubers. Other societies kept them close to human settlements and fed them on kitchen waste or shared with them the roots and tubers eaten by the people themselves." Pig meat was relished as often as it was forbidden. The relationship was complicated as some "treated piglets as pets, even to the extent of women letting them suckle at their breasts. Others considered them embodiments of filth" (90). Both the human and the other animal beings had to feel comfortable around each other and even come to take comfort in the presence of the other for these relationships to form.

For many humans it feels good to be around other animal beings. While it is not often discussed, until the advent of industrialized intensive animal agriculture, most livestock caretakers truly knew and liked (or disliked) the individuals in their care. Many studies look at how being around cats and dogs improves the physical health and social well-being of humans. In fact, hanging out with other animals is credited with increasing human sociality and making it possible for humans to settle down. However, when humans settled down, so too did the animals living with them. This settling had consequences and some have been problematic. As with pets, human-controlled breeding has resulted in a number of health problems for livestock animals. Confinement, too, has harmed the well-being of many, giving rise to physical and psychological problems (lameness, self-mutilation, and stereotypies such as weaving and bar biting). It also resulted in conditions that harm both human and other animals—spread of disease, contamination of water, air and ground pollution, antibiotic-resistant bacteria, and tainted food, to name a few.

In the past, and in some places still, humans and the animals on whom they depend for food and fiber are truly friends. They lived in close proximity and shared shelter and nourishment. The animals were slaughtered and eaten by someone who knew them and whom they knew. At the other extreme there is a now near-complete separation of lives—with the animals confined, artificially bred, fed and milked by machine, and slaughtered on a mechanical line, the physical and emotional contact between the human and other animal beings is minimized. With the increasing specialization and separation of the various parts of the animals' lives, the person who breeds the animal doesn't raise and feed the animal, and neither of these people is part of the animal's death. The animals are slaughtered and eaten by humans who have never known them and rarely (if ever) think of them or their kind.

Further consequences fall on free-living animals such as deer, elk, elephants, whales, wolves, coyotes, rodents, insects, and birds. Classified as predators, problems, or pests, they are seen as nuisance animals from the perspective of many invested in raising livestock. Free-living horses are seen as competition for grasslands; seals as competition for salmon; coyotes and wolves as marauders; and birds, rodents, and insects as competition for the crops that feed humans and livestock. Because the ways that humans relate to nondomesticated animals are so limited, the response to these situations has often been simply to move or kill the animals.

For several years students and I have been visiting farms and talking with farmers who are grappling with these (and other) issues. How they view the natural world, their place in it, and the place of their farm and livestock will be the framing context for examining how to better live together with other animals. The experiences of the animals themselves will also be a focus. This approach developed over three separate summers of research. Our first task was to figure out how to approach the work. We wanted to understand how one's metaphysical views translated into practice. Then we wanted to examine the ethical implications of these practices and, by extension, the ethical implications of the metaphysical views. Here I'm using the term *metaphysics* broadly to mean the study of "being." What we wanted to know was how various farmers thought about "nature"—that is, about what is it to be a cow, a chicken, or a pig. How do those beings interact with the rest of their environment? How do farmers interact with those beings and the rest of the environment? We came up with two questions for the farmers in our study: (1) How do you view the human relationship with the rest of nature (animal and nonanimal)? (2) How do these views affect how you choose to farm? Our goal was to get at some of the metaphysical assumptions held by the farmers—for example, their views of what it is to be human, their views of what is and is not a part of nature, and their views on how farming fits within natural environments. We then examined their answers in light of some of the ethical and political implications of the positions that emerged.

Of course, it wasn't simple to understand or categorize the answers to these questions. Our conversations with the farmers were wide-ranging and complex. Generally I can say that most of the farmers did not see the domesticated animals they raised for meat, milk, or eggs as part of nature. However, they did think that the livestock animals impacted "nature," by which they meant wildlife, streams, and the ecosystem as a whole. Most, but not all, thought domesticated animals had been artificially created to serve human purposes, and this resulted in a different way of understanding them and so of treating them. I can also say they were all generous with their time and genuinely interested in talking about the issues raised in this book. Other than that, there is very little I can generalize. The farms and farmers in the study are varied. Some have a long history with livestock animals, others are just learning. Some approach it purely as a business, some as a kind of steward-ship (of land and animals), some as a spiritual endeavor. Some focus mainly on human health concerns.

Just to whet your appetite, I would like to give you a taste of what one farmer had to say in an email correspondence. Wendy and Erick Haakenson run Jubilee Farm, a biodynamic farm in Carnation, Washington. While they focus on produce, they also have a herd of beef cattle. The Haakesons origi-nally purchased the cattle to supply manure for fertilizer, as they wanted their farm to be a closed system. Over time, they have also come to focus on what kind of cattle are best, given their land and purposes. We were not able to visit this farm, but Erick responded to our questions. He began with a response to our second question first. How do these views affect how you choose to farm? He wrote, "I like this question because I have long believed that there is an inviolate relationship between the way a people farm and their beliefs about the ultimate nature of reality. I suppose it's possible for people to act in ways incongruous with their underlying beliefs for a time, but if people ever really grow up, what they believe will be reflected in what they do (farming or what-ever)." Here Erick nicely expresses the idea that one's metaphysical beliefs play out in how one relates to the rest of the world.

In his response to our first question—how do you view the human rela-tionship with the rest of nature (animal and nonanimal)?—he presents some of his metaphysical beliefs and how they impact his view of ethics: "It's hard after Darwin to not recognize the continuity within all living things. Even from the narrow perspective of self-interest most of us recognize that failing to nurture every manifestation of existence will lead to potential harm to us. A departure from self-interest could, and in my case certainly does, strengthen the notion of developing a caring relationship with the rest of nature." Here Erick argues that given the connectedness of everything even prudential self-interest should lead people to care for the rest of nature. Further, though, he thinks that same connectedness should help people develop a relationship of respect and reverence for the rest of nature: "I treat the earth with respect, and the soil with care and even reverence. I try to make myself as knowledge-able as possible about how the soil functions and try to provide what it needs, and avoid what is harmful. This has led me to be an organic farmer—and now, over the last six years, a 'transitioner' into biodynamic farming. . . . Thanks for the questions. I haven't thought about these things for a while—too many 14 hour days!"

By seeing the earth, and the plants and other animal beings living on it, as persons deserving respect, care, and reverence Erick has set some clear parameters for what he is and is not willing to do in order to produce food and has become committed to biodynamic farming. Rudolph Steiner started the biodynamic farming movement in the 1920s. It is a spiritual, ethical, and ecological approach to farming that stresses developing a healthy, balanced, and diverse ecosystem when farming. On their website the Haakensons say, "Biodynamic farming treats the farm as a complete living entity and so focuses on the relationships between various plants and animals. Nature takes advantage of this synergy by never growing one thing, so we emulate that diversity on the farm by growing a wide range of vegetables, fruits, and grains. We also raise different livestock, each serving a unique purpose." As with the methods of many of the farmers discussed here, this approach to farming requires particular attention to "the land"—the soil and the microorganisms that keep it healthy. Their website points out that "the most important group of living things on the farm are the millions of micro-organisms found in the soil. They consume plant and animal waste and make nutrients available to plants. . . . We can achieve self-produced fertility only by recognizing the natural relationships between living things." This one example of the rich responses we got from farmers points to the importance of how one understands the human relationship with the rest of nature. My goal was to listen to a variety of farmers think and talk about what they do and why they do it. Erick's comment about fourteen-hour days is a good reminder of the time-consuming nature of the work of farming and ranching. Time to think and talk is a bit of a luxury, but it is essential to developing relationships of care and respect.

As a pragmatist and an ecofeminist, I feel it is important that I say something about who I am as it relates to this topic. Soon after I was born, my family moved to a citrus ranch, where we had horses, dogs, and cats. We raised a few cattle for beef (their hides served as rugs in our house), and we raised chickens for meat and eggs. One of my older sisters raised rabbits for meat, and the other raised sheep. I helped feed the sheep and collected eggs. The rooster did not appreciate the theft of the eggs and would chase me. One day my mother went in with me and he attacked her; he soon went into a soup. My father killed the chickens and the rabbits and we helped. For some reason I didn't mind killing chickens, but I wanted nothing to do with killing or eating rabbits. When it came time for the sheep to be slaughtered the butcher came to the ranch. Desperate to save at least some of the sheep, I took two and we hid under an orange tree. We were found and I had to deliver the sheep to their death. I had to be forced to eat them.

I did not like eating meat other than chicken and hamburger. I would be kept at the table and told to eat some amount of the meat I had been served. I would sneak the meat to one of our dogs, or try to hide it in my napkin. My father had said, "You need to know where your food comes from so you can make an informed decision." I wanted to not eat meat. My parents thought I needed to eat meat. And so I did. When I went to college I ate less meat, but by then I was fully habituated to the cultural norms of our meat-based culture. I majored in philosophy, but no one taught about animals. I decided to go to graduate school in philosophy, but before I did that I taught philosophy for a year at a private high school. One of the books I was assigned to teach was Peter Singer's *Practical Ethics*. In the middle of a discussion of his chapter on animal welfare a student asked me whether I was a vegetarian. I said no and she asked why not. I had no real answer. I told them about my upbringing and early aversion to meat. By then I had philosophical concerns about the status of animals and the human treatment of other animal beings. So, I decided to become a vegetarian. That was in 1987.

I have continued to have a variety of concerns about the human treatment of other animal beings and I am still a vegetarian. I do not pretend that a vegetarian diet is without many ethical problems, though, and this book does not take the position that everyone should stop eating meat and consuming other animal products. I do argue that there is much wrong with our current treatment of livestock animals, even while I realize there is no unproblematic way to eat and live. No matter one's dietary habits, I do think there are many moral and existential problems when one eats without thinking. The same is true for other kinds of consumption as well. I hope this book can start some new ways of thinking about the human relationship with those livestock animals who have long provided humans with food, fiber, and friendship.

To do that I engage a number of philosophical perspectives throughout the book: the land ethic, deep ecology, animal rights, animal welfare, ecofeminism, and pragmatism. I work from the pragmatist and ecofeminist understanding that theory and practice are not separable, and that metaphysical views impact ethical and political choices. I take up the pragmatist and ecofeminist insight that no one person has a take on the whole; we each offer only partial and situated understandings of particular situations. For that reason, we need a community engaged in discussion if we hope to make any particular situation better. This means working with people with whom we might disagree (because they have some valuable insights) and entails embracing the democratic commitments that run through most pragmatist and ecofeminist work (the commitment to inclusiveness). Participation and consultation of all impacted parties is important for any real change to be possible. Such a process can be slow and uncomfortable as it acknowledges that no one is completely right (we are all fallible), and that we must be genuinely open to learning from one another. This usually means that more moderate (less extreme and universalistic) positions prevail, and that is not a popular position in the current political and media-driven culture of the United States, but it is one to which I am committed in this work.

I propose that a pragmatist ecofeminist perspective provides an important approach to these issues that is grounded in experience, evolutionary history, and actual relationships. It accommodates complexity and change, and it respects other animal beings as individuals in their own right. As I have discussed, the very process of domestication was, and is, a *transactive relationship*. I borrow this term from John Dewey, who believed that organisms grow and develop in transactive relationships with their environments—physical and social. While many have willfully misinterpreted the concept as referring to an economic transaction, this is not what Dewey meant. He meant that organisms shape their environment even as they are shaped by it, and that environments are shaped by various organisms even as they shape the growth and development of the organisms. These are mutually transformative relationships. Writing in the late nineteenth century and the first half of the twentieth century, Dewey was influenced by theories of evolution and the idea that beings and environments are not static, but rather changing, entities. This notion of a dynamic universe doesn't just allow for change but rests on the inevitability of change. Since organisms and their environments are mutually transformative, change in one will effect a change in others. This is what happened, and is still happening, with the domestication of various animal beings (including human beings).

All life is connected in the evolutionary process. The evolution of human beings is connected to the evolutionary history of all mammals. The evolution of mammals is connected to the evolutionary history of reptiles, insects, plants, and so on. *Your Inner Fish* is a recent book that provides some interesting examples of these relationships and shared histories. Here Neil Shubin discusses examples such as how the pattern for primate limbs and hands can be found in fish: "We are not separate from the rest of the living world; we are part of it down to our bones and ... even our genes" (43). The very possibility of humans emerged from past conditions and the continuing pressure and process of human evolution influenced the conditions in which all the life we know exists. Human beings are not outside of nature but very much a part of it. This is one reason to examine our choices and actions very carefully. Our actions impact the possibilities for life in general, not just human life. We have long manipulated other life-forms in our environment for our purposes. For example, we have domesticated plants and animals for the purposes of supplying us with food to eat, fuel to burn, fertilizer to replenish the land, canvas on which to write, and cloth and skins to wear. In the case of animals it is also clear that they have provided friendship (many also have experienced such relationships with various forms of plant life, and interesting work in this area is growing).

These various forms of life have also taken on religious significance. Plants and animals have been offered in sacrifice, worshiped for their power and fertility, and feared for their ability to harm and hurt. Human lives are physically, socially, and culturally intertwined with other plant and animal life.

Donna Haraway (and others) discuss this in terms of coevolution. Various beings constitute themselves and each other through their relationships. In understanding domestication we tend to focus on the ways human beings have impacted the physical and social natures of other animal beings and forget to examine how we too have been transformed. Here I am focusing on relationships between human beings and those other animal beings we call livestock. As already mentioned, livestock changed the possibilities of being human through their use as labor, transportation, food, fertilizers, clothing, and other materials. Living and working with livestock also changed humans more intimately, as it changed the microbes that help make up humans' physical nature and it altered immune response as we shared diseases, bacteria, and parasites such as SARS, brucella, and anthrax. Consuming the milk from these animal beings, probably in the form of cheese, made it possible for more humans to be able to digest milk products as the processing helped remove the lactose. As groups adapted to such a diet, a mutation occurred that allowed for the digestion of lactose that was passed on to offspring. Some argue that eating meat helped increase the brain size and intelligence of humans as well. Others suggest that the ability to cooperate, which made human hunting possible, was a by-product of an increased brain size that arose with humans' increased sociality.

Humans changed those animal beings who became livestock as well. These animals were bred for docility and tractability, which changed their social nature; they were bred for the amount of meat and milk they could produce, which changed their physical shape and size; they were bred to produce meat and milk with varying fat content, which changed their physical and emotional constitution in the process. More recently they have been bred not only in traditional ways but also using artificial insemination, and most recently they have been genetically altered by the insertion of genes from other species. The first genetically modified animal approved for human consumption is now on the market—AquAdvantage salmon. But there have been consequences to these changes that are not always good for the animals involved. Congenital health issues arise when breeding becomes too focused on a few specific traits. Breeding for docility sometimes has the consequence of producing animal beings without the intelligence to think for themselves, increasing their dependence on humans to an extreme level. The increased docility has also changed the possibilities for housing, and the animals are now kept in increasingly cramped conditions that increase the physical and social ills they experience. It is clear that not everything about these relationships has been beneficial.

To get to a working philosophy that can help guide the various relationships among human beings and other animal beings, humans need an understanding of themselves that includes the evolutionary realities of their relationships while acknowledging that these evolutionary histories do not fully determine or constrain the possibilities going forward. I think a pragmatist ecofeminist framework is well suited to do this work and I would like to reiterate a point I made in *Pets, People, and Pragmatism*. Human life is intertwined with all other life and very intimately intertwined with the lives of domesticated animal beings. While many suggest that domesticated animals are somehow unnatural, and many suggest that the best way to approach the ethical difficulties that come with human relationships with such beings is to stop breeding and raising them, I believe that "*to try to withdraw from relationships with domesticated animal beings would be to deny something central about who and what human beings, and other animal beings, are*" (19).

Some of the key insights of the pragmatist tradition of philosophy are that humans are natural creatures situated within natural environments. There is no nature/culture dualism since human culture is part of the natural development of the world. This notion of development is also important as it points to the dynamic nature of a world that grows out of, and is still involved in, an evolutionary process. Many other philosophical approaches set humans outside of, and above, the rest of nature. This usually rests on either religious assumptions about God creating humans in God's image and giving them the rest of creation to use, or on philosophical positions that point to the human use of language and reason to set them apart from the rest of the living organisms.

But humans are mammals and share mammalian physical, social, emotional, and reasoning processes. There is a continuity, and strong resemblance, among mammalian creatures of all kinds. That does not mean there are no differences between humans and other mammals, but so too are there differences among all the other mammals. There is no reason to see the ways that humans differ as making us somehow exceptional and superior. In fact, some of the differences show that humans lack some useful capacities that other mammals have. Humans are not as fast or strong as many other mammals; humans lack the sonar capacity of whales and dolphins; humans can't use their sense of smell (at least consciously) to detect disease and find friends.

And this continuity is not limited just to mammals. Mammals share structures and capacities with other forms of life. This means humans share DNA with plant and animal life of all kinds. Some are more closely related in this way to be sure, but there is no sharp break between one life-form and another. There are differences, as different creatures have evolved at different times, under different pressures, in different environments. But often these differences also hide similarities. For instance, even when there are obvious differences in the physical structures—such as the avian brain as compared to the mammalian brain—there is often a functional equivalence. The evidence that is often used to set humans apart from the rest of life is the presence and size of the human neocortex. As it became clear that this was something shared with other big-brained, social mammals, human exceptionalism lessened a little. And now there is evidence that many birds use the dorsal ventricular ridge (DVR) part of their brain in much the same way as the neocortex functions in mammals (chickens were the birds used in these experiments).

While many individuals working within the pragmatist tradition have engaged in various forms of human exceptionalism, this perspective is not warranted by the pragmatist insight that humans are part of nature and that the same developmental processes are at work in all life. More consistent is the insight that there are many ways of being that have value and many perspectives that provide useful information for successfully navigating within one's environment. This pluralistic perspective is another hallmark of pragmatism, and is one shared by most in ecofeminist philosophy as well. Rather than pick one way of being (human, male, European) as the norm, and then measuring everything and everyone else by the supposed norm, a pluralistic approach finds differences to be natural (not deformities or deficiencies). While pluralism obviously does not deny differences, it does tend to avoid understanding those differences in terms of hierarchical dualisms that privilege some in terms of power, rights, and the freedom to be.

When one is open to the differences, one can learn from others. Human observation of various animal beings is one important instance of this kind of pluralism, combined with a willingness to experiment with other ways of doing things in order to make things (hopefully) better in one way or another. It is quite likely, for instance, that early humans learned to find various forms of plant food by following and observing other animals and then being willing (or forced by hunger) to experiment with what they saw those animals eating. Most anthropologists agree that humans scavenged meat before they themselves became hunters. This required observation of animals such as lions, wolves, chimpanzees, coyotes, hawks, and vultures. While some of these relationships evolved into partnerships—with the domestication of some wolves leading to the partnership between humans and dogs—there was also an element of exploiting those relationships for the benefit of the humans. The dogs were useful as hunting partners and protectors. Their hunting abilities could be trained in a different direction, though, as humans used their observations of their prey to begin to domesticate and keep these animals as well. Rather than hunt wild ruminants, humans began to keep them and raise their off-spring. Dogs became herding partners as the humans moved domesticated livestock to fresh grass.

The move to humans keeping livestock was one based on experimenta-tion—all did not go well for the humans or the other animal beings. Humans were trampled, gored, and bitten; cattle, sheep, goats, fish, and poultry suf-fered and died as their needs were not fully met by these new conditions. Hu-mans (and other creatures) are fallible—another important insight of prag-matism—and the willingness to accept that mistakes will be made opens up greater possibility for experimentation that leads to real learning and the pos-sibility of making things work better (to ameliorate a situation). It also means, however, that every "solution" raises a host of new problems that need to be addressed. This is life in process; there is no fixed end point where everything works perfectly.

Human relationships with other animal beings are always in process. At any given time some things work well for the human or other animal beings and others do not; at any given time some of the living conditions and uses are fair and reciprocal and others are not; at any given time some of these relationships are respectful of the needs and desires of the various animal be-ings and others are not. *At no time, however, is there an option to just stop be-ing in relation with one another.* Even the cessation of all livestock production (which is not really a live option anyway) would not end humans' connected-ness to these creatures. Given this, the focus should be on how to improve the relationships humans have with various other animal beings. This requires an openness to new understandings and real change in how we live together and relate. Not everything is fine as it is. For example, in "Pragmatism and the Production of Livestock" I presented a pragmatist take on the history of humans living with livestock. In brief, starting with the human need for cal-ories, some people eventually moved from following animals (to scavenge or hunt) to controlling the movement of flocks and herds. Once plant agricul-ture resulted in some surplus, some humans began confining and feeding the sheep, goats, and cattle instead of moving the animals to the food. Each sys-tem has costs and benefits—herding can require less human labor and result in healthier animals, but it comes with the risks of predation and exposure to the elements. Confinement can mitigate concerns about weather and preda-tors but comes with increased mortality due to disease. It also requires more human labor to bring food and water to the animals and remove their waste. Today drugs help mitigate disease, but this use of drugs results in health con-cerns for those who consume the meat and environmental issues of water contamination. The concentration of manure presents environmental issues as well. At this juncture, industrial animal agriculture seems to create more problems than it solves, and in that article I suggested that we need to explore alternatives: "When habits fail to be productive and satisfactory, then those immersed in the method of critical intelligence apply critical thought and experimentation to alter or replace them. We need to see ends-in-view that promote growth and open up possibilities. Those who refuse to examine habits are fixed and rigid. Dewey speaks of the ossification of the brain. Our culture seems ossified with regard to our habits of consuming animals and animal by-products. Today plenty of alternatives are available that require less reliance on animals. We need to start exploring these possibilities" (172). Pragmatism can help with this ongoing examination, and so I turn to some key figures in the founding of that tradition who addressed animal issues over a century ago.

Charles Sanders Peirce (1839–1914), one of the "founders" of pragmatism, focused on the idea of human ontological continuity with the rest of nature. Everything is related, and this entails the possibility of understanding and communicating with the rest of nature. He also focused on the fact that life is always in process. This view places humans in a shared evolutionary process with other animal beings, which enables shared communication and mutual modification. He says, "I can tell by the expression of the face the state of mind of my horse just as unmistakably as I can that of my dog or my wife" (Peirce 379). This allows for joint activities like herding sheep or riding a horse. The communication may be mysterious but it is real. "In riding a horse, I understand him and he understands me; but how we can understand one another I know hardly better than he" (456). As Doug Anderson writes, "our relations with animals constitute an ongoing experiment that needs to be informed by a full understanding of animal life. Peirce is not blind to the viciousness of animals or humans; on the contrary, he is well aware of animal fallibility. Furthermore, he understands that community requires reciprocal relations. It's not just that we must be nice to animals; animals too must come to join in the community's well-being to the extent they can" (93). Domesticated animals in particular are in reciprocal relationships with humans, but all animal beings have personalities for Peirce, and we need to be attentive to these and take them into account in our relationships with them.

Along with this continuity, William James (1842–1910) calls for an approach that entails respecting others who are different. Continuity does not mean sameness, and much can be learned from stretching oneself and encountering other perspectives. While James himself sometimes failed to remain open to the differences of other animal (and human) beings, his view definitely calls on us to include such perspectives in our understanding in order to engage the world around us in satisfactory ways. In "On a Certain Blindness in Human Beings," James famously notes that humans need to remain open to the experiences of other human and animal beings. He points out that dogs enjoy bones more than books, and humans should recognize and respect what makes life significant for dogs. In "Is Life Worth Living?" written in 1895, he points to the failure of humans to take into account the experience of cattle and comments on the moral complexity of life in mixed-species communities. He writes, "When you and I, for instance, realize how many innocent beasts have had to suffer in cattle-cars and slaughter-pens and lay down their lives that we might grow up, all fattened and clad, to sit together here in comfort and carry on this discourse, it does, indeed, put our relation to the universe in a more solemn light" (James 232). One cannot ignore the perspective of the cattle, nor the complexity of the relationships involved.

Charlotte Perkins Gilman (1860–1935) also saw the continuity among mammalian life and often used this continuity to support her views on the need to change the lives of human women. Gilman engaged in actual experiments with changes in living conditions in order to improve the position of women in society and so to allow for the continued growth of the human species. She connected this work to improving the position of domesticated animals and called for a move to vegetarianism on ecological grounds. While the position she arrived at in regard to such animal beings (to end all domestication) may not ultimately fit with the pragmatist view I present here, her method and approach to experimentation does, and much can be learned from looking at her work in this light. In making her point that species should trump sex distinctions, she noted how the ram and the ewe were more alike than different. Under domestication, however, the females of such species were changed in some of the same ways human women had been changed—they were shaped by male human desires. Their femaleness became the whole of their being.

> To make clear by an instance the difference between normal and abnormal sex-distinction, look at the relative condition of a wild cow and a "milch cow," such as we have made. The wild cow is a female. She has healthy calves, and milk enough for them; and that is all the femininity she needs. Otherwise than that she is bovine rather than feminine. She is a light, strong, swift, sinewy creature, able to run, jump, and fight, if necessary. We, for economic uses, have artificially developed the cow's capacity for procuring milk. She has become a walking milk-machine, bred and tended to that express end, her value measured in quarts. The cow is over-sexed. (Gilman 43–44)

Written in 1898, long before the development of the modern industrial dairy, Gilman's observations remain an important touchstone for contemporary ecofeminist views such as those found in Carol Adams and Val Plumwood (discussed in later chapters). Her work (and the work of other ecofeminists) adds an important gender component to a more general pragmatist analysis that will be taken up here to examine human relationships with a variety of livestock animals. For Gilman, domestication is an experiment that has gone wrong, just as the limitations placed on human women failed to promote growth and development of humans and their environment. She argues that humans should admit to these errors (to their fallibility) and change.

But this fallibility and uncertainty should not stop attempts to ameliorate situations. Jane Addams (1860–1935) exemplifies this trait of American prag-matism in her work to improve the living conditions of recent immigrants in Chicago in the late 1800s and early 1900s. While less directly concerned with the livestock animals themselves, she was concerned about the diseased milk and tainted meat being sold in the city. She was involved in improving garbage collection in the city, and some women with whom she worked brought in pigs to eat garbage (more on this role of pigs in chapter 8). The Chicago stockyards were a mark of the city during her lifetime, and the conditions faced by the workers in Upton Sinclair's novel *The Jungle* are the kind she worked to improve. She is actually the model for a character in *The Jungle*. Addams drew attention to the plight of immigrant labor in the emerging meatpacking and factory sys-tems. This concern remains today and will be discussed in chapter 10.

John Dewey (1859–1952) took up this Peircian naturalism and Jamesian pluralism as well as Gilman's experimentalism and Addams's amelioration and emphasized the indeterminacy of things with the insight that life is devel-opmental. Life is always changing and generally seeks growth and "improve-ment." Such growth, if it is to be successful, engages any particular aspect of life or situation as being in a web of relationships with other life. No one and no thing stands alone. Taking up the new science of the time, Dewey saw indi-viduality to be a function of relationships in time. Using Abraham Lincoln as an example, he notes that his individuality was not wholly shaped from with-out, nor did it simply unfold from within. Dewey wrote, "The career which is his unique individuality is the series of interactions in which he was created to be what he was by the ways in which he responded to the occasions with which he was presented" (*Later Works* 110–11). Dewey notes that many see this to be the case for humans but not for other animals, plants, or "inanimate" objects. But he pushes back on this point. There are differences between the animate and inanimate "but no fixed gaps between them." He continues, "The principle of a developing career applies to all things in nature, as well as to hu-man beings—that they are born, undergo qualitative changes, and finally die, giving place to other individuals. The idea of development applied to nature involves differences of forms and qualities as surely as it rules out absolute breaches of continuity. The differences between the amoeba and the human organism are genuinely there even if we accept the idea of organic evolution of species. Indeed, to deny the reality of the differences and their immense significance would be to deny the very idea of development" (*Later Works* 14:108). Problems arise, however, when one reads such development as "necessarily proceeding from the lower to the higher, from the relatively worse to the relatively better" (108). Potentialities are those things that develop in interactions *with* other things:

> Hence potentialities cannot be known till after the interactions have occurred. . . . Potentialities of milk are known today, for example, that were not known a generation ago, because milk has been brought into interaction with things other than organisms, and hence now has other than furnishing nutriment consequences. . . . With the use of milk as a plastic, and with no one able to tell what future consequences may be produced by new techniques which bring it into new interactions, the only reasonable conclusion is that potentialities are not fixed and intrinsic, but are a matter of an indefinite range of interactions in which an individual may engage. (109–10)

He further notes that freedom of thought and expression "have their roots deep in the existence of individuals as developing careers in time. Their denial and abrogation is an abdication of individuality and a virtual rejection of time as opportunity" (113). This happens to humans when they "become imprisoned in routine and fall to the level of mechanisms" (112). One argument of this book is that this is exactly what happens to animals (human and other than human) in industrial farming—they lose their individuality and their freedom.

While sometimes Dewey seems to lean in a more mechanistic direction that might justify industrial agriculture, those passages need to be understood in the context of his larger commitments. For instance he writes, "When chemical fertilizers can be used in place of animal manures, when improved grain and cattle can be purposefully bred from inferior animals and grasses, . . . man gains power to manipulate nature" (*Middle Works* 12:120). This sounds like animals and plants are inert things to be manipulated at will. But his larger point is to argue against the separation of mind and materiality and the separation of means and ends in both science and morality. A few paragraphs later he says, "Until the dogma of fixed unchangeable types and species, of arrangement in classes of higher and lower, of subordination of the transitory individual to the universal or kind has been shaken in its hold upon the science of life, it was impossible that the new ideas and methods should be made at home in social and moral life" (122–23). His optimism that the tendency to separate and rank had been outgrown was premature, as we still see this mentality working in racism, sexism, classism, and speciesism, but his call to rethink the nature of types and species as fluid and changing is important. Ironically the example of changing cattle and grasses proves his point and raises new problems. We now know that chemical fertilizers create a host of problems and that genetic manipulation of animals and plants (through conventional breeding or more technological genetic modification) comes with many unintended consequences that do not fit the needs and desires of those organisms and fail to respect their individuality.

For Dewey, individual and species development depends on transactive (mutually transformative) relationships with the rest of the environment (living and nonliving). His theory (if not his personal views) committed him to seeing a continuum of traits such as intelligence, emotions, and consciousness in all animal beings. Interestingly it was a relationship with a goat that finally got Dewey to see other animals as personalities in the way Peirce suggested and to consider relationships from their perspectives as James suggested. Dewey's correspondence is filled with reference to the animals in his life: horses, dogs, cats, fish, rabbits, pigs, and a special goat. His correspondence with Arthur Bentley often focused on the nature and intelligence of animals. Over time Dewey's position that language is something that clearly separates humans from other animals shifted as he admitted that we can't know when animal signaling becomes animals using signs (Dewey and Bentley, letter dated March 12, 1946). In 1949 his correspondence became filled with discussion of a goat from whom he "gets three quarts a day." He describes her as "very clearly an intelligent animal" who forms strong attachments; she even tried to go into the house (letter dated August 14, 1949). Dewey played with the goat and came to know her as an individual. He called her a person and wrote that this should not be denied to plants and animals (letter dated December 29, 1949). Here Dewey began to move in the direction of panpsychism despite earlier worries about Peirce (and Whitehead) for doing the same.

This openness to seeing other animals as having personalities and individuality and being creatures with "developing careers" that need to be respected is an important insight. It is the insight developed in this book, using a largely Deweyan pragmatism augmented and expanded by ecofeminist theory and practice. The next chapter will develop a Deweyan ethic, based in the more general pragmatist and ecofeminist perspective presented here, to examine what such respect might entail. To begin, that chapter will further explore the current conditions faced by fish. Fish are connected to poultry, pigs, and cattle, though, so that discussion will only serve to launch the larger exploration of living with livestock.

CHAPTER TWO
_____

Fish and Pragmatist Philosophy

DEVELOPING A DEWEYAN ETHIC

When asked about livestock most people don't think of fish. When asked about fishing they tend to think of people catching fish with a line. Others, aware of the realities of the fishing industry, might think of big trawlers scraping the ocean floor and pouring the contents of their nets on the deck of a boat—much of it just thrown away as unintentional bycatch. But, in fact, many fish are regularly farmed and have been for quite a while. Carp were farmed in China at least as far back as 4000 BCE, and in Europe written records point to carp farming nine hundred years ago with very large operations existing by the 1500s (Lichatowich 115). Carp are the most commonly farmed fish, but others include trout, catfish, tilapia, seabass, seabream, yellow tail, oysters, clams, and shrimp. Large-scale fish farming is just the most recent transformation of more traditional ways of raising animals and procuring animal protein. While more and more people are aware that the overwhelming majority of cows, pigs, and chickens don't spend their lives roaming fields, nesting in straw, or scratching in the dirt, fewer people seem to be aware of the conditions so many of the fish they are eating have faced throughout their lives. People seem even less aware of the environmental impacts of industrial farming, whether of fish or of fowl.

Salmon are the most commonly eaten farmed fish in North America, but the artificial propagation of salmon is a more recent development that goes back only 250 years (Lichatowich 115). In the United States, salmon and trout were first raised in hatcheries in an attempt to stock lakes, rivers, and the ocean. The focus shifted from hatcheries to farming the fish for direct human consumption. Today over a third of the fish who are consumed in the United States are farmed fish. In *Meat: A Benign Extravagance*, Simon Fairlie points out that "only a tiny fraction of the world's terrestrial meat is hunted, but almost all of the marine fish that provide five per cent of the world's protein are wild animals, captured in the chase. . . . But that frontier, too, is under threat" (Fairlie 123). As big corporate fishing fleets developed, fisheries began to collapse—herring fisheries in the North Sea in the 1960s, anchovy fisheries in Peru in the 1970s, and cod fisheries in Newfoundland in the 1980s. Although fishing has long been a way for the poor to make a living, feed themselves, or both, this way of life is endangered when corporations move in and ignore long-standing practices that have served to sustain the fisheries (123–25). Rather than change fishing practices to recover and sustain local fisheries, corporations have turned to fish farming to feed the worldwide appetite. Fairlie writes, "Until recently it was difficult to fence fish in, but the farming of fish has changed that. The ultimate form of marine enclosure is fish-farming. In the 'cage' system, areas of ocean or inland waters are literally fenced off to provide an area for the private rearing of fish or other sea creatures; in other cases fish are reared in excavated lakes or ponds. Like terrestrial farmers, fish farmers supply their stock with feed, and protect them from disease and chemicals" (124n17). Aquaculture takes the model of intensive animal agriculture and applies it to fish. The industry works to find the optimal stocking rate—the number of fish that maximizes yield and minimizes inputs. There is an acceptable mortality rate, and fish are medicated to keep them alive long enough to slaughter. This model has been lifted from the poultry industry, and, ironically, many of these fish are fed chicken and chicken by-products from industrial chicken operations. The industrial farming of fish multiplies the number of animals harmed and killed to produce food and raise environmental concerns.

While fish are farmed in a number of ways—in tanks and ponds on land or in floating cages in the sea—as fresh water becomes scarcer, more of the focus turns to saltwater farming. Pumping seawater to on-land tanks is expensive and consumes a great deal of energy. This has been a common way of raising halibut and turbot. Cages in the sea are less expensive and less energy-intensive and, unlike shellfish production, they do not occupy desirable coastline. But cage farming needs locations that have a good tidal exchange of water while being sheltered from large waves and storms. The best locations have been found in British Columbia, Chile, Norway, and Scotland, and fish farming is firmly established in these areas. Newer areas where this kind of farming is growing include Greece, Japan, Australia, and Washington and Maine in the United States.

Jim Lichatowich, in his book *Salmon without Rivers*, notes that salmon in the Pacific Northwest provide an interesting example of the developments in the fish industry. Pacific salmon are now extinct in 40 percent of their historic range (54). As overfishing, the building of dams, and other disturbances to the salmon's rivers from the timber, mining, and agricultural industries pushed various species of Northwest salmon to the brink of extinction, various plans emerged to rebuild the native stock. To get around the dams, fish ladders were built in some places, and in others the fish were captured and trucked around the dams to be released on the other side (not without stress, injury, and death). Some attempts to clean up the rivers and restrict the damage done by logging, mining, and ranching were also made. The main push, however, was to increase the number of fish, and to do this the hatchery system was developed. The hatcheries had to capture wild fish, kill them to take their eggs, inseminate the eggs with sperm, raise the fry, and release them at the appropriate time. Mistakes were made along the way—releasing the fish at the wrong time or not monitoring the water flow from the dams as the young fish tried to make their way. Even when all went according to plan, however, return rates for hatchery fish rarely made up for the number of fish taken by the hatcheries. Given the need to kill salmon to hatch salmon, the hatcheries were generally an additional stress on wild populations rather than a way to help them recover (131, 144).

Salmon hatcheries began in 1763 in an attempt to increase the number of Atlantic salmon and were more seriously taken up in the early 1800s. Even then a farming metaphor and mentality was used. Writing in *Harper's* in 1868, two French fisherman, Joseph Remy and M. Gehin, make this clear: "Does not man sow his entire field with the single sort of grain he wished to culti-vate? What then, is there to hinder us from stocking bountifully our streams with fish, by aiding the process of hatching, and protecting the young from destruction by the innumerable enemies?" (quoted in Lichatowich 117). The first commercial hatchery was called a piscifactory, or fish factory, and salmon were viewed more as a product than as living animals with complex life cycles. The first salmon hatchery in the West was built in 1872, but those eggs were shipped back east to try to populate rivers there. As more hatcher-ies opened in the West, they traded eggs as well. There was no thought given to the complexity and specificity of salmon's lives in particular rivers, at par-ticular seasons. They were seen as interchangeable things. Without local adaptation most of the young fish did not survive (126). Lichatowich writes, "Hatcheries fit nicely in the nineteenth-century view that ecosystems were warehouses of commodities that existed solely for human use and benefit. The earth itself was seen as a giant factory. . . . People had the mission of sub-duing the wild elements, of ridding the land of animals and plants that were useless to humans, and of bringing the whole system under efficient control" (128).

My students and I visited one hatchery near Winthrop, Washington. Rather than catching salmon to harvest eggs, this hatchery was getting eggs from its own fish. While this relieves the pressure on the wild fish, it raises concerns about genetic diversity. The hatchery employees said they released about two hundred thousand fry for eight hundred fish to return. The hatchery was also involved in "ridding the land of animals and plants that were useless to humans" by trapping "nuisance" beavers. Nuisance beavers are "any beavers who are where they aren't supposed to be." They said they tried to trap families together. When that wasn't possible they put them in social groups and tried to release them somewhere where there weren't any beavers. Ironically, these "nuisance" beavers are part of the reason for the decline of salmon, but it was their removal, not their presence, that caused the problem.

Beavers help make the rivers of the Pacific Northwest habitable by salmon. By the early 1800s fur trading was big business, and beavers were a big part of that trade. The Hudson Bay Company sought to take as many animals as they could so that the expanding United States would find little of value in the country. By 1843 there were many local extinctions of beaver, and by 1900 beavers were nearly extinct throughout North America. Beaver and salmon had coevolved, and the beavers "enhanced salmon habitat. Beaver dams create pools that store sediments, organic material, and nutrients, releasing them slowly to the stream. They reduce fluctuation in flows, increase dissolved oxygen in the outflowing waters, create wetlands, and modify the riparian zone. All of which stabilize the ecosystem and buffer the effects of natural disturbances such as floods and droughts" (Lichatowich 55). While the importance of beavers for the health of the river system is now acknowledged, humans still determine the beavers' value by what they see as the direct impact on the lives of humans. Inconvenienced by flooding caused by beaver dams, the humans had removed the beavers we saw that day instead of rethinking their own placement in the river system. These beavers were treated in much the same way that the "predators" mentioned in chapter 1 are treated in order to protect farmed fish—they are some "thing" humans see as in the way of their own desire to use and consume.

Given the limited success of hatcheries some have turned to fish farming to "relieve the pressure" on the wild native salmon. Fish farms are defended as an important tool for preserving the wild stock. Cypress Island American Salmon sent us materials which read,

> By the late 1950's and early 60's people were beginning to realize that the stocks of wild fish in the oceans were limited and that eventually there would not be

enough of them to supply the world's needs. They realized that it would be necessary to farm fish or we would over-fish and deplete our natural stock in the
oceans and that consumption of seafood would have to be reduced. So they
built on what had been learned in the early hatcheries. They improved rearing
techniques and developed methods for growing fish to market size. In so doing,
they started what can now be thought of as "modern fish farming."

It is important to note the assumption that the human desire to consume
something should be met. Not only is the *desire* to consume not questioned,
but it is turned into a *need*. While there are many places where seafood con-
stitutes the main part of a subsistence diet, this is *not* the market being served
by most fish farms. Nor are the fish those people rely on being preserved. Further, since fish do not use carbohydrates well they are fed protein. This comes
from a variety of sources, such as fishmeal, soybean meal, animal by-product
meals (poultry in particular), and corn gluten. Some of these protein sources
could feed humans directly.

Being located in the Pacific Northwest, we had hoped to focus on the controversial practice of fish farming, but with the exception of a shellfish farm
(discussed later), no one we contacted wanted to participate in our study.
One responded by email to say that our questions were basically questions
about sustainability and were answered in the packet that was attached. This
was Cypress Island American Salmon (quoted above) which is the marketing
arm of American Gold Seafoods. The materials they sent state that they are
the "only American owned and operated salmon farm in the United States."
They write that their low-density approach to farming reduces stress and that
they are a sustainable fishery that lessens the pressure on wild sources of seafood. They note that public relations is an important element in their future
success as an industry and a company. Consumer concerns with "the ethical
aspects concerning food production such as protection of the environment
and animal welfare" are their focus, with the harvest being of particular import. They write, "A slaughter method is considered to be humane when the
animals concerned are rendered immediately insensible and unconscious-
ness lasts until death. Percussive stunning is now widely used and considered
to be one of the most humane methods of slaughtering animals." Most of their
discussion about the slaughter process, though, is in terms of the effect on the
"textural quality, color, appearance and shelf-life" of the product, not of the
animals' experience. To reduce the adverse effects of stress on the meat of the
fish, humane slaughter methods are preferred.

Their practices have been guided by the *Interim Guidelines* set by the Washington Department of Natural Resources. The guidelines don't allow pens near
protected habitats or "nutrient-sensitive" areas; require monitoring of "waste,

feed, feces, and bacterial growth"; and allow only nonlethal forms of predator control. These guidelines were set in the 1980s in order to gather data for
future regulations. Further study resulted in the first permits being issued in
Washington in 1996. It was reported that in 2005 all commercial pens met or
exceeded the Department of Ecology's standards. These standards apply only
to a one-hundred-foot perimeter around the pen. Given the fluid nature of
water, though, waste, feed, feces, and bacterial growth can move further than
one hundred feet, but the industry argues that any polluting effect is confined
to the footprint of the pen. At the same time, however, in an effort to claim
that they have a form of "waste treatment" that exceeds that of most industrial and municipal waste treatment, they point to the high waterflow rate in
the areas where the pens are placed. Because of this waterflow there may be
less waste product in the area of the pen and the one-hundred-foot perimeter
in which the testing occurs, but that does not mean a high volume of waste is
not being dispersed. To handle that possibility they argue that since the waste
products of fish farms "are of an organic nature (i.e., carbon-based) and do
not include the toxic material homeowners and some industries flush down
their drains or apply to their properties" there is no need to worry. Being less
bad than other waste, though, does not make this waste good. To mitigate
that perception they say that fish waste is available for others in the food web
and can act like fertilizer, and Integrated Multi-Trophic Aquaculture (IMTA)
is something that the industry is trying to develop. The Canadian Aquaculture website says IMTA farms bring "different aquaculture species together
in a way that allows one species' wastes to be recycled as feed for another.
Typically, IMTA systems combine an aquaculture species that requires external feeding (e.g., salmon and other finfish) with species capable of deriving
nutrients from the wastes of the 'fed' species." This system is praised for both
its positive impacts on profits and its environmental benefits: "By recycling
nutrients that would otherwise be wasted, IMTA systems offer aquaculturists
the potential of increased economic gains. IMTA systems could also lead to
'greener' aquaculture practices through the reduction in waste products in the
marine environment—as well as a decreased risk of algal blooms and cloudy
water" ("Integrated Multi-Trophic Aquaculture"). This description is interesting because it acknowledges the dangers of fish farming even as it proposes a
"solution" that offers increased economic gain for the corporations.

Concerns over antibiotics in the feed and the waste are pushed aside by
noting that their use is strictly monitored and has declined with the use of
vaccines. Fish growth rates decline with the use of antibiotics, and the industry is proud of how their limited use compares with the high volumes of use
in the rest of industrial agriculture. There is no discussion of the effect of the
vaccines in the wider web. Parasites and fungi are treated with formaldehyde

(a substance regulated by the EPA due to its "adverse health effects"). Noting that most anything humans do has an environmental impact, they argue that fish farming can be done with very little negative impact and some positive impact. The materials sent by Cypress Island come closest to answering our two questions about their view of nature and how those views impact how they farm when they say that the

> impacts can be very limited and there are typically positive effects of well-sited mariculture, such as food-web enhancement of diversity and abundance found around the perimeter of fish farms. Of course everything human beings do has some environmental effect. Agriculture, fisheries and now fish farming inevitably interact with the natural environment, because they are such an integrated part of it. In some cases the interactions may be significant; in others they may be minor or even positive. The challenge for our human society is to figure out how we can maintain the standard of living to which we have become accustomed in the developed countries, and advance that of those in undeveloped countries, while ensuring that changes in the natural environment are minimized. We believe that this is the course on which the fish farming industry is set and that what it has achieved up to now has been accomplished with an impact that is both minimal and acceptable.

Again, there is an assumption that "we can maintain the standard of living to which we have become accustomed in the developed countries, and advance that of those in undeveloped countries." The possibility (much less the desirability) of that goal is not questioned. There is clearly a perspective of seeing the earth (the oceans in this case) as a "giant factory" that humans can control and manipulate to produce a consumable product. This factory element of such fish farms became clearer when we visited the salmon farm in Canada.

Salmon farms are mostly open-pen farms. Most salmon farms raise Atlantic salmon, no matter where the farm is located. This is because Atlantic salmon were one of the first farmed fish (their farming began in Norway in the 1960s). They are referred to as the "cows of the sea" because they are docile, gain weight easily on the processed food they are fed, and withstand high stocking densities (Robson 34). One problem is that with open-pen farming, fish can escape. In the Pacific Northwest, this leads to nonnative fish being released into already stressed and delicate ecosystems. Other concerns include disease, lice infestation, vulnerability to plankton blooms, and pollution. Farms use food that contains antibiotics and other medicines to deal with some of these problems. When free-living fish come near these pens they run the risk of contacting the parasites, the diseases, and the medicated food (though the food is monitored closely to minimize waste). Predators (eagles, seals, sea lions, and bears) who are not successfully discouraged by predator nets and site cleanliness also risk consuming diseased and drugged fish, not to mention being killed or relocated to prevent their predation.

Our visit to the salmon farm began with finding the tourist pamphlet in our hotel. The public tours were advertised as "a new way to see salmon in the wild!" This is technically true, if wildly misleading, as the fish pens are out in the "wild" open waters. So, we took that rather exciting boat ride discussed at the start of the book. On the ride out we were able to speak with our guide. When we asked about lice, we were told that the lice problem found in Norway and Scotland does not exist in the waters of British Columbia. There is a kind of lice present, but they've never had unacceptable levels of lice reported (Robson 47). Nonetheless they feed the salmon Slice (a form of avermectin). Though the drug is not approved by Health Canada, its use is made possible by Health Canada's Emergency Drug Release Program (163). When we asked about waste, we were told that the pens are carefully placed where currents can redistribute the waste from the fish and help with decomposition. If sulfides exceed the threshold they fallow the farm for several months (47, 91). Our guide did admit there is a concern when farms are located on the migration routes of wild salmon. She said antibiotics are added to the food only with the prescription of a veterinarian to address specific problems. Since salmon are fasted prior to "harvest," all drugs are supposed to be out of their system. This is monitored and enforced by the Canadian Food Inspection Agency and the U.S. Federal Drug Administration. Further, to avoid the cost of administering drugs, every attempt is made to keep the fish healthy and disease-free.

When asked about the loss of food value involved in feeding fish to fish our guide said that was a problem. Seven of the top ten farmed fish are predator fish (tilapia are herbivores but are generally seen to be less healthful for humans) (Simon 154–55). Salmon and tuna eat five pounds of fish to produce one pound of food for humans. Our guide said they want to be a net producer of fish, so they look for vegetable sources for protein and oil. Some fish farms have started to mix in the by-products of the slaughter of chickens to replace some of the fish—involving fish farming with the industrial farming of chickens. When we asked about feeding the original protein source (whether fish or poultry) to people, rather than feeding it to fish, we were told that the source is fisheries specifically used for the production of meal and oil (not food), and that this is used in other animal foods—pig, chicken, and pet food. Turkey heads and feet that would otherwise be wasted are fed to fish (A. Smith 99).

When we asked about stress and disease in the fish we were told the fish aren't stressed, since stocking density is controlled to avoid stress and disease. Seeing scrapes on some of the fish, we asked about fighting and were assured the fish do not fight but might get scraped on the nets during feeding time. During our visit they could not get the automated feeder to work. Cameras are placed in each pen to monitor the food dropping through the pen and prevent food waste. In addition to the many fish on the surface, when we looked in the camera the water below was packed with fish. They apologized that there were only a few fish visible since they weren't feeding. If we were seeing "a few," it's hard to imagine the true density of the fish. The literature says, "Farmed salmon are typically stocked at densities of 5–12 kilograms per cubic metre (8.5–22 pounds per cubic yard). If the fish have too much room, the company won't realize the full potential of its netcages. If the fish are too crowded, they will have to compete harder for feed, and the stress associated with crowding may make them more susceptible to sickness and infection" (Robson 78).

The BC Salmon Farmers Association notes that since escapes represent money lost to the producer they work to reduce, if not eliminate, any escapes. Improving the materials that make up the nets, improving the anchoring systems, and sending divers down every month to inspect the nets help to make this happen. Nonetheless, the week before our visit there had been an escape. Our guide said an unusual current had dragged a net anchor out of place but that the company would do everything to prevent anything like this happening again. She was confident that the escaped fish would not thrive, or even survive, in the free-living conditions and so presented no competition to native fish. Further, she asserted, there was no danger to native fish as inter-breeding would not be possible.

The fish at this farm used to be transported to the processing plant alive, but now they are dead-hauled. That meant the farm needed to be located within an acceptable distance from the processing plant in order to maintain the quality of the fish. Our guide said it was important for people to connect to the whole process, so we did visit the processing plant. That day, however, weather had diverted the load of fish they had expected, and so the plant was quiet. The tour emphasized the safety of the workers and the efficiency of the automated systems. There was nothing said about what made it better for the fish or the environment.

While most of our questions received reassuring answers, the issues re-main controversial. The point here is to see fish farms as an interesting case for exploring how particular views of nature impact choices about how to farm. The stated purpose of salmon farming is to provide market-sized fish year-round (74). But salmon are seasonal, and until the advent of farmed salmon, salmon were not available year-round; different salmon were har-vested at different times of the year. The salmon farmers also say they want to provide a consistent product, but different kinds of salmon have different textures and tastes. Our guide told us that people generally prefer the milder taste and texture of Atlantic salmon. The farmers see themselves as feeding the people and feeding the people what they want. But that "product" does not mirror the nature or the life cycle of the salmon beings themselves.

What about their relationship with the rest of nature? The relationship with potential predators is a hostile one. Predators are at risk for being killed or relocated to "control a problem." The industry tries to minimize the need to harm other wildlife and does acknowledge this as a public relations problem. For example, sea lions are often blamed for the diminishing number of salmon available to be caught for human consumption. About twenty sea lions were found shot in Washington and Oregon in 2012. It is widely surmised that they were shot because relocation efforts had ended after several of the protected sea lions died in the relocation attempts.

When pressed, our guide said that for the most part people in the industry do not think about the fish as individuals. As mentioned, Atlantic salmon are considered the "cows of the sea" and they are thought of as a resource (there was no reflection on whether seeing cows this way is appropriate). She said people who raise small groups of sturgeon are known to talk about their individual personalities, but that once one is raising large numbers of fish on a farm, one generally thinks of them as a population and not as individuals. She also noted that fish are cold-blooded and live in a different medium (water) and suggested that this difference adds to the distancing that is experienced, the belief that "they" are not like "us," and the difficulty of seeing them as individuals. Just saying the words to us seemed to give her pause. Rather than thinking about the fish, she mostly had thought about preserving the natural environment into which the fish are placed. The reasons for this were clearly focused on human use and values. The view is that the environment should be preserved in order to have a place to farm, to have other thriving industries such as timber, and to maintain the recreational use of the water and islands. These multiple uses, however, result in polluted water. Given the state of the rivers and oceans, eating wild-caught fish, or fish farmed in the open ocean, comes with the risk of consuming a variety of contaminants. While mercury is a special concern connected to river fish, PCPs are a concern for ocean fish, so water pollution is an environmental concern for the fish industry. Some turn to shellfish farming as a way to improve water quality.

We visited the Shelton location of Taylor Shellfish Farms, which is a one-hundred-year-old family farm. Their website says they hope to run the business for another hundred years: "Our mission is to sustainably farm quality shellfish from larvae to table while being responsible community citizens and active stewards for our marine environment." At the time of our visit in 2010 they had hired a new sustainability manager. He said, "We are doing most of what we can in growing and harvesting since we have to stay in business. We need clean water. But more can be done with our packaging. We use bleach because it is required by the Department of Health. We also use lots of water—we could use less, but we have to do what is required by law." They use 150,000 gallons a day from their well. They clean the water they use by putting it back into their forest so that it can filter.

It is a big operation. They have about four hundred employees working at their nine farms. Washington is one of just two states where private individuals can own tidal flats, and Taylor Shellfish Farms owns more than ten thousand acres of tidal flats and lease more. They think it is important to be a good neighbor and a steward of the land and the water. "One thing we've learned over the years is that consistently producing the most delicious shellfish requires a long-term commitment to people and place. You need healthy watersheds, healthy estuaries, healthy communities, and healthy business practices. We're proud to have had a hand in all those things, and we plan to keep it up for many more generations" ("About Us").

The Olympia oyster crop became a major "resource" starting in the 1800s, and the Taylor family started farming Olympia oysters in the 1890s. They added Pacific oysters in the 1920s and 1930s when Olys started to fail due to pollution from the timber industry. Pollution from pulp mills in the 1950s and 1960s hurt the Olympia oyster crops again, and in the 1970s a cleanup began. The Taylor family works with other farms, regulators, and conservation groups to help maintain clean water. "Today," our guide said, "the biggest issue is development." Runoff from lawn and yard chemicals is one issue; fecal coliform from pet waste and failing septic systems is another. Nitrogen from farm waste is also a concern, as plankton and algae blooms can smother fish or cause low levels of dissolved oxygen that result in fish kills. Shellfish crops are seen as helping to improve water quality, as they remove excess nitrogen. They write, "By cleaning the water they grow in, shellfish are environmentally restorative by nature" ("About Us"). Silt from erosion is also a problem, and our guide said that maintaining wetland buffers is the biggest help in preventing erosion. There are also concerns over a number of invasive species, and they work to control drill snails and crab. They are also facing lost harvest as a result of carbon dioxide emissions. Since they already suffer loss from ocean acidification that results from rising global carbon dioxide levels (which prevent baby oysters from forming their shells), their focus is on producing stock that can adapt to the emerging conditions. They argue that retaining shellfish production provides good habitat for other species and so makes the Pacific Northwest a good place for trout and salmon.

Our guide referred to the various shellfish as their *crop* as she took us to see the *nurseries*. This demonstrates an interesting tension in the view of shellfish—they are an animal, but are often seen as more like a plant. Our guide talked about planting "seed" and then caring for the floating nursery.

But then there is the hatchery, where the young are born, setting the shell-fish apart from how most people see and understand plants. It generally takes them one and a half years to bring mussels to harvest, three years for clams, two to four years for their five varieties of oysters, and four to six years for geoduck. They plant in the spring and summer and need a good summer for the shellfish to hibernate successfully. If they miss the window for harvesting, they suffer "summer mortality" as the shellfish get too big, too old, and too thick, and die. The right timing is essential in this kind of farming, and the tide drives everything. Our guide said, "We go with the rhythm of nature. We have to work with nature since we depend on clean water. The intertidal area is very dynamic and demands that we have a tight relationship with nature." If it rains one inch or more in twenty-four hours they must stop the harvest for five days because such a rain brings pollutants down from the surrounding lawns and farms. They have to pick up and move the crop if the water quality becomes a problem; they also have to find, pick up, and move back the crop if winds move the shellfish from where they were planted.

Some of the growers we talked with seemed to see the shellfish as animals. They said, "The Kumamoto oyster can be finicky," and, "Clams move around—they go for a walk." When our guide dug into the mud they spit water at us and moved away. While there is nothing like a mammalian brain at work in these animals, there is still an experience and reaction. This made us won-der about the processing they go through. The plant is very cold, bright, and noisy. We know these conditions impact the human workers and we assume the shellfish react to these conditions too. And what about the ones who are frozen alive? Eaten alive? We were told they have a shelf life of at least three to four days in the summer and ten to twelve days in the winter. How do the shellfish feel about this? The workers also talked about the shellfish having preferences and being happy: "By constantly experimenting and challeng-ing ourselves, we've been able to match the right sites with the right shellfish species and growing methods," and, "Some tidelands are perfect for Olympia oysters; others make Kumamotos happier, and still others grow the most de-licious clams" ("About Us"). All oysters can be tracked with a harvest tag re-quired by the Department of Health (this is similar to the method of tracking conventional livestock with identification tags and chips). Such tracking is an effort to ensure human health. Nothing about government regulations in the fish industry is about the welfare of the fish themselves. Fish welfare is not a concern. But fish do have negative, stressful, and painful experiences that should be taken into account. The growers at this farm know this, even as the system as a whole operates by denying it.

In his book *Meatonomics*, David Robinson Simon analyzes the growth of fish farming and the pain the fish face. He notes that there are eighteen pain receptors in a trout's head and that pain management has been shown to affect their behavior (demonstrating that pain makes a difference in their lives). Farmed fish also suffer from fear and anxiety. This is especially true for solitary fish like salmon when they are crowded into pens. These crowded conditions also contribute to a high rate of diseases and parasites, causing further suffering. If they are slaughtered by using carbon dioxide to stun them they often thrash around for as long as nine minutes before dying, and they bleed out while conscious. Sometimes the fish are frozen while they are dying to keep them fresh. They take longer to suffocate at lower temperatures (137–40).

Fish are complex and diverse. So are the ways they are caught, farmed, and killed. The needs of salmon differ from those of catfish, and both of those differ from the needs of the oyster. I cannot discuss the great individual variability that fish as a whole present, but I do want to point out that this is something every aspect of this industry should be addressing. On top of the stress to wild fish and their ecosystems caused by the production of fish for food, there is the additional stress of catching fish for sale as pets. In her book *Do Fish Feel Pain?* Victoria Braithwaite notes that "certain fishing practices used to capture wild tropical reef fish … are taking a serious toll on the world's coral reefs. In South East Asia illegal fishing with cyanide strips reefs of their inhabitants and kill the corals too. The majority of the fish caught this way survive only long enough to be transported to pet stores where they are sold to customers, but many die quickly afterward from slow cyanide poisoning" (Braithwaite 15). These pet fish can also suffer and be stressed.

Questions about fish welfare rarely surface, but they should. Fish do feel pain; they suffer and can be stressed. Braithwaite cites studies that confirm that "developmentally and functionally there is evidence of a limbic-like area in the fish forebrain" and that this means that "fish have an area specialized to process negative, fear-related stimuli" (101–02). She notes that there is species variability among fish's tolerance of pain and fear and that context can make a difference as well (105). This complexity is also reflected in the intelligence of fish as they solve puzzles and coordinate a hunt. Braithwaite argues, "If we already accept that mammals and birds are sentient creatures that have the capacity to experience positive and negative emotions—pleasure or suffering, we should conclude that there is now sufficient evidence to put fish alongside birds and mammals. Given all of this I see no logical reason why we should not extend to fish the same welfare considerations we currently extend to birds and mammals" (113). She acknowledges that this is starting to happen with squid, octopus, and cuttlefish in Canada and the United Kingdom. Accounts of their intelligence abound. Other invertebrates, such as crabs, lobsters, prawns, and barnacles, are thought to feel pain, but there is less certainty that they are self-aware, but "fish, like birds and mammals, have a capacity for self-awareness" (135).

Braithwaite is concerned that certain aspects of aquaculture fail to respect this but thinks this is beginning to change. As an example she points to the practice of netting and handling the fish to size them being replaced with a less stressful process that uses hoses of different sizes to move different-sized fish to separate tanks. Cod, who like to chew, have been found to benefit from enrichment items that provide an outlet for their natural tendency to manipulate kelp and other objects with their mouths. Some operations now have feeding systems that let the fish operate the feeders themselves. Others are studying issues of water quality, optimal stocking density, and fin health (156–60). These issues are all complicated by the fact that the answers differ depending on the species of the fish, the location of the pens, the age of the fish, and the quality of the water and feed. She writes, "A very real problem faced by those trying to devise guidelines and protocols to promote the welfare of captive fish is the sheer breadth of species that we use—this diversity makes it tricky to create generic guidelines. Different species have different requirements; they behave in different ways, they have different specialized sensory systems, and some are better at coping with the captive environment than others. Furthermore, fish are much more variable than their terrestrial cousins" (162). In Europe they are working to develop species-specific guidelines that cover the care of the fish and their environment. While here my focus is on farmed fish, similar welfare concerns carry over to how fish are handled when they are caught—whether this is by a trawler (which is especially painful for the fish) or by an angler. They also apply to fish who develop stereotypies when kept in captivity in aquariums. New research supporting this need to understand and address the needs and desires of fish can be found in Jonathon Balcombe's *What a Fish Knows*.

The variability of conditions and species' needs is why I think it is important to bring pragmatism into the conversation. While sweeping bans or general guidelines are easier for people to embrace, they fail to do justice to the complexity presented by these animals. Pragmatism is not itself a singular view but a pluralistic philosophy that is still developing as it works in the world. It might best be described not as a set of doctrines but as a style or attitude that entails the critical engagement of philosophy with problems of the world. This requires an openness of mind and an experimental spirit. It deals with the reality of change, development, and the temporal dimension of existence.

Six basic dimensions of pragmatism will be examined here: *naturalism,*

pluralism, developmentalism, experimentalism, fallibilism, and *amelioration.*
Putting these in terms of our relationship with livestock means we need to
understand the evolutionary history of the various animal beings and we
need to examine the ways we have influenced and transformed each other
(naturalism). We need to be open to seeing the world from the perspectives
of all the animal beings (pluralism) with whom we live if we want to develop
mutually satisfactory relationships. We need to recognize that these relationships are always in process as is the nature of both the human and other animal beings (developmentalism). We need to experiment (experimentalism)
with new and different ways to sustain and improve (ameliorate) the relationships, and we need to be willing to admit when we make mistakes (fallibilism)
in understanding ourselves, other animal beings, and our relationships with
each other.

As discussed in chapter 1, the philosophical perspective of pragmatism is
not just about what is practical or expedient, though this is how the word is
commonly understood. Rather, it is a view that understands humans as natural creatures already in interactive and transactive (mutually transforming)
developmental relationships with the environment and the other creatures
in it. Recognizing that humans are limited in perspective and prone to error
(fallible), pragmatism calls for a pluralist and experimental approach to living
that focuses on trying to improve conditions (ameliorate). Following Peirce, a
pragmatist analysis of fish farming would start with the understanding that
human beings exist on a continuum with fish. There is plenty of evidence for
this biological connection. We share structures of arms and hands, feelings,
and intelligence. At the same time we need to respect the differences fish
present. They see and experience the world differently than humans do and
have a different bodily comportment in the world. There is also a pluralism
among fish, the developmental histories of specific species of fish, that needs
to be better understood and respected. For example, the view of various kinds
of salmon as interchangeable fails to take the specific developmental histories of salmon seriously and by doing so jeopardizes the complex riparian ecosystems in which specific salmon exist as well as the fish themselves. While
pragmatism endorses experimenting with different approaches to improving
the lives of fish, such experimentation must be embedded in this understanding of the complex life histories and relationships. Hatcheries, trucking fish
around dams, and denying fish can escape are not such experiments. Mistakes must be admitted and not allowed to sediment into policy. The denial
of human fallibility seen in the denial of fish escapes, for instance, is a kind of
human arrogance that often accompanies moves to industrialize the human
use of livestock animals and to make the lives of individual animals invisible

and inconsequential. Instead, improving (ameliorating) the various lives and relationships should remain a primary focus. This includes providing a good death.

Aquaculture has had to look not only at the lives of the fish but also at their deaths. As mentioned, fish who are stressed produce a "poor quality product." Carbon dioxide, used to kill poultry and pigs, has been used to kill fish as well. The fish struggle and become immobile from lack of oxygen, but they are not unconscious when they are taken out and have their gills cut so they can bleed out. The ice they are on simply slows their metabolism and prolongs the process and the suffering. As a result, some processors have moved to using electric stunning or percussive stunning. Braithwaite again draws a parallel between fish and other livestock animals when she says, "If more humane harvesting methods can be found, then aren't we obliged to invest in these? In large part, that has been the conclusion for terrestrial animal industries" (183).

This is one of the main concerns of this book. I believe our current production of livestock actually is very limited in its concern for birds and mammals, so it is no surprise to find that fish are not considered beings who can suffer, have needs and desires, and demonstrate intelligence and sociability. Even with acknowledgment of the capacity to suffer, the variety of needs and desires found in cattle, pigs, and poultry are not respected in fish. I think an ethic rooted in pragmatism generally, and the work of John Dewey in particular, can help change thinking and behavior around these issues.

A pragmatist ethic based on the work of John Dewey builds on a dynamic understanding of life to develop an approach to morality that is rooted in the natural and social histories of organisms and their environments. As Mark Johnson notes in *Morality for Humans: Ethical Understanding from the Perspective of Cognitive Science*, when we call something a value what we mean is that actual organisms act to achieve that state of affairs. He writes, "To speak of something as 'valued' is to say that some organism has a predisposition to seek to realize a certain state of affairs, namely the 'valued' or desired state of the organism-environment interaction. Values are therefore relational because they require a relation between an organism and the environments with which it actively engages. Some state of affairs is valuable for or to some organism, animal, or person" (49–50). This means all living beings are valuing beings. What these various beings value is formed by the evolutionary histories of the various species, is based in needs that help these species survive and flourish, and is a state of affairs that these beings will seek to fulfill or achieve as they grow and develop. Some of these values are shared among human and other animal beings, such as the ability to sustain life and the need for interpersonal engagement. The ability to achieve such valued states of affairs is rooted both in biological capacities and in learned behavior (50–51).

Johnson writes, "An organism's preferential directedness toward the realiza-
tion of certain states of organism-environment interaction is an evaluative
process, and the 'state' toward which the organism is preferentially directed
can be selectively and abstractly described as that organism's values." (52).

Some of the most basic of these values are those that allow life to exist
and flourish. These are connected to the dynamic cluster of physical needs
that every organism has: appropriate food and climate, clean air and water,
care, nurturance, and protection (from predators and disease). Equally important, however, are those values related to interpersonal relations. Sociality
is an evolutionary aspect of most life and is a necessity for mammalian life.
The physical, psychological, emotional, and social well-being of mammals requires attention to this aspect of life since their very existence relies on extended care, nurturance, and learning from others. The neuronal organization
of mammals and social birds promotes bonding, distress when separated,
and nurturing behaviors directed at others, even others beyond kin (56–59).
Johnson writes, "The care that is necessary for survival and flourishing is for
the most part predicated on the possibility of empathy, which is our capacity
to experience the situation of another person—an ability to feel with and for
them" (60). We come to be, and to understand ourselves, through and with
others in our environments. Interactive social creatures find value in things
that help with cooperation, cohesion, and harmony. Some of the common vir-
tues that result from this social need include truthfulness, integrity, courage,
loyalty, acknowledgment of authority, and civic-mindedness (63–65). With the
possible exception of civic-mindedness, there is evidence that animals other
than humans value these same traits. Johnson acknowledges this possibility
when he writes, "Morality concerns our well-being—of ourselves, other people, and, some would argue, even the more-than-human world" (66). While
Johnson argues that the human capacity for creativity and language gives
humans an advantage when it comes to critical inquiry and problem-solving
(69), this does not mean that other animal beings do not share in the capacity to have meaningful lives. This meaning is generally found in work, play,
and love—activities in which those animal beings seen as livestock all participate. There is work, play, and love within the various species communities,
and between species. This includes relationships with human beings. Dewey's
relationship with the milk goat is one example of such a relationship, while
Peirce's relationship with his horse is another (see chapter 1). Literature (fiction and nonfiction) is rife with meaningful and poignant human relationships with various animal beings—pigs, chickens, and cows included. Such
connections entail understanding that there are relationships and activities
that are meaningful to these other animal beings and so should be respected.
This does not require a stance of noninterference, though. Human children

have meaningful relationships and activities in their lives, but adults often intervene in these either accidentally or on purpose. What would be wrong is to act as if these did not have meaning for the children or that the children's needs, preferences, and desires didn't matter at all. I think the same holds for other animals. For example, I have argued that horses develop meaningful relationships and that humans should consider this when making decisions that involve moving horses around. This does not mean it is never ethical to move a horse (or a child) from a familiar place and friends. Similarly, dairy cows develop long-standing relationships within a herd and thoughtful, respectful husbandry practices acknowledge and work with these relationships. These animals and their relationships are morally considerable.

While the capacity for rational thought and action is what is usually held up as the distinguishing human feature, especially when it comes to being seen as a moral agent or a being worthy of moral respect, Johnson's account of morality undermines this notion. The research makes it clear that most cognition is unconscious and is laden with emotions (73). Emotions are responses that work to restore the dynamic equilibrium of conditions that sustain life. Johnson says, "Emotions are . . . bodily responses to our mostly (but not exclusively) nonconscious, automatic, ongoing appraisal of how things are going for us as organisms. . . . This quest for well-being (ourselves and others) is the very core of morality, even though it is often carried out beneath the level of our conscious acts of moral reflection" (78). Feelings are our awareness of these changes. He continues, "We share this life imperative with all other animals, and there is compelling evidence that some of the emotions and feelings that underlie human social behavior are present in other (non-human) species" (83). This would imply that other animal beings are themselves moral agents—at least in regard to their relationships with others of their own species and with their environment—and that this capacity is something that humans (with their more complex understanding of their relatedness) should acknowledge and respect. Johnson writes, "The false presumption that morality applies to humans alone is typically predicated on the erroneous assumption that humans possess an autonomous reason and will, which is regarded as the supreme necessary condition of morality. Once we recognize how morality is present beneath and before explicit rational reflection and how emotional/feeling responses are the primary engine of our moral judgments, we are forced to abandon exclusivist claims about morality being a strictly human affair" (83). While Johnson quickly adds that human morality has "achieved a complexity and richness that seem unavailable to other animal species" (83–84), my point still holds. Other animal beings are themselves moral agents—at least in their relationships with others of their own species and possibly with their environment—and this capacity is something that humans (with their more complex understanding of their relatedness) should acknowledge and respect when we engage in moral deliberation about actions that impact other animals' well-being.

For Dewey moral deliberation involves experiencing a situation as problematic. Problematic situations are those in which our habits no longer work to put us into a satisfying relationship with our environment. Satisfying relationships with our environment leave open the present and future possibility of further growth and flourishing. In response to such tensions the inquirer can try to ignore the tensions and continue with past habits, but this is not an intelligent or moral response for Dewey. Instead, he requires that people wrestle with the experience (with the situation) and develop various possible responses to try out (in imagination and in practice) and continually revise as experience suggests. This is an ongoing task. As Gregory Pappas writes in *John Dewey's Ethics*, we must engage life where we find ourselves:

> The only choice available to us is between modes of participation. As Dewey says, "one cannot escape the problem of how to engage in life, since in any case we must engage in it some way or another—or else quit and get out" (MW 14:58). This does not mean we are trapped—unless we presuppose a non-relational, non-contextual notion of ourselves. However, it does mean the question of how we should live cannot be answered once and for all; there is no final resting place, and no final answer, because our options and conditions can change. . . . Therefore the pragmatic approach has to be tentative. (72)

The ability to engage in heartfelt deliberation but remain open to being mistaken and to being corrected by other experiences is not easily cultivated. Dewey's focus on a kind of education that teaches intelligent and open inquiry is essential to creating people capable of working together in a democratic fashion to ameliorate concrete situations.

Given that morality has to deal with actual complex problems it is important to see that "moral principles are never absolute laws, but are instead tentative guides to a reasonable process of inquiry" (Johnson 100). The problem is that humans tend to develop "sedimented patterns of emotional response," responses that rely on "biological makeup, cultural factors, and personal history" (102). I believe that the current habits of meat consumption in the United States are such "sedimented patterns of emotional response" and that these habits have resulted in problems related to human health and environmental sustainability and an estrangement from other animal beings. Pragmatism offers one line of possible inquiry into diagnosing and defining these problems, deliberating about possible responses, and creating the possibility for new habits. To be more effective, however, I believe it is important to augment the insights of pragmatist philosophy with the theory and practice of ecofeminism. While Gilman did this kind of work early on, contemporary ecofeminist writing is an important resource to explore. This will be done in the following chapters as the interviews with farmers provide possible new habits for consideration.

These new habits won't be easy to develop given the complex interconnections among various kinds of industrial farming. I have already mentioned that industrialized poultry are fed to farmed fish. On the flip side, industrialized pig farms are often cited as sources of river pollution and so kill fish. In 1995 an eight-acre lagoon of pig manure burst and dumped into the New River in North Carolina. According to Simon's *Meatonomics*, "it was the worst hazardous waste spill in North Carolina's history and one of the worst ever in the United States. After the spill, extraordinary levels of nitrogen and phosphorus in the New River caused persistent, toxic algal blooms and a massive hypoxic region—a dead zone in which oxygen levels were too low for the waterway's bass, trout, muskei, walleye, catfish, sunfish, and bluegill to breathe. The incident killed ten million fish and closed five hundred square miles of wetlands to shellfishing" (111). These seemingly separate forms of farming, and different species of farmed animals, are actually intertwined in many ways.

Grazing cattle provide another example of how the lives of livestock interact with those of other animals as grazing puts added pressure on the diminished beaver populations. It is hard to return the beaver, and so improve the rivers for the fish, when the cattle remove the food the beavers need. As Lichatowich notes, "riparian zones once consisted of extensive galleries of cottonwoods and willows—food for beavers, which the grazing cattle have all but eliminated. 'Cows and beavers don't mix.'" (56). In the next few chapters I turn to cattle to show the long and complex history of importing livestock to the United States, to discuss the impact of livestock on Native Americans and the land, and to explore the ways human relationships with livestock can be improved.

CHAPTER THREE

Beef Cattle

ANIMAL WELFARE AND
LEOPOLD'S LAND ETHIC

"Beef: It's What's For Dinner."
"Beef: It's What You Want."
"Beef: Real Food for Real People."

These three advertising slogans from the Beef Council are all designed around the idea that beef is central to what one eats and who one is. In fact, beef consumption has been in decline in the United States. According to the United States Department of Agriculture (USDA) website, U.S. annual consumption increased from 28.1 to 25.5 billion pounds over the last seven years. In 2014 people in the United States moved from eating beef more than any other meat to eating chicken more than any other meat. Most attribute this change to a combination of health concerns on the part of consumers and rising beef prices (which reflect rising corn prices). This means the United States still averages about fifty pounds of beef per person per year—not an insignificant amount of consumption.

While the U.S. population may consume less beef than they did before, this in no way diminishes the cultural role of beef and cattle in the United States. Whether it is hamburger or high-end steak, beef is seen as "real food for real people"—well, actually, real food for real men. Beef has been, and despite advertising efforts continues to be, linked to masculinity. While the Beef Council has aimed many of its advertisements toward women, even those ads are based on the premise that women can join the world of men by eating beef, and just a brief look at the rest of the advertising tells a different story. Women are more the object of consumption, rather than the consumer. From

Hardee's numerous ads using images of highly sexualized women eating burgers and dripping with sauce to Burger King's "It'll Blow Your Mind Away" print ad to Carl Jr.'s ad with the X-Men female shapeshifter transforming into a man when she eats a burger, it's pretty clear who the burgers are for and who the intended audience is.

Ecofeminist theorist Carol Adams has written a great deal on the links between masculinity and meat—and beef in particular. She notes that the "association between attractive human female bodies and delectable, attractive flesh appeals to the appetitive desires as they have been constructed in the dominant culture in which we interpret images from a stance of male identification and human-centeredness. Thus, animals who are available for corpse eating are represented in one menu as doing the cancan. In such an image...animals become neither man nor beast, but are rendered as consumable feminine entertainment" (Adams, *Neither Man Nor Beast* 30–31). Real men consume meat and real men consume women. Not surprisingly, then, the cowboy has long been used in advertising beef. Many of the ads show images of cowboys, while others use the voices of actors who have played cowboys. The cowboy, and the image of cattle grazing on the range, are part of the allure of beef. But the majority of cattle do not spend many months there anymore, and cowboys have been replaced by computers.

The history of cattle in the United States is long, as cattle were among the first animals transported from Europe by colonists. In the Northeast in the 1600s, the first cattle were mostly Devons from England. This was a very old, dual-purpose breed, used for both beef and milk. Devons were known for their thriftiness—their ability to fatten under normal feeding practices—and as good draft animals. There were also Danish cattle and some from the Spanish West Indies (Bidwell and Falconer 22). In the South, the first livestock came to the Mississippi region (probably with the Spanish), and by 1619 there were some two hundred cattle in the area (Bidwell and Falconer 19). By the 1700s numbers in both regions were on the rise from increased importation and domestic breeding. There were legal limits on the number of cattle that could be slaughtered so that there would be enough left for breeding (79). Whereas in 1684 there were four hundred cattle slaughtered in the Northeast, in 1698 that figure was three thousand. In the Northeast cattle were grazed on common pastures, but by 1747 soil depletion was noted, and pressure from land development pushed the cattle west (Bidwell and Falconer 57, 70). In the South, livestock were mostly free-range. Here, property owners legally had to fence out livestock rather than fence them in on their property. This system entailed more loss to predation, some hunting by Native Americans, and increased theft (Gray 138–45). To help prevent theft, animals were marked, registered, and checked at sale. As the numbers increased there also began to be some regulation of the range—ten cattle per one hundred acres. Generally, however, there was not much focus on the health of the land. As in the Northeast, grazing land began to disappear and the practice of confining and feeding cattle started to grow (143, 198, 200).

The 1800s saw increased interest in stock societies, fairs, and shows as efforts to "improve" cattle began. A cattle show in Lexington, Kentucky, in 1816 was the first west of "the mountains" (784), and by 1822 Ohio had an institute to train farmers (which would later become a state agricultural school). Ohio had become a cattle state because it was close enough to the growing eastern market that cattle could be driven there on the hoof. While the growing industry in the East provided demand for the meat and milk (with fewer people there keeping animals of their own), it also took up the bulk of the labor supply. Finding themselves shorthanded, farmers sought to improve the breeds and so get more meat, milk, or both per animal (Bidwell and Falconer 194, 178–79). As part of this effort, in the North they imported Herefords, Devons, Alderneys, Guernseys, and improved Durhams (shorthorned) (220). The shorthorned Durhams (known as Teeswater cattle until they were imported to Virginia in 1783) were developed in England in the 1600s and, like the Devons, were known as being good milk, meat, and draft animals. By 1854 imports of these cattle to the United States were largely focused on beef production, and crosses with the Spanish longhorns (to improve that breed) made them an important part of the U.S. beef industry. The American Shorthorn Association was established in 1872 ("Shorthorn Cattle").

Of these early imports, along with the shorthorn, the Hereford was and is among the most influential in the United States. The Hereford was developed in 1742 in England and the first breeding herd came to New York in 1840. These cattle were tough, thrived on limited grass, and kept their weight during drives and transportation by railcar. They were often crossed with other cattle to improve the stock, but by 1881 breeders established the American Hereford Association, which promoted the breed. Through its attention to stock selection and breeding, the association has done much to change the beef industry as a whole ("Breeds of Livestock—Hereford Cattle"). Farmers in the South bought improved stock from northern farmers. Many focused on the Devon, but some focused on breeds known as good dairy cows such as the Ayrshire and the Holderness. Others included the Lincolnshire, Herefords, and shorthorns (Gray 850).

The prevalence of Herefords and shorthorns can still be seen today. The first farm my students and I visited was one that raised horned Herefords, with some shorthorn and Angus breeding in the mix. At the time of our visit in 2008 (and still in 2016), Joann Hutton had twenty-eight cows, one bull, and twenty-four yearlings. Since she works the ranch by herself and wants to know her cattle, she keeps it small. She slaughters on a seasonal basis (late fall/ early winter), when the cattle are eighteen to twenty-two months old. Hutton comes from a fourth-generation cattle family and has been raising cattle since she was five. Unlike many in the industry today, she breeds her own stock and raises and feeds them from gestation to slaughter. She chose the Hereford breed because their temperament makes them easy to work with. They are good breeders who calve independently—that is, care for their calves without human help—an important trait for a one-woman operation. Being good for-agers, they were a good choice as she started with less than ideal land.

When we visited she told us her interconnectedness with the land and animals was important in shaping her practices. She took classes in holistic management before starting Grass Fed Beef–J. Hutton, based near Ellens-burg, Washington. Holistic management involves grazing livestock in a way that mimics the grazing of native wildlife. Hutton practices planned grass ro-tational grazing, moving pastures about once every three to ten weeks. This system allows the cattle to graze on the best forage, interrupts parasite cycles, and keeps the grasses healthy. During our visit she was particularly proud of the fact that the land—hardly surviving when she bought it—was now begin-ning to thrive. Her interests are not simply to see herself survive but to see the land thrive as well. This focus on the land is also noted on the Animal Welfare Approved website page describing her farm:

> Letting her pastures rest fully between grazing allows them to bloom, provid-ing food for pollinators, adding fertility to the soil and nutrients for her cattle, and helping to seed her pastures year after year. The key, she says, to improving pastures without using pesticides is to improve the soil. "First, focus on rais-ing many varieties of grasses and legumes, by proper watering and grazing," she says. "Test the soil regularly and check the types of weeds and other plants that are growing in the pasture. Check to see if there are pollinators, dung beetles, earthworms, reptiles, birds, raptors and other wildlife in the pastures and keep records." ("Grass Fed Beef")

Healthy cattle require healthy land; healthy land requires a complex healthy ecosystem. Hutton talked about the land having an energy she desired to know better in order to work *with* the land instead of against it. She has learned to observe and listen to the land—something she described as a feel-ing or spiritual practice. "Weeds," she said, "are there because the land needs them. Killing the weeds just kills the soil." Hutton is proud that her cattle graze on pastures that have never been treated with pesticides or chemical fertilizers. Using such products is "going to war with the land." She doesn't think it's healthy, and in the end it doesn't work. She made the observation that men (as opposed to women) assume they have "power and control" over nature. She thinks this attitude will be humanity's downfall. She was particularly proud that her land does well for her because she does *not* assume that she is in control of nonhuman nature. Instead she works with nature and sees her livestock as part of nature. The cattle have never been fed grain, given hormones or growth promoters, or treated with antibiotics. Instead of resorting to these methods, she has worked to promote healthy land as a way to produce healthy cattle.

Her ideas about the land have much in common with Aldo Leopold's land ethic. Leopold (1887–1948) argued that we must care for the land in order to flourish. Like Hutton, Leopold thought that our desire to control nature and make it into a commodity for human use and profit was the central problem facing society. He also thought that an overly individualistic mindset caused humans to miss the fact that they are members of the biotic community. While working for the Forest Service, Leopold saw the detrimental effects of the human impact on the environment. Soil erosion from overuse, damage from flooding caused by altering waterways, and loss of biodiversity from the introduction of invasive species all threatened to create a future with fewer natural resources. He was particularly concerned about farming. While farming was increasingly taking a "scientific" approach to "improving" soil, "eradicating" pests, and "controlling" weeds, Leopold suggested a more ecological approach. Like Hutton, he saw the land as a complex interactive system that one should get to know and work with rather than try to dominate and control. "Land, then, is not merely soil," he said. "It is a fountain of energy flowing through [an open] circuit" in which "some energy is dissipated in decay, some is added by absorption from the air, some is stored in soils, peats, and forests; but it is a sustained circuit, like a slowly augmented revolving fund of life" (*Sand County* 253). Leopold thought humans needed to see themselves as part of this community rather than as being outside of it.

Even more, he believed, humans need to recognize our dependence on the land. While humans might think they are in control, their role as an apex species means that the things that humans eat eat other things that eat other things and so on. Someone who eats a cow, for instance, is depending on the health of the cow. The cow depends on the health of the grass and water. The grass depends on the health of the water and soil. The soil depends on the health of insects and microbes. If humans poison insects and microbes, they are in fact poisoning themselves. If they eradicate the organisms who build the soil, they are undermining their own future as well. Leopold wrote, "We abuse land because we regard it as a commodity belonging to us. When we see land as a community to which we belong, we may begin to use it with love

and respect. There is no other way for land to survive the impact of mechanized man, nor for us to reap from it the esthetic harvest it is capable, under
science, of contributing to culture" (xviii–xix).

Leopold's concerns about the attempts to control and "improve" nature as
part of farming proved to be prophetic when the Dust Bowl drought occurred
in the Midwest from 1934 to 1941. The government responded by passing the
1934 Taylor Grazing Act (which created grazing districts and regulated grazing on public land to maintain the health and long-term usefulness of these
lands) and the 1935 Soil Conservation and Domestic Allotment Act (which
enacted changes in practice in order to conserve soil and ensure the future
production of food and fiber). I will discuss these acts more in the next chapter, but here it is enough to say that while they did attempt to push people to
think in the long term rather than focus only on immediate economic gain,
they still understood "the land" mainly as a resource humans could exploit if
they used science to control and improve it.

Leopold warned that the conservation strategy of the day "defines no right
or wrong, assigns no obligation, calls for no sacrifice, implies no change in
the current philosophy of values. In respect of land-use, it urges enlightened
self-interest" (208). He worried specifically about agriculture. In 1936 he wrote,
"Agriculture has assumed that by the indefinite pyramiding of new 'controls'
an artificial plant community can be substituted for the natural one. There
are omens that this assumption may be false. Pests and troubles in need of
control seem to be piling up even faster than new science and new dollars
for control work" (Callicott 278). In 1945 he pointed to two competing views
of the farm—it can be viewed as "a food-factory" and the criterion of its success as "salable products," or it can be viewed as a place and way to live, and
the criterion of success as "a harmonious balance between plants, animals,
and people; between the domestic and the wild; between utility and beauty"
(278). He wanted "a scientifically informed agro-ecology" (279). While artificial, such a system tries to mimic aspects of natural systems by including a diversity of species and utilizing the by-products of production to replenish the
system. It should use aspects of the natural ecosystem in which it is located.
"Agro-ecosystems . . . substantially reduce, if they do not eliminate altogether,
the application of chemical fertilizers and pesticides" (281).

Elaborating on Leopold's views, J. Baird Callicott's *Beyond the Land Ethic*
notes that the practices of modern agricultural threaten the survival of species and ecosystems. Soil, water, plants, and animals are all negatively impacted by the practices of plowing and irrigation; the use of chemical fertilizers and pesticides harms living organisms—farm workers and consumers as
well as the other-than-human parts of nature. He attributes the prevalence of
such practices to the dominance of a metaphysical view of nature as mechan-

ical: "On this chemico-mechanical conception of growing food, a chemico-mechanical conception of production technique is overlaid. Processes are reduced to their simplest elements as on an assembly line. Products are standardized; scale is magnified; and crops are specialized and monocultured. Food 'processing' is automated" (268). Like ecofeminists such as Carol Adams and Carolyn Merchant, he attributes much of this view to the philosophical views of Descartes and the notions of science that grew along with that view. Like Adams and Merchant (and Dewey) he suggests the need to get beyond the view of classical liberalism, which posits atomistic individuals in conflict as they pursue their own self-interest.

Specifically we need to understand the environment as more than the sum of its parts. The reductionist view needs to be replaced with a holistic view, and Callicott suggests four tenets of such a holistic view: (1) systematic wholes have emergent properties—"properties that are neither reducible to nor predictable from the properties of the parts"; (2) systems affect individuals—"when an individual organism is located in a particular ecosystem, the resulting phenotype is shaped partly by its genes and partly by its environment"; (3) parts are systemically related—"components of societies, organisms, and ecosystems are causally related to one another in multiple and interacting positive and negative feedback loops"; (4) parts are internally related—"they are what they are because of their relationships with one another" (273–75). Seeing "land" as a set of interrelated systems, involved in Deweyan "transactions," would challenge much about contemporary conventional farming, which is increasingly separated and specialized.

Leopold's concern for the "land" included concern for other animals, as they are members of the biotic community on which humans depend. In particular he developed a concern for wolves. Early in his life Leopold had hunted wolves as part of the government's wolf eradication program. As a hunter he saw wolves as competition and bought into the idea that eliminating the wolf would result in more big game for him to hunt. While he remained an avid hunter throughout his life, and sought to conserve nature primarily so that ecosystems would be healthy enough to ensure a variety of species to hunt, hunting wolves changed how he understood things. One particular encounter with a dying wolf (dying by his gun) and her dead and wounded pups was transformative: "We reached the old wolf in time to watch a fierce green fire dying in her eyes. I realized then and have known ever since that there was something new to me in those eyes, something known only to her and to the mountain. I was young then and full of trigger-itch; I thought that because fewer wolves meant more deer, that no wolves would mean hunters' paradise. But after seeing the green fire die, I sensed that neither the wolf nor the mountain agreed with such a view" (138–39). Leopold came to understand that the wolf played an important role in the health of the ecosystem and that the wolf had a life of its own that deserved respect. As wolf eradication proceeded, Leopold saw deer and elk herds grow in size and forests become decimated: "I now suspect that just as a deer herd lives in mortal fear of its wolves, so does a mountain live in mortal fear of its deer. And perhaps with better cause, for while a buck pulled down by wolves can be replaced in two or three years, a range pulled down by too many deer may fail of replacement in as many decades." Leopold went on to connect his observation with cattle ranchers as well: "So also with cows. The cowman who cleans his range of wolves does not realize that he is taking over the wolf's job of trimming the herd to fit the range. He has not learned to think like a mountain. Hence we have dustbowls, and rivers washing the future into the sea" (147). The desire to protect livestock from predation was, and is still, a central threat to the lives of many nonhuman predator species. I will discuss the relationship between livestock and wolves more in the final chapter, but here I would like to point out that raising animals for humans to kill and eat has always meant finding ways to keep those livestock animals safe from other animals who would also eat them (as already discussed in chapter 2 with regard to fish). In this sense, many ranchers find themselves "at war" with those predators, even as they protect and care for livestock animals. That was evident when we visited Hutton.

When we arrived at Hutton's ranch she invited us into her house. One of the first things she said to us was, "My rifle's in the laundry room and the safety's off." While my mind flashed to the safety of the students (as in the boat), she explained that a raccoon had been killing her cats and she intended to be ready to kill it. For Hutton all animals are part of the natural system in which we live. She had a strong relationship with her dog, Jo, and her twelve remaining cats. When the raccoon next came through the cat door she ended its life. Since then she has experimented with ways of discouraging the raccoons from coming around the house and her cats. She didn't like the idea of killing a raccoon, but she needed to protect herself, her dog, and her cats. A similar tension can be found between her business of killing cattle and her caring very much about their happiness and well-being while they are alive. She told us of her interest in various animal welfare standards. She is now certified by Animal Welfare Approved. When asked whether she thought the standards went far enough, she said they went "further than most are ready to go."

The standards for the Animal Welfare Approved certification are extensive. They begin by requiring farmers to be committed to the health of the land, the animals, and their local community. Some of the highlights include the following: that animals must be raised on pasture or range; that animals never be fed animal by-products; that hormones or growth promoters never be used; that animals be seen and attended to regularly; that animals be slaughtered in an approved facility; and that animals be able to express natural social behaviors and undertake natural physical activities. The well-being of the animal must come before its marketability, so if it is in need of treatment with antibiotics they must be administered. Not treating sick and injured animals is grounds for removal. Euthanasia must be performed if pain and suffering cannot be alleviated.

The bulk of the standards, though, are species-specific—recognizing that different animal beings have different needs. The Animal Welfare Approved (AWA) standards say, "All standards address every aspect of each species' lifecycle needs from birth to death" ("Standards"). Their standards for beef cattle deserve a brief description so that they can be contrasted with more common practices used in the beef industry today. For beef cattle one of the first standards is that the breed used must be appropriate to the use and to the environmental conditions of range life. Cloned or genetically engineered stock are prohibited, as are any breeding practices that have negative health impacts. No use of artificial insemination or embryo transfer is allowed, and the cows must be capable of independent live births. The farmer must work with a qualified expert to develop a health plan that focuses on preventive care and addresses nutrition, pasture management, manure management, and the avoidance of stress. The cattle must be kept in stable social groups. Calves should be reared by their mothers and not weaned until eight months of age; weaning should occur as naturally as possible. Tail-docking and dehorning are not allowed in cattle, but castration and disbudding (the inhibition of horn growth) are allowed within certain parameters. Ear cuts and branding are prohibited, though ear tags and tattoos are permitted.

There are general directions that the cattle must have access to sufficient food and water, free from competition. Importantly, however, the standards acknowledge that there are differences from farm to farm: "A pasture management plan must be in place that addresses the specific farm site" and ensures clean, nutritional pasture that is not overgrazed or otherwise eroded. No specific grazing method is mandated. In extreme weather conditions housing of the animals is permitted, with specific requirements for bedding, light, and ventilation. The livestock must be protected from predators. The use of guard dogs and live traps is allowed for this purpose. Rats and mice must be controlled, though some methods of control are prohibited. Any dogs used for guarding or herding purposes must be kept and handled according to AWA standards as well. Cattle must be handled in a calm manner, with no use of electric prods or abuse. Transportation of cattle must limit stress, not expose them to extreme weather, and not exceed eight hours (unless no approved slaughterhouse is available at that distance). No injured or sick animals, or young calves, may be transported. No cattle can be sold to feeder operations.

On-site slaughter in a mobile unit is preferred and AWA is working to make that more available. Their requirements for slaughterhouses include calm, non-abusive handling, safe flooring, appropriate lighting and ventilation, limited noise to reduce stress, and complete stunning. Hutton became Animal Welfare Approved because their philosophy matches her own: "I am trying to do what is best for the animals—including people—and the earth—from the soil to the air. Letting nature do the work, by harvesting the solar energy, makes my life more enjoyable" ("Grass Fed Beef").

Hutton refers to her connection with her cattle as something akin to ESP, saying that she can be away from the animals and know she is needed. She attributes this ability to a kinesthetic personality and the quiet and solitude of the land she lives on with her cats and cattle. While she is concerned about animal welfare, and very attuned to her cattle, she does hold the opinion that "these animals are sacrificing themselves for us." She views animals as having legitimate lives that humans must respect. Since she truly believes that the animals are sacrificing themselves, when she says that an animal gives its life for human use, she does not mean to imply that humans have the right to dominate other animals. Humans must respect other animals while they live and when they die. When we went out in the field, she discussed different individuals. When our presence started to make the cattle uneasy we left the field. We were able to look around and ask questions, but she did not want our visit to disturb the cattle.

One of her main concerns at the time of our visit was the slaughter of her cattle. With the increasing centralization of meat processing over the last sixty years, the number of slaughterhouses declined. Between 1980 and 1999 the number of slaughter plants for cattle in the United States decreased from more than 600 to about 170 ("Summary of Meat Processing"). Most will not take in the smaller number of animals from independent producers like Hutton. This means increased transportation time for the animals. Transportation is stressful, and various weather conditions can cause them to suffer in a number of ways. Hutton is lucky to be located fairly close to the Livestock Processing Cooperative in Odessa, Washington, but her cattle still have to travel a minimum of 120 miles to a slaughterhouse. This was something she wanted to change but it's hard for the small abattoirs to compete and stay in business.

Hutton's ranch represents an alternative to the main beef industry in the United States. Little about the life of her cattle—other than the end they meet—is shared by the animals that provide the beef found in most stores and restaurants. The AWA standards are at odds with most current mainstream practices and require that the cattle produced under their standards do not emerge from mainstream production or end their lives in that system. While Hutton is working with cattle bred to excel in beef production, she has chosen not to participate in the increasing specialization of cattle and the increasing segmentation of the life and death of cattle. A little more history will help provide a fuller understanding of most contemporary beef production.

Along with the diversity of breeds imported to the United States in the 1800s, there also came increasing specialization. Cattle that were dual-purpose began to be crossed with the goal of creating cows that were better at producing either milk or beef. This was seen as a way to increase output and profit. In addition to improving the stock, farmers looked to husbandry practices as a way to increase their profit. While grazing cattle requires less input of labor from the farmer, it results in limited weight gain and it takes longer for the cattle to fatten. So the practice of grazing cattle on specifically grown crop lands began to increase. Eventually this moved to confining the cattle and bringing the food to them, but more on that later. The point here is that as the East Coast became more settled and industrialized, farming and grazing were pushed west. Grazing was largely not compatible with farming since animals damage crops. So livestock were pushed even further west. This migration was enabled by the development of railroads, which made it possible to ship the cattle to market rather than drive them on the hoof.

Beef cattle are part of the mythology of the West, along with the horse, cowboys, and American Indians. In fact the stories of these groups are very intertwined. In her book *Creatures of Empire: How Domestic Animals Transformed Early America*, Virginia DeJohn Anderson argues that the cattle the European settlers brought and bred disrupted the American Indians' way of life and understanding of the world. Cattle transformed the local flora and fauna and so interfered with Native hunting and cultivation practices; they introduced new parasites and diseases with which both the Native peoples and other native animal beings had to contend; they confounded the Indians' understanding of other animal beings. For the Indians, other animal beings were powerful spirits in their own right, not things that could be owned. The first cattle (and other livestock) brought by the settlers were mostly allowed to roam freely because the settlers did not have the wherewithal to fence and feed them. And yet if an Indian killed one of these beings, they were punished for violating someone's property rights. The early colonists would often send their cattle ahead of them into Indian territory they wanted to settle and use any killing or theft of the cattle as an excuse to do violence to the Indians. In this way, the cattle who were initially intended by settlers to serve as way to help "civilize" the Native populations by helping them learn to settle down and be industrious farmers actually served to further disrupt and unsettle them. Anderson writes, "As it became clear that colonists intended for Indian livestock-keeping to spawn a host of other changes, the animals provoked even more native resentment than what was already generated by the creatures' prodigious ability to make nuisances of themselves. Symbols of civility to the English, livestock threatened to become symbols of cultural annihilation to Indians" (206).

As European settlement pushed west, farms replaced the rangeland where ranchers grazed their cattle and sheep. The "removal" of Native peoples, and the bison on which they depended, was seen as necessary in order to make room for the cattle. Edward E. Dale published *The Range Cattle Industry* in 1930. There he wrote, "As population increased settlers advanced steadily westward, pushing before them not only the Indians but also those livestock raisers who wished to keep near the border of settlement in order to pasture their animals on the unoccupied and unclaimed lands beyond. . . . For a century and more it was there, a kind of twilight zone with the light of civilization behind it, and the darkness of savagery before. The livestock raisers could not move too rapidly nor push too far out into the wilderness because of the savage tribes of Indians that occupied it" (xii–xiv). When the book was reissued in 1960 as *The Range Cattle Industry: Ranching on the Great Plains from 1865 to 1925* he repeated this statement. This is not surprising, as it wasn't until the 1960s and 1970s that growing American Indian activism began to change how non-Natives wrote about Native Americans and the genocide of Native Americans. It does, however, provide a look at how the story of the West was, and often still is, told and understood. General Nelson Miles, a military leader in the late 1800s who was involved in the massacre at Wounded Knee (1877), said, "When we get rid of the Indians and buffalo, the cattle . . . will fill this country" (Rifkin 73). As Native Americans and bison were seen to stand in the way of the cattle industry, today environmentalists and various endangered species are seen to do the same.

According to Dale, in the 1800s, constraints posed by the shrinking of what was perceived as unoccupied (and so available) land pushed ranchers to "reduce their herds and market animals at an earlier age to feeders in the corn belt to be finished for market on grain" (xiv). When cattle were driven to market, they lost weight on the long walk, and so it was common to fatten them up on corn right before going to market to help mitigate the lost value. As the corn belt expanded it became more profitable for ranchers to sell their cattle to a feeder in the Midwest who would then market the cattle. The industry started to separate into specialties: the raiser, the grazier, the feeder, and the packer. Stall-fed cattle became common. By 1860 the railroads made it possible to move the grazing cattle further west and still have them return east to fatten and kill. By 1891 Chicago, the railroad hub, was the packing center of the nation. Texas and Missouri became prime sources of cattle, while Illinois and Iowa became cattle-feeding centers (Bidwell and Falconer 391, 397–98).

With railroad transport removing the need to focus on the hardiness to survive the drive to market, breeding of cattle began to focus on other traits, such as faster maturity. This meant it became profitable to slaughter cattle at younger and younger ages. This could again make it possible to raise some cattle on grass and give the range cattle industry new life. According to Dale, this created two parts to "cow country": cattle were bred in Texas, New Mexico, and the Indian Territory (present-day Oklahoma) and then they grazed in the central and northern plains in Kansas, Nebraska, the Dakotas, Montana, Wyoming, and Colorado (71). Ironically, this system profited from U.S. government contracts to supply meat for the Indians who could no longer hunt for themselves due to policies set by that same government. As refrigeration became possible in the 1880s, U.S. beef became a craze in England, and cattle interests grew in size and power—for example, the Wyoming Stock Growers Association operated as a part of the territorial government (Dale 102). With the pressure for land on which to graze cattle increasing, many ranchers moved cattle onto Indian and public lands—sometimes with permission, often without. When President Cleveland ordered cattle removed from these lands it resulted in the overstocking of already highly grazed lands. Combined with a bad winter in 1886–87, the overstocking resulted in many dead cattle. Ranchers had to decrease the number of cattle and increase the amount of feed and care provided to them. Again, improved stock was needed to make this a profitable arrangement (108–11).

Dale remarks that when the Indian Territory was opened to settlement in 1889, the cattle being grazed there had nowhere to go: "When the great Indian reservations were opened to settlement it is popularly believed that the land was taken from the Indian and given to the white man. As a matter of fact the Indian did not use the land so as an economic factor in the history of the region is negligible. The man who really used these lands was the ranchman, and what really happened in the opening of the large Indian reservations to settlement was that the land was taken from the cattleman and given to the farmer, or its use changed by governmental action from grazing stock to the growing of crops" (156). Blind to his dismissal of Indian rights and culture, Dale focuses only on the loss of space for grazing cattle. As pasture became too expensive, corn states became the feeding ground for cattle. He writes, "Forced off the Indian lands, these cattle must either be marketed or thrown upon the already over-stocked ranges of the North. The scarcity and increased cost of pasturage brought the ranchmen of the plains into still closer relationship with the corn belt. Instead of attempting to mature and fatten animals for market upon the grass alone, they began more and more to ship young steers to the corn belt to be finished upon hay and corn" (113). A division of labor was set in place with one region rearing cattle and another fattening them for market. Given increasing land prices, it was cheaper for those in the feeding region to pay the freight to ship the cattle than to raise them themselves. Both groups desired better breeding to help increase their profit. They wanted breeding that, on the one hand, would produce cattle that grew larger faster, and, on the other, would allow the cattle to put fat on easily.

To do this, breeders focused on high-grade shorthorns and the hardy qualities of Herefords—the very cattle we saw on Hutton's ranch. With "better" breeding and the feeding of corn, slaughter weights went up even as slaughter age went down. Slaughter ages went from five or seven years old down to two (162). Feeding no corn or other grains, Hutton slaughters at eighteen to twenty-two months of age. These changes in breeding and feeding were just the start of a major shift in the U.S. cattle industry. One of the effects of the change was a fattier, more marbled meat that people like to eat. The corn diet, however, has consequences for the cattle and for the humans who eat them. Some ranchers, like Hutton, have tried to provide an alternative for both the cattle and the consumer. Two other operations that try to do things differently are those of Lee and Joe Markholt—uncle and nephew.

Lee Markholt raises organic cattle near Tacoma, Washington. His choices about how to farm were influenced by his concerns for the health of the land and for the health of the people eating his animals. When speaking about his motivation for switching from a conventional to an organic ranch he said that it was important to maintain a balance between humans and the earth, thereby creating "better" or reciprocal conditions: "It is better for both human health and earth health." He wanted to use methods that were radically different from the chemicalization and artificialization common in commercial, corporate U.S. agriculture. He said, "Better taste, better for the earth, healthier—one turns the clock back fifty years with organic. Better than 'advancement.'"

His operation is unusual in that the cattle's whole lives are spent under the care of one set of people. The broodstock live a few counties south of Lee's meat shop and ranch. He has one Piedmontese bull and a herd of Angus breeding cows there. His pastures have been certified organic for over fifteen years. When it becomes necessary, the cattle eat certified organic hay from eastern Washington. This is a big expense, with the organic hay costing $605 per ton versus $150 per ton for nonorganic hay. Their diet is supplemented only with oats and barley, which he feeds so that he can move the cattle from pasture to pasture calmly and on his own. (When we went out into the field, Lee was immediately surrounded by friendly cattle who took an interest in meeting us.) There is straw in the barn where the cattle can go for shelter. This straw is also certified organic—just in case they eat it. With a closed herd he has had no need to inoculate any of his cattle. While the brood cows are allowed to be wormed in the third trimester, Lee had not wormed in the four years prior to our visit. He uses fecal tests to monitor his cattle and rotates them among his pastures to cut the parasite cycle. Lee's farm was one of the first twenty in the state of Washington to be certified organic. He noted that there is a lot of bureaucracy involved in being certified organic, but he thinks it's worth it.

The main reason Lee promotes organic products is human health. "Humans can't be healthy unless the land on which their food is produced is also healthy." Over the last decade or so there has been growing criticism of how food is produced in the United States. As Peter Singer (along with many others) points out, the standard American diet is heavy in meat, sugar, and fat; we consume large amounts of processed foods and fast food. Films like *Supersize Me, King Corn, Forks over Knives,* and *Food, Inc.* have all served to raise public awareness. Some concerns are environmental—depletion of topsoil, contamination of water with chemicals and manure, use of water and oil in production, and the clearing of forests for crop production and grazing to name a few. Some concerns focus on the well-being of animals: the level of confinement in Concentrated Animal Feeding Operations (CAFOs), the inability of livestock to express natural physical and social behaviors, unnatural and unhealthful diets, and the pain and suffering involved in transport and slaughter. Still others focus on human health: the chemicals used in producing food (herbicides, pesticides, fertilizers), the use of hormones and antibiotics, increasing reliance on genetically modified organisms (GMOs), and various foodborne illnesses and diseases.

Some of these concerns overlap. It turns out that if one is concerned about getting sick from the meat one eats, one should probably pay attention to the welfare of meat animals while they are alive. Some of the main concerns connected to beef include E. coli 0157:H7 and Bovine Spongiform Encephalopathy (BSE)—better known as "mad cow disease." These have been highly publicized and much discussed. Most people became aware of E. coli 0157:H7 when it sickened and killed people in 1993—starting with a Jack in the Box in western Washington not far from Lee's ranch. E. coli from corn-fed cattle is resistant to acid and so more dangerous to humans. It turns out that feeding cows corn changes the pH balance in their stomachs, causing acidosis. The rumen (that is, the first section of a cow's stomach) can then ulcerate and allow bacteria to enter the bloodstream. This allows the virulent strain of E. coli to populate the cattle and increase the risk of contamination of the meat during the slaughter process. Further, since most of these cattle are housed in confined feedlots, they stand in each other's manure and pass the organism around the herd. Manure gets caked on the hides of the cattle as well. Given the speed at which slaughter lines work, it is not hard for the E. coli to get on the meat from either the hide or the stomach. Once it is on some part of the meat it can be spread further if that meat goes for hamburger. In the highly centralized slaughter industry we now have, one hamburger usually contains meat from at least one hundred cattle. So a few cattle can contaminate a very large quantity of meat. Interestingly, the response to the 1993 outbreak was new regulations for processing and cooking hamburger meat. There were few if any suggestions for changing how we feed, house, or slaughter cattle. Mad cow disease changed that to some extent. BSE is a variant of the human Creutzfeldt-Jacob disease known as vCJD. There is also a variant currently found in farmed elk. The origins of the disease are found in a longtime disease of sheep called scrapie. Although the first case of BSE in UK cattle was recorded in 1986, the first signs of a problem came in the 1990s, not long after there was an outbreak of hoof and mouth disease. Eventually it was determined that feeding practices had included feeding animal parts to cattle. Since cattle are herbivores this qualifies as an unnatural diet.

Less ominous-sounding than mad cow disease and E. coli 0157:H7, but equally troubling to many, is the ubiquitous use of antibiotics and other growth promoters in cattle-feeding operations. There is growing concern about the overuse of antibiotics in livestock production resulting in antibiotic-resistant strains of microbes. There is also concern about trace levels of antibiotics and hormones in meat causing health issues. It is interesting that just as humans are experiencing rising levels of food allergies and sensitivities, the same seems to be true of many dogs and cats who are fed products made from industrial livestock.

This account provides a picture of some of the motivations people have for raising and consuming organic cattle. It is important to note, though, that organic certification for beef requires no particular attention to most issues of animal welfare. The organic label is focused on what does and does not go into the cattle—food and medications. To yield meat that can be labeled organic, they cannot eat food that was produced using synthetic fertilizers and pesticides, and they cannot be given antibiotics and hormones. Often, in order to keep the cattle alive and healthy without the use of antibiotics and hormones it is necessary to raise fewer cattle and allow them a more natural environment. But this is not required and does not always happen. The animals used to produce organic meat (and dairy products) can be raised in very confined conditions that frustrate their natural physical and social behaviors even though organic standards call for the accommodation of natural behaviors such as grazing. And, in the end, most still end up at USDA-approved slaughterhouses where the meat will be mixed with that of feedlot cattle more likely exposed to lethal E. coli and BSE. Salmonella, campylobacter, and listeria can also be added to the list. According to the USDA, in 2014 there were ninety-eight meat recalls (these are voluntary)—for a total of 18,675,102 pounds of meat. There have been numerous meat recalls in 2015, one of which involved 13.5 tons of beef. Recalls are common enough that they are reported on the news as just an ordinary event.

Concerned about his health, Lee no longer drinks or uses Copenhagen. Ironically, he also eats less beef. But he wants good meat when he does eat it, as do his customers. He said films like *Food, Inc.* have increased his customer base and made them more informed. Since his customers are educated about the food industry there are few questions or complaints about the higher prices for his meat. Since they are informed, though, they do have questions about how he treats the land and the animals. "One's word must be backed by practice," he says. The animals' well-being is a concern, and health (of both human and other animal beings) is important too.

In responding to our first question about how he views the human relationship with nature, Lee spoke of a human partnership with nature: we have a responsibility to "treat this great earth with respect." "Pure, wholesome, natural food" is good: good for us, and good for the earth. He tested the meat from his cattle once and found that it was close to salmon for providing omega-3 fatty acids. Grass-fed meat is generally lower than grain-fed meat in total fat and saturated fat. It is also higher in omega-3 fatty acids, which are considered helpful with heart disease, rheumatoid arthritis, and depression. Given these benefits, Lee can make a profit with a niche market and remain committed to his principles. The formation and implementation of a philosophy or set of beliefs is very important to Lee. He noted that economic sustenance through farming is difficult. He believes that conventional farming is "on the way out" but organic farming is here to stay. The "economic recession" proved difficult (we visited in 2010), but with the exception of the previous two years Lee had turned a profit and hoped to do so again soon.

To help make a profit, Lee ran The Meat Shop of Tacoma. Here he cut his meat, processed wild game, and sold organic products from other farmers. So while he no longer raises pigs or chickens for meat, he sells pork and chicken produced by others who share his principles. He sells cheese from Organic Valley (a cooperative of family-owned farms who focus on producing organic dairy products and eggs). He also sold eggs from his own hens—four dollars a dozen. Unlike their counterparts in commercial egg operations, Lee's chickens eat an organic feed, and he keeps the hens "until they expire." He said a prolific egg-layer lays about two hundred eggs per year (as opposed to "an egg a day" in most commercial operations).

When it's time to take the animals to slaughter, Lee said, he tries not to think about the animals or the process. To help reduce the stress for the cattle, Lee helped start the cooperative USDA-approved mobile slaughter truck in Pierce County, Washington. He uses that truck to slaughter his cattle whenever he can. He usually slaughters about six cattle at a time when they are eighteen to twenty-four months old and said he'd never get involved with veal calves. He feels attached to his land and his animals, and many have names. While he repeated that he didn't like to think about it, he did say, "This process involves killing. It *is* killing." Seeming to sum up his commitment, the following quotation hung on a sign in the meat shop:

> Have a heart that never hardens, a temper that never tires,
> and a touch that never hurts.   —CHARLES DICKENS

However, this can be a hard philosophy to live by when dealing out death. Like Hutton's, Lee's operation faces the tension between raising animals to kill them and treating them well while they're alive—and it again raises the issue of killing some animals in order to protect livestock. Reminding me of our visit with Hutton, Lee told us about a raccoon who had gone after his chickens; he "ended" its life with his thirty-thirty. Protecting the well-being of his livestock entails harming other animals. In the end, what he does means the death of cattle and chickens. Before that death, however, he tries to use "a touch that never hurts." Most of his cattle are naturally polled (born without horns), so he does not dehorn. He does use ear tags for identification and to let him know who each one's mother is (ear tags are permitted by the AWA standards Hutton uses). He moves them between pastures and onto and off trucks with grain, not cattle prods. He talks with them when he's out in the field and "gives them a good scratch."

His story adds another twist. The money to start his organic, grass-fed beef operation—a business that respects the land and animals—comes from working in construction, logging, bull-riding, and bull-wrestling. He also raises racing quarter horses. When we asked how he felt about the treatment of the bulls (and other cattle) in rodeos he expressed that he did not have concerns. He noted that they travel a lot but since the animals are worth a lot they are treated well. He said they "get accustomed to that way of life." This demonstrates the complexity of the moral issues regarding animals and the environment. Lee's ability to embark on this grass-fed beef business relied on practices many see as exploiting the land and environment (logging and construction) and exploiting other animal beings for entertainment (racing and rodeos).

Joe Markholt is Lee's nephew and often helped his uncle with his business at the Meat Shop. He also helps train his uncle's race horses. Joe is a specialist in butchering and cutting meat and raises some twenty-five beef cattle of his own. They are Limousine, Angus, shorthorn, and Hereford crosses, chosen for their calm temperament, height (they can clear brush), and hardiness. Along with his wife, Sona, they run Salmon Creek Meats in Mossy Rock, Washing-

PHOTO 1. Cattle at Salmon Creek Meats. Photo by Sona Markholt.

ton. Since our visit with Lee, he has closed The Meat Shop. He still raises organic grass-fed cattle, though, and sells them through Salmon Creek Meats. Another family connection is that Joe too was a bull rider and still judges local bull-riding events. He also uses his knowledge of anatomy, garnered from his meat-cutting experience, to the advantage of horses in equine massage. By combining the massage business with cutting meat for customers and selling the meat from his own cattle, he and his wife make a living. There are several motivations for the work they do: one motivation, as it is for Lee, is a focus on human health; another is to provide themselves and their daughter with a certain kind of life. They live in a beautiful spot, and their daughter Uriah rides the ranch horses in roping and barrel-racing competitions. While we stood in the field with the cattle, Joe talked about the importance of preserving open spaces and knowing the origin of one's food. As their website says, their central belief is "Respect your body, respect the animal, respect the earth you are borrowing."

PHOTO 2. Cattle at Salmon Creek Meats. Photo by Sona Markholt.

Their cattle are not certified organic since the cost and bureaucracy is prohibitive. Joe said that if your customers know you well and know your practices, that is more important than any label: "Often a label can be just for
show; the practice is the most important thing." The cattle are out on pasture;
Joe grows the hay they eat when they need it. Like his uncle, he does not dehorn his cattle. He said, "Dehorning is more stressful than castration." He does
tip their horns, however. As opposed to dehorning, which removes the entire
horn either by a band or using a tool that slices through the base of the horn,
tipping involves using a handsaw at the point of the horn that is 1.25 inches in
diameter to remove only the tip. While the procedure causes some discomfort, studies have shown it is much less than that involved in dehorning. He
castrates the cattle using bands and does it at a young age—something most
animal welfare standards allow. He contrasted this with the pain the cattle feel
when banded at six months—a common industry practice. He weans them at
six months of age and tries to limit the stress of that event. He moves his cattle
among several pastures, and during the summer "they go up the mountain."
Joe uses horses to move his cattle and to go up to check on them. Predation is
a risk, but one of the reasons he has the cattle he does is that they can and will
protect their young. Mountain lions, coyotes, and wolves are known to be in

the area, but with a herd, the risk of loss is limited. The elk share the pastures with cattle—coming and going as they please. While several of the farmers we interviewed have put up fences to keep the elk out, Joe did not. He noted that "it takes a lot of time and money to build a fence to deter elk, and they have a right to be out there too." He enjoys seeing them. "It's all about balance. A few wolves can be a good thing—they keep the elk numbers down." He does worry that government regulations sometimes go too far, though, and "too many wolves gets out of balance, too."

Since Joe does not sell his meat in the way most people these days buy meat, he has a close relationship with his customers. Most of his customers come out to his place to pick up their meat. This is because Joe sells the cattle live. This is a legal option used by smaller farmers. If customers buy the cattle "on the hoof," then they can pay Joe to have it slaughtered and the meat cut. This entails buying a whole animal, or going in on shares—a half or a quarter. Joe said that he grew up farming, working with horses, riding bulls, and cutting meat. It's the life he knows. He's glad he's been able to share that life with his daughter as "this type of farming is the only way to go. It's a lot of work—haying, fencing, butchering—but it's good work." It allows his family to live in a beautiful spot, do the things they like to do, and they always have food. In addition to the beef and chicken they raise, they have three goats (all of whom have names), which they used to use for milking. Sona grows produce and they have fruit trees. They raised broiler chickens for five years. The barn, which held one thousand chickens at a time, is still there. Doing the slaughtering and processing on that scale did not fit the lifestyle they had in mind, but he didn't think the chickens suffered. "They live in the moment," he said. But the mess and the hours were not worth it.

Joe would not want to raise cattle on the industrial model. He said, "The feedlots are not pretty places to be—for cattle or humans. You don't get to know your animals." The cattle at Salmon Creek Meats have names and the people all have relationships with them. When it's time to butcher them, it's a sad day. Joe talked about the reaction of his daughter when she was very young. She cried and would not speak with him for days—that was hard for him. But now she is part of the operation and understands how it is possible to love and care for animals even as one uses them. "We're on top of the food chain," he said. "That's how it's always been. It's fine to choose to not eat meat. I've got no problem with that. But it's natural for us to eat meat." He noted that often the reasons people choose not to eat meat include how the animals are treated and what goes into them. Those aren't an issue on his ranch, though. He is happy to see more alternatives developing and lasting, maintaining that the industrial system of raising cattle is bad for the humans who eat the meat, bad for the humans who raise the cattle, and bad for the cattle and the land.

He believes that "inexpensive meat" is bad all the way around and it is not sustainable. It is also part of a system of government (USDA) and corporations that limits people's choices. Choice is an important issue for Joe, but the choices need to be meaningful: "Big organic is just words. Most certification just creates another bureaucracy and does little for the land and the animals. But that doesn't mean this kind of ranching can't feed more people."

When asked whether this kind of ranching was sustainable on a large scale, Joe pointed to Country Natural Beef. This is a cooperative of ranchers who share a philosophy. Their webpage leads with "Our Product is More than Beef." Like Joe, they talk about the relationship among the health of the people, the land, and the cattle. Their billboards depict the wildlife that coexists with their cattle. They also discuss the importance of relationships with consumers: "Our consumers know where the cattle come from, and they know the people who produce it. . . . They know what the producers' land ethics are. They know the product will taste good every time. They know that the cattle are treated well. They know that we embrace humane animal-handling practices" ("The Country Natural Beef Story"). Like Joe and Lee, they have a desire to work with educated customers to find economically and ecologically sustainable ways to produce beef. The ranchers choose breeds of cattle adapted to their local conditions and capable of birthing calves on their own. The ranchers get training on low-stress handling techniques, and, when possible, this includes designing facilities that respect the natural behaviors and instincts of the cattle. This is most important when it comes to loading and transporting the cattle. They write, "Humane processing is a priority and is carried out with great respect. It is sudden, immediate and complete without generating fear or pain in the animal's final moments" ("Raise Well").

Country Natural Beef does finish their cattle in feedlots, however, on a low-corn diet. This makes their method a kind of hybrid approach to raising cattle and allows them to produce enough beef, on a predictable timetable, to supply stores and restaurants. They sell beef to the Northwest Burgerville chain and the McMenamins chain of brewpubs. Their meat can be found in a number of grocery stores, including many Whole Foods stores. Given that most people don't want to give up their fast food, and most don't want to buy their beef half a steer at a time, many find this kind of approach a good middle ground.

To better understand why some people are motivated to seek out ranchers like Hutton and the Markholts (and CNB), I return to what that industry is like today. These first three cattle ranchers all represent some version of what many people like to think of when they imagine the life of cattle. Peaceful cattle grazing in a pasture. They are raising what is now called grass-fed beef. Since cows are designed by their evolutionary history to eat grass, and people who ate beef through most of human history ate cattle who ate grass, it is a bit odd that this is now a specialty market and far from the norm for the over thirty million beef cattle in the United States.

An operation with a foot in both worlds is "Coho Creek Ranch" (this is a pseudonym) in Lewis County, Washington. This ranch, which advertises itself as raising grass-fed beef, has been in the same family for over 150 years. They are doing much to recover segments of prairie and restore the creek to being a salmon run. "Coho Creek" consists of 550 acres where about 115 head of cattle are raised. Forty percent of the grassland is protected under a 2002 Grassland Reserve Program certified through the USDA. We saw native camass flowers in abundance, indicating the return of the prairie ecosystem. While they have not used any commercial herbicides, pesticides, fungicides, or fertilizers for about six years, they use chicken manure that comes from industrial chicken farms.

Their main goal is to keep the farm fertile and intact. They did recognize the interconnectedness of the grass, trees, soil, animals, and plants and said that "the operation depends on nature's symbiotic mechanisms." To borrow a distinction from Lichatowich's *Salmon without Rivers*, they rely on the natural economy rather than on the industrial economy to preserve the land. The natural economy consists of the sun, soil, water, decay processes, and the like, while the industrial economy relies on oil, chemicals, drugs, and the like. The ranchers at "Coho Creek" have a strong relationship with the land because of the long family history on the land. The connection to the land, however, seems to outweigh relationships with the cattle. They do practice cross-wire weaning, with mothers and calves able to see and talk to each other across a fence, because this reduces stress for the animals. But the reason for this didn't seem to be a direct concern for the animals but rather a desire to reduce stress-related disease and weight loss. Similarly, they do not use pesticides on the animals but rather cull any animals prone to succumbing to parasitic infestations. Since they do not breed all their own cattle, there is a risk of importing disease with the new arrivals, so they vaccinate. They say their goal is "for the cattle to enjoy their life while they are on the ranch." Again, however, this seems to be mostly because happy, unstressed cattle are healthier and thrive. They manage the cattle for profit, with the main goal being to keep the ranch intact and in the family. At no time did they speak of the cattle as part of nature. Instead the cattle are seen as a tool to help restore the natural prairie while also providing a food resource for humans. There was a focus on utilizing symbiotic relationships with the flora and fauna and on preserving the land. That the cattle are seen as a resource is also evident in the fact that the bulk of the cattle are sold to industrial operations to finish in a feedlot. Only five or six of the calves are held back each year to be sold when two years old as grass-fed beef.

So while "Coho Creek" markets grass-fed cattle they also participate in the more common, and more segregated and specialized, approach of raising beef cattle. Today some ranchers focus on producing seed stock—those cattle who will breed. Others focus on raising and grazing the babies—as "Coho Creek" is doing. Still others focus on finishing the cattle in a feedlot—they are feeders. From here the cattle are sold to processing plants where they are slaughtered and butchered. Often one company will have arms in more than one part of production. For instance, some who supply the bull for breeding buy back those offspring to finish and sell for meat. In this way the cattle industry is beginning to approach something like the arrangement found in the poultry and swine industries. As will be discussed later (chapters 8 and 9), in these industries many farmers are really just contract workers, raising livestock for someone else who owns the animal. It has not gone that far with cattle yet. The rancher still owns the cattle and the fact that the breeders buy the offspring of their bulls ("their genetics" as they say) is seen simply as confidence in how the cattle produced from their breeding stock will "finish" and do on the market.

This highly segmented and specialized approach to beef production is an example of the contemporary scientific and industrialized approach to meat production. As discussed above, though, there is a long history of such segmentation and specialization. First made possible by the railroads and refrigeration, this specialization has gone further with the advent of antibiotics, artificial insemination, computers, and the internet. For instance, before effective vaccinations and the advent of antibiotics, it would not have been possible to keep as many cattle as CAFOs do. As discussed earlier, in the 1800s stock associations began keeping records of breeding and production in order to find the crosses that would improve the market value of various cattle. Today, with those records on computers the level of analysis available is quite sophisticated. That, combined with the use of artificial insemination, can allow one bull to breed a countless number of cows. Today, breeders sell "genetics." Other companies sell the service of inseminating the cows; some specialize in doing this out in the field. Hormones are used to bring all the cows in season at the same time (synchronization) so that they can be inseminated with one visit. Embryo transfer has become its own highly profitable industry.

As has been documented by many contemporary writers (Michael Pollan, Eric Schlosser, and Jeremy Rifkin, among others), today, as in the 1800s, cheap corn is the engine of the cattle industry. Corn-fed cattle produce meat that is fattier. The meat-eating population of the United States is hooked on corn-fed beef, as is much of the world. Another perceived advantage of corn is that when it is cheap, so is beef. However, beef prices rise as other uses of corn are developed (e.g., using corn in the production of ethanol). As mentioned at the start of this chapter, rising prices offer one explanation for the decline in beef consumption in the United States (though there is increased consumption in many parts of the world). Another is that too much red meat is not good for human health. This is more true of corn-fed beef than of grass-fed beef. Even with grass-fed beef, though, too much can be a problem. While vegetarianism and veganism are still minority diet choices, reducing one's meat consumption is very mainstream. For example, health care companies such as the Washington-based Group Health Cooperative openly suggest eating less meat as a way to improve one's health. And red meat is often the main object of concern. Eating too much of anything can be a health problem; for humans, eating too much of any kind of meat is usually a health problem. But some of the concerns with beef are as much or more about what the cattle are eating than they are about the fact that the humans are eating the cattle. There is evidence that grass-fed beef, such as that raised by Hutton and the Markholts, is lower in total fat than grain-fed beef but higher in omega-3 fatty acids. It is higher in vitamins such as B and E, as well as in calcium, magnesium, potassium, lutein, and zeaxanthin. But little is likely to change for the majority of cattle in the United States, as people like the taste of corn-fed beef, and they like that this beef costs them less (at least on the face of it) than the grass-fed alternative. Grass-fed cattle can't supply the fast food and supermarket industries. To change the lives of cattle would require that humans reorganize much about their lives.

"Coho Creek" represents one step in such a reorganization by going beyond the reductionist view found in the mainstream cattle industry, working to see how parts are systemically related and understanding that the whole is more than the sum of its parts. On this ranch the ecosystem comes first, not the individual species or animals. This is reminiscent of an approach rooted in deep ecology, which will be discussed in the next chapter. The restoration of the prairie ecosystem entails the return of the native camass flower, and so the family relies on the cattle to graze down the fields and allow the flower to flourish. The restoration of the salmon necessitates keeping the cattle away from the stream, so the family arranges their pastures accordingly. The return of the salmon will help improve the health of the creek and bring back more wildlife. Not wanting to hunt potential predators, the family leaves the younger cattle in with the cows who will protect them—mimicking the natural ecosystems. They do not generally talk about individual animals, or even individual species. It's about the whole system. They have modified the land, as all creatures do, but they have not taken a dominating approach. They are trying to integrate the agricultural use of the land into the natural ecosystem of the area in order to protect it from other kinds of development. They have clearly rejected the notion of farm as "food-factory" and have taken on Leopold's view that "the criterion of success is a harmonious balance between plants, animals, and people; between the domestic and the wild, between utility and beauty" (Callicott 278). Nonetheless, in order to be economically viable, they continue to participate in the industrialized food-factory model with the majority of their cattle. It's not easy to pull out of the system—for farmers or consumers.

Another way some farmers have found it economically viable to raise cattle and restore the land is to partner with groups like Ducks Unlimited to restore and preserve wetlands. Scott Myers of Sweet Grass Farm, located on Washington State's Lopez Island, is committed to raising cattle, improving the health of the land, and supporting wildlife. The use of the word *farm* here is important. Myers says that ranches usually focus on the livestock while farms focus on plant crops and soil health. His focus is on the health of the land and grass; the cattle are a harvesting tool that helps maintain the health of the land. The presence of healthy wetlands for birds is an added benefit.

We were not able to visit this farm, so we conducted our interview by phone. Meyers began our conversation by pointing to the difficulty of changing the Western European relationship with land and nature. He described this relationship as a "conquering, subduing relationship of humans over nature." "On this view," he said, "nature presents difficulties for the health of crops and fruits" and one must attempt to avoid such problems. He had grown up in a family that raised fruit trees, and he described that life as a "battle with nature." Myers raises grass-fed cattle because this can be done in cooperation with, rather than in opposition to, nature. He has a holistic approach to his farm, capitalizing on symbiosis within the land ecosystem.

Myers raises Wagyu cattle because they are a hardy breed who are able to store fat in their muscles and so produce the desired marbling effect even when raised solely on grass. Myers's herd is a closed herd and he focuses on improving "the genetics." The quality of the beef is dependent on the health of the soil and the quality of the grass but is also dependent on having comfortable cattle who are not stressed. He says he and his family are out with the cattle every day, so the cattle are comfortable and curious around humans. He said, "We select for quality physical attributes supported by carcass data. Emotional stability is another key quality in creating a zero stress herd. Breeding alone doesn't produce the quality we expect, management makes a critical difference. Our lives are integrated with our herd. They are not simply a commodity to us; they are companions and often teachers" ("Wagyu Beef"). Videos on the Sweet Grass website demonstrate the relaxed nature of this herd and show the personal relationship Myers has with the cattle.

Myers's ultimate goal is to increase the fertility of the land, as he considers himself a custodian of the land. He uses no commercial pesticides, herbicides, fungicides, or fertilizers; the cattle provide the natural nutrients and fertilizer for the pasture. He believes that raising cattle using rotational and organic methods promotes land fertility. He is critical of plowing and molesting the land to grow grain, because it leads to water contamination and land erosion and decreases the land's fertility and lifespan. He explained his sentiment that to improve the health of the planet, or at least the health of the land in the United States, humans must learn to coexist with plots of land and develop close relationships with the inhabitants and elements of the land. He believes this can be accomplished through sustainable farming methods. The cattle are an important element in his approach, and he has a very intimate relationship with the animals as well as the land. He knows the cattle as individuals and calls to them to move them from pasture to pasture. He participates in a cooperative that manages a mobile USDA slaughter truck that comes to the farm. During the slaughter Myers personally walks his animals into the truck; he thinks he owes this to the cattle.

He says that "harvest" day is the hardest day. It was especially hard the first time, but he acknowledges death as part of life. He is not concerned or worried about his own death and recognizes his small role in a larger, organic whole. He believes that farming gives one such a realistic perspective and provides experience and knowledge based on integrity, observation, and contemplation. This kind of recognition allows him to appreciate and recognize the worth and beauty of nature's systems and to see the cattle (and himself) as part of this system. Further evidence of this respect for natural systems can be found in the fact that this farm maintains wetlands that attract migratory birds. He has a relationship with Ducks Unlimited in order to try to maintain habitat for the birds who belong in the ecosystems and to limit the damage of invasive bird species. Too many birds can damage the land he is trying to restore. For similar reasons Sweet Grass does not raise other animals. Doing so would require Meyers to feed grain and he believes this requires once again entering a battle with nature that results in a less productive use of land, requiring one to grow a product to feed an animal to feed a human.

The relationship with Ducks Unlimited adds another twist to this story, though. This is not the hunting of predators for protection, but sport hunting. This kind of conservation effort is focused on saving wildlife in order to have a sufficient population for hunting. As their website says, "Ducks Unlimited is the world's leader in wetlands and waterfowl conservation. DU got its start in 1937 during the Dust Bowl when North America's drought-plagued waterfowl populations had plunged to unprecedented lows. Determined not to sit idly by as the continent's waterfowl dwindled beyond recovery, a small group of sportsmen joined together to form an organization that became known as Ducks Unlimited. Its mission: habitat conservation." They took to heart Aldo

Leopold's argument that a focus on ecosystem health is the most important element in species conservation. They partner with private landowners, including many ranchers and farmers, to protect wetlands and wildlife habitats on their land. To help with this effort they take advantage of government programs such as the Wetlands Reserve Program (WRP) and the Conservation Reserve Program (CRP). Ducks Unlimited says, "These partnerships support what is known as the North American Model of Wildlife Conservation, which has its roots in more than a century's work by sportsmen and other dedicated conservationists. At the heart of the model is the idea that wildlife is public property and as such is a shared resource that must be conserved for the greater good." The idea of wildlife as a resource fits well with most people's view of livestock as a resource. While Leopold's land ethic promotes the health of ecosystems, the lives of individual animal beings within those ecosystems—domesticated and nondomesticated—is not a focus. Overall balance is the focus.

Ducks Unlimited uses the words of Aldo Leopold to promote their work. "Conservation is a state of harmony between men and land" (*A Sand Country* 189) appears on some of their materials. Further, Leopold's joy in hunting is celebrated by citing key passages from his writings: "a lone black duck came out of the west, . . . set his wings and pitched downward. I cannot remember the shot; I remember only my unspeakable delight when my first duck hit the snowy ice with a thud and lay there, belly up, red legs kicking" (129). Similarly, Leopold writes about the first partridge he shot on the wing. His father insisted that he not shoot the birds while in a tree, but only in flight—an ethical code he supported. But there was no limit to his joy when he did kill: "I could draw a map today of each clump of red bunchberry and each blue aster that adorned the mossy spot where he lay, my first partridge on the wing" (129). Describing the different ways different hunters watch the wilderness, Leopold says, "The non-hunter does not watch" (224). He continues, "A man may not care for golf and still be human, but the man who does not like to see, hunt, photograph, or otherwise outwit birds or animals is hardly normal" (227). Further he speaks of the importance of learning to work with dogs and horses (common companions of hunters) and learning to follow an ethical code when alone in the woods, unwatched by other humans (232).

For Leopold hunting is essential to the formation of good human beings, and so we need to preserve ecosystems to help keep hunting possible. Even his famous description of hunting wolves, described earlier in the chapter, works in support of maintaining healthy ecosystems for the hunter to enjoy. It is not that the wolf, or her injured pups, called out to Leopold, but that he took the perspective of the mountain who needs wolves to keep the deer in check so that they don't destroy the trees and shrubs. He encouraged ranchers to take the same view. Bears were seen by many as predators who needed to be removed to make the land safe for cows. But removing the top predator (who might take a cow a year) upsets the overall balance. Ironically, in many places what was cow country has become tourist country "and as such [has] greater need of bears than of beefsteaks" (145). As with the bobcat, there is something lost with their removal: "By this time the Delta has probably been made safe for cows, and forever dull for adventuring hunters. Freedom from fear has arrived, but a glory has departed from the green lagoons" (152). Leopold goes on to question the sense of progress involved in the removal of these predators: "We forest officers, who acquiesced in the extinguishment of the bear, knew a local rancher who had plowed up a dagger engraved with the name of one of Coronado's captains. We spoke harshly of the Spaniards who, in their zeal for gold and converts, had needlessly extinguished the native Indians. It did not occur to us that we, too, were the captains of an invasion too sure of its own righteousness" (145). Leopold is able to be critical of actions that seek to remove a group of human or other animal beings in the pursuit of personal gain, encouraging a view that encompasses the many and complex relationships among all life in order to find ways of cooperating for the benefit of all kinds. But at its root, his desire for the healthy, functioning ecosystem is to ensure that hunters, both human and nonhuman, have game to pursue.

On his view, ranchers who seek to remove animal predators do not fully understand how the raising of livestock should fit with other elements in an ecosystem. While their actions have been justified by profit and progress, Leopold says they have been short-sighted: "Man always kills the thing he loves, and so we the pioneers have killed our wilderness. Some say we had to. Be that as it may, I am glad I shall never be young without wild country to be young in" (157–58). He laments the loss of the wilderness and wildlife that he himself helped to remove. He does not think humans are changing their ways of thinking and being, so soon there will be little left to appreciate and few left capable of such appreciation. He writes, "The life of every river sings its own song, but in most the song is long since marred by the discords of misuse. Overgrazing first mars the plants and then the soil. Rifle, trap, and poison next deplete the larger birds and mammals; then comes a park or forest with roads and tourists. Parks are made to bring the music to the many, but by the time many are attuned to hear it there is little left but noise" (159). Leopold was critical of farming and ranching for causing much of the damage to ecosystems and the loss of biodiversity, but he did see some trying to change: "The discontent that labels itself 'organic farming' while bearing some of the earmarks of a cult, is nevertheless biotic in its direction, particularly in its insistence on the importance of soil flora and fauna" (260). Some of these farmers "have learned from experience that the wholly tamed farm offers not only a slender livelihood but a constricted life. They have caught the idea that there is pleasure to be had in raising wild crops as well as tame ones. They propose to devote a little spot of marsh to growing native wildflowers" (203). For this revolt to become more widespread there needs to be a larger change in outlook. Instead of a focus on the amount of food produced, the focus should be on the quality of the food. Depleted soils, even when "enhanced" with chemical fertilizers, cannot increase food value. Part of the reason for this failure, on Leopold's view, is the overreliance on those at the universities who dissect and separate seeds, plants, and animals in order to understand and improve instead of working to understand and build on the relationships among species (162).

One of these failures of understanding has resulted in damage that ranchers still live with today. Plant and animal species move around the globe with the intentional and unintentional help of humans. When such species find a hospitable spot, they can often take over. For example, Leopold noted that cheat grass found a home in the "ready-made seedbed prepared by the trampling hoofs of range livestock" (165). Had the grasses been healthy cheat grass would have had a difficult time making inroads: "The cause of the substitution is overgrazing. When the too-great herds and flocks chewed and trampled the hide off the foothills, something had to cover the raw eroding earth. Cheat did" (165). As it spreads it pushes wildlife and livestock to higher elevations to feed. While the livestock can be fed in the winter, the wildlife find the snows returning them to land with little available food. Leopold lists some of the problematic consequences of this takeover: starving deer, sores in the mouths of cattle, degraded alfalfa fields, trapped ducklings, choked pines, and higher fire danger (167). However, the cheat grass at least stops the erosion that overgrazing would have caused had nothing taken over. At the time he was writing Leopold wondered whether cheat grass would simply be accepted as inevitable, or whether efforts would be made to restore the land. Today cheat grass still presents a challenge to cattle ranchers in the western United States.

Leopold noted that the scientific progress of the time could not "abide that the farmland and the marshland, wild and tame, exist in mutual toleration and harmony" (172). But this is indeed what Ducks Unlimited encourages farmers and ranchers to do. Leopold was not uncritical of Ducks Unlimited, though, and eventually withdrew his membership. In "Conservation Esthetic" he wrote, "When we conclude that we must bait the farmer with subsidies to induce him to raise a forest, or with gate receipts to induce him to raise game, we are merely admitting that the pleasures of husbandry-in-the-wild are as yet unknown both to the farmer and to ourselves" (293). In the end, then, he saw a need to promote a different way of seeing and being in the world. This way of being needs to respond to something deeper than short-term advantage and the profit motive.

I think Leopold's land ethic was an important step toward a new way of seeing and being in the world and remains a valuable resource. But his work remains rooted in a masculine idealization of hunting and a managerial model that is limiting. I think a pragmatist ecofeminism provides more resources for developing a new way of seeing and being in the world. While industrial agriculture frustrates most moves to this different way of seeing and being in the world, I use the following chapters to show there is hope.

CHAPTER FOUR

In Mixed Company

DEEP ECOLOGY, MEAT CONSUMPTION, AND CONSERVATION

Today, all mainstream animal agriculture is highly specialized and segmented. One of the ideas behind this approach is the view that it is more efficient to focus on one kind of production, and even one aspect of that production. For beef cattle that means specializing in breeding, birthing and weaning, feeding and finishing, or slaughtering and processing. Most of the farmers discussed in the previous chapter stray from the norm by taking on all aspects of the life (and death) of the cattle. They do, however, specialize in cattle. Another approach involves mixing species. This used to be commonplace.

One person who spoke strongly against the specialized and segmented approach was Keith Swanson. When we spoke he was part of Thundering Hooves Ranch in Walla Walla, Washington (which has since closed), and he now runs Blue Valley Meats. When we met with Swanson at his meat shop he said, "It is hard to break out of being segmented. However, there is only a small profit margin in the segmented paradigm and the people involved in that kind of production have no idea of the quality of their end product. Their only goal is to produce heavy animals fast." He went on to discuss the hidden costs of unhealthy animals' reliance on grain and medication and the need to grow and harvest corn and other grain on a large scale. The segmented system results in soil degradation that then necessitates fertilizers, which require a great amount of oil and water. He said, "There is no sustainability in that system because it is only ever taking organic matter from the soil. When the farmer depends on fertilizers the soil becomes like a drug addict—every year it is more depleted and needs a bigger 'hit' than the last year. In that system nature is the enemy." He thought farmers should instead see themselves as part of nature and work with the natural processes. Swanson said, "If you utilize the laws of nature as your friend then half the battle is over. Leave the ecosystem alone—the soil has micro-organisms and worms that will do the plowing for you. It pays to treat the land right, and you don't have to be organic to know that." Since any health benefits from meat are connected to the quality of the grass available for the livestock, the more segmented and grain-based system is bad not just for the land and animals but also for human health.

Part of any meat system includes the death of the animals. Swanson said, "Something will eat them, whether it's wolves, bears, or humans. If you want cattle to be alive (because without humans they'll go extinct) we have to kill them." Thundering Hooves did try to keep the process as stress-free as possible. The cattle were not confined until right before the slaughter truck arrived. Since the cattle were regularly moved as part of their pasture rotation, they came when called. When asked whether there was any sense of betraying the cattle in doing this, he said no. "The cattle don't ponder their fate as they're waiting in the pasture before slaughter so as long as they don't suffer while they wait there is no betrayal." He did note that humans are also food for nature. Swanson mentioned an image of a casket with tree roots trying to get inside. He said he'd "rather be part of that tree's system than not" and that this applied to all life.

While death itself wasn't a problem for Swanson, he did think there was a problem with the specific breeds of cattle and chickens they used. It took longer to finish their cattle on grass because they were using cattle bred to fatten quickly on corn and yield as much meat as possible. Swanson said it would be better to get back to smaller-framed genetics in cows if they are going to be grass-fed. He thought breeding should return to a focus on hardiness and independence as well. The same applied to their chickens. They used a Cornish Cross chicken in their broiler production. The Cornish Cross is the meat chicken most in demand, since it is the industry standard. Mechanized slaughter processes demand a standard-sized bird; warehouse production demands a bird that will gain weight in the high-density living conditions; customer preferences demand more breast meat. To achieve this, those involved in industrial chicken farming bred the bird for big breasts and fast weight gain. They are ready to slaughter in six weeks or less. It is important that this time be short so that they don't die from the polluted conditions in which they live. Customers are used to a certain taste and certain size of bird, so raising a different breed could cost them their customer base. But Swanson said the Cornish cross is not well suited to being pastured, and raising these birds added about a 25 percent death loss over raising a more hardy breed of chicken. This is also clearly a welfare concern.

Swanson admitted that even though they tried to do things "the right way," Thundering Hooves was far from the ideal they hoped to achieve. They were trying to "create a system with the right amount of land and the right amount of ruminants." Because they outsourced the chicken and pig production they couldn't rotate grazing among different animals. Swanson said that would be "marvelous to do but it's a time issue." Rather than becoming more integrated this ranch became more of a meat distributor and retailer. According to Bruce King, "moving from a crop-oriented farm to a livestock-oriented farm required quite a bit of investment. The meat shop was a big part of this initial debt. As they added each different type of product there was a substantial investment in the equipment, facilities, and learning curve required for each one. Chickens, Turkeys, Cattle, Lamb" ("Thundering Hooves Postmortem"). King suggests that the family lost its focus on farming and that the founding farmer, Joel Huesby, become more interested in mobile slaughter facilities.

Thundering Hooves provides a good example of the complexity faced by livestock farmers today. The norm is to be a livestock producer rather than a farmer. A producer simply warehouses and feeds as many animals as she or he can. A farmer or a rancher, however, tries to raise animals in ways that are consistent with the well-being of the animals and the land on which they depend. At Thundering Hooves they were cattle ranchers, but with the increasing number of chickens and pigs, and the outsourcing of the work, they become more like producers. Often those critical of the industrialized meat industry focus their critiques on those producing the animal—that is, the farmer or the rancher. Animal husbandry—the practice of caring for the well-being of the livestock—is very time-intensive. Most farms small enough to manage in a way that truly cares for the animals need to charge more for their meat and milk to stay in business. If customers are willing to pay more it is possible to do, but people often say they can't afford to buy organic or humanely raised animal products (or produce). (This is the same logic discussed in chapter 2 by those who say fish farming is necessary to meet consumer demand.) People in the United States spend relatively little on their food—an average of 11 percent of a family's disposable income (Ogle 211). It's more that they aren't willing to pay higher prices for *the amount* of meat and dairy products they'd *like* to consume. Most could at least spend no more on these products but buy and consume less meat and dairy. That choice is rarely considered given the current cultural habits of consuming animal products at every meal.

This extravagant diet is a recent development. In the United States in the

1950s average annual meat consumption was 138 pounds while in 2000 it was 195 pounds. That increase of 57 pounds consisted of 7 more of red meat, 46 more of poultry, and 4 more of fish ("Profiling Food Consumption" 15). Commercials push burgers, bacon, and cheese. Such consumption only became affordable for most people with the industrialization of meat, dairy, and egg production. But with the changes in how the livestock were bred, raised, and killed, the animal products also changed. Growing *concern* about some of these changes means consumers need to take some *responsibility* as well. One way some consumers have started to put their money where their mouths are is joining a CSA (Community Supported Agriculture). CSAs are a way for consumers to share the risks and rewards with the farmer. Consumers buy shares, and this money is used to raise and harvest the food. Whatever is produced is then shared with the CSA members. Produce CSAs are very common now, and meat and egg CSAs are growing in number. CSAs are usually focused on raising healthful food in ways that improve and sustain the health of the land and any animals they raise. It is the commitment of the consumers that make it possible for these farmers to live by their own commitments as well. The Crown S Ranch is an example of such a place.

The Crown S, in Winthrop, Washington, is run by Louis Sukovaty and Jennifer Argraves. During our visit Sukovaty showed us around. An engineer by training, he called himself a "scientific observer" rather than a "creator." The 105-acre farm includes pastures, forests, and streams. He said there must be special attention paid to "learning the systems [from soil to cattle] on top of each other" in order to maintain a small-scale farm with a diverse population of livestock including cattle, sheep, hogs, broilers, laying hens, and turkeys. He sees grazing ecosystems as being as much a part of nature as other ecosystems, and their website says, "On organic pastures, we humanely raise cattle, pigs, sheep, and poultry without toxic drugs or chemicals. We protect and enhance the environment and maintain a balanced ecosystem by integrating traditional animal husbandry with innovative technology and utilizing natural cycles. Better for the Animal. Better for the Environment. Better for You."

Sukovaty and Argraves use their engineering knowledge to make every aspect of this farm moveable. This enables them to take full advantage of their land and keep it as healthy as possible. For instance, the chickens spend the winter in the greenhouse so that the manure is there when it's time to plant. The greenhouse is relocated as needed. Young chickens and the broilers are kept in an enclosure to protect them from predation, but it's on wheels. Solar energy moves it very slowly around the pasture allowing the chickens to graze on fresh pasture (they obtain 30 percent of their dietary needs from insects, grass, and even mice!) and distributing their feces. There is no accumulation of ammonia and the feces can help build topsoil by feeding various microorganisms. When older, laying hens are left to roam freely in the pasture. They have a wagon they can go into for shelter and protection from night predators. Their pasture diet is supplemented with organic grain harvested and milled on the farm. For the laying hens, there is some loss due to predation, but Sukovaty said this is more than offset by the fact that they don't lose chickens to illness caused by confinement. Having the chickens in the pasture also helps with the cattle. The cattle rotate among the pastures regularly—Sukovaty whistles and they follow. They mob graze eighteen to twenty-six cattle per acre. This can be done given the diversity of grass, clover, and herbs used to seed the pastures. The chickens go through the cattle's manure and eat parasites and insects that would be a problem for the cattle. They also help spread the cattle manure, further increasing the health of the land. The pigs are in the same pastures, but enclosed in pens that Sukovaty moves around. Their wallowing area is moved annually and the old area becomes a garden—"the pigs have dug up the dirt and fertilized it already." The chickens help break up the pig manure too. The pigs and sheep follow the cattle and, because they graze and use the land differently, this allows the pasture to recover even while it is supporting animals.

The Crown S now has a Washington State Department of Agriculture (WSDA)–certified poultry slaughter and processing center. They are very proud of the fact that the offal and wastewater from the slaughter facility is composted and used to nourish the land—one way of completing a cycle. Another is their use of passive flytraps. The cattle walk through a chute on their way to water and insects such as horn flies and face flies fly into a container where they die. They are then fed to the chickens or composted and fed back to the land as well. The idea is to work with the various parts of the ecosystem and keep things in balance. This balance is key to the Crown S, but while Sukovaty stressed the importance of his connection with the land during our visit, he was also concerned with utilizing this connection so that they could stay in business. He did not specifically mention welfare concerns or respect for the animals unless it was related to the quality of the product. Several times he proudly compared his finishing times and mortality rates to those of factory farms, to demonstrate that a more sustainable approach is possible and profitable. Further, he said, this balanced way of farming "works with nature, requires less energy, creates clean air and water, is a carbon sink, and builds topsoil." While industrial farms damage the environment, this way of farming can improve it. In this context, the livestock sometimes seemed to be viewed mostly as economic investments. Sukovaty obviously has relationships with them, but he is very practical and honest about their fate and purpose. The cattle are numbered and not named; however, their health and well-being are a top priority. He runs the ranch as a business, taking pride in his operation's ability to compete with the finishing time of industrial operations even though his cattle are on an all-grass diet. Their cattle average a weight gain of two to three pounds per day—"just 5 percent below the rate of gain in grain fed feedlot animals." Similarly, he is proud of the fact that his birds' mortality rate is much lower than that of industrial farms. Industrial farms do not let their chickens outdoors, but he believes "sunlight is a great sterilizer." Even while he made comparisons with CAFOs, though, it was clear Crown S's practices are more labor-intensive and they cannot produce as much meat. That means the Crown S has to charge more for their meat, but their products are so highly sought after that they routinely sell out.

Sukovaty is critical of industrial operations' abstraction from the relationship with the land and the animals. He believes that industrial operations simplify the complex relations among various natural systems and dumb down the labor required to care for fruits, vegetables, and animals. This is done so that money can be saved on labor costs. The scale of the farming is a big part of the equation. The large industrial farms make it impossible to know the individuals or to work with the relationships among the various crops being raised. Sukovaty and Argraves enjoy the challenges this complex farm presents and have come up with many inventive ways to handle the labor involved. At the time of our visit, the Crown S paid for itself but didn't generate enough income to expand, but now it has.

The Crown S raises an interesting question of whether it matters *why* people engage in environmentally responsible modes of farming and raise livestock animals in ways that respect the animals' natures. Farmers may do this because they are primarily concerned for human well-being (an anthropocentric view) or because they see humans as just one member of the biotic community whose health is part of the health of a larger ecosystem (a biocentric view). Anthropocentrism is generally understood as a human-centeredness that gives human beings priority over other animal beings or the rest of nature. Animal rights and welfare activists and theorists, as well as environmentalists, are usually critical of anthropocentrism. It is seen as an obstacle to changing human behavior toward, and thinking about, the rest of nature— animal and nonanimal. Anthropocentrism is often connected with the view that humans have dominion over the rest of nature and so can do with it what they please. While there are interesting critiques of this understanding of dominion in books such as Matthew Scully's *Dominion: The Power of Man, the Suffering of Animals, and the Call for Mercy,* this view usually understands human beings as somehow being outside of nature and, even if dependent on nature in some ways for food and other forms of sustenance, enough in control of nature to not be affected by what might happen to nature as a result of human actions. So most animal rights and welfare theorists argue that we need to get beyond an anthropocentric outlook if we hope to change the lives of other animal beings in any meaningful way.

There are some who argue that we can't get beyond anthropocentrism, though, since every animal sees, understands, and uses the world she or he inhabits from the point of view of that species. In fact, many animal welfare theorists make this very claim when arguing that humans need to respect how other animal beings perceive and use their environment: since humans are one species of animal among many, humans too have a human way of perceiving, understanding, and using their environment. In this way, we cannot escape anthropocentrism—at least not entirely. But the human capacities for reason and imagination do make it possible for humans to gain some insight into how others negotiate the world as well. Many argue that this capacity results in a moral obligation for humans to do their best to respect other animal beings and the natural world on which all life depends. But this may not result in any kind of obligation to abandon anthropocentrism entirely (even if we could).

One problem with most anthropocentrism is that what humans see as being in their interests does not always coincide with what might be in the interest of the environment or other animal beings. If the belief system one has is based on the idea that human interests matter most (or are the only thing that matters) this can pretty regularly result in actions that harm other beings. A quick survey of environmental literature and philosophy can serve to make this case. On the other hand, a view that puts the biotic community above all else often has the consequence of ignoring the interests of individuals—humans and otherwise. This kind of biocentric view is often related to deep ecology, promoted by philosophers such as Arne Naess, Bill Devall, George Sessions, and Holmes Rolston III.

Briefly, deep ecology makes a case for the intrinsic value of nature as opposed to the instrumental value humans find in nature when they take an anthropocentric stance. Specifically, what matters most from this perspective is the health and well-being of the whole of an ecosystem, not how it can be used by humans. Deep ecologists argue for ecological holism and say that the value of an ecosystem or species trumps the needs and interests of individuals. Ecological holism is usually to be understood, however, within the context of a biocentrism that respects all living organisms. According to Devall and Sessions, in such a view human beings are just one organism among many in an ecosystem in which "all organisms and entities in the ecosphere" are "parts of the interrelated whole, are equal in intrinsic worth" and have "inherent value . . . independent of any awareness, interest, or appreciation . . . by a conscious being" (67, 70). Deep ecologists see no bifurcation between human and nonhuman realms. Species are conceptualized as being on a continuum rather than as being on a pyramid (as in Leopold's land ethic) in order to eschew the perception of a hierarchy with human beings at the pinnacle. Once an ecological consciousness and identification with nature have been attained, deep ecologists believe, necessary shifts in behavior will automatically follow. They tend to believe that actions in harmony with wild species and the land will be a natural outcome, and actions that harm the planet would be no more likely than for a person to cut off his or her own finger.

Naess formulated eight basic principles for deep ecology to help guide and direct the self-realization process. These principles are basically that (1) the flourishing of all life has intrinsic value that is independent of any possible human use for that life; (2) biodiversity is itself a value; (3) humans should not reduce biodiversity except to satisfy vital needs of survival; (4) the flourishing of nonhuman life would be aided by a decrease in the human population; (5) human actions interfere with the nonhuman world too much; (6) this interference is getting worse, so economic, technological, and ideological policies and practices must change; (7) we need an ideological shift that results in an appreciation of the quality of life over and above increasing one's standard of living; and (8) humans who agree with these points have an obligation to work for change (Devall and Sessions 70). Many adherents of deep ecology also talk about learning to be more "place-specific" and building harmonious relations with the land.

In many ways this sounds very much in line with what is happening at the Crown S. The land has been in the family and they know it well. They farm in ways that respect and try to build on the biodiversity of the ecosystems on the ranch and in the surrounding area. They use technology to lessen human interference with the ecosystems. Sukovaty and Argraves, and their customers, value their quality of life as much as or more than any particular standard of living. They could make more money with less labor as engineers, and their customers could spend less of their money on the meat they buy. They and their customers are working to change the systems they see as interfering with a healthy ecosystem and good quality of life. However, it is not clear that they see the flourishing of all life as having intrinsic value that is independent of any possible human use for that life. Sukovaty and Argraves are not aspiring to be labeled deep ecologists; they obviously value their animals as useful to humans. The animals function to make the land healthier, to make the grazing ecosystem work, and to provide food for humans (and probably some dogs and cats). The livestock are treated respectfully, but this is more a consequence of their instrumental value for humans than any intrinsic value. Interestingly, though, this may not really put them at odds with most deep ecologists. Deep ecologists don't see domesticated animals as part of the ecosystem and so don't see them as deserving respect for their intrinsic value. In fact, unlike pragmatists, deep ecologists see domesticated animals as destructive agents and seek their removal in order to protect an ecosystem. Some examples include killing feral goats or pigs who are damaging forest or island ecosystems, eliminating cats because they kill wildlife, and removing cattle from public lands where they graze. I think this is a major limitation of deep ecology and results in a position that does not see livestock as morally considerable. This perspective also takes humans outside of nature and sees all human impact as unnatural. But, as Dewey noted, all organisms modify their environments. Any particular form of agriculture will have positive and negative impacts, but agriculture itself in not unnatural. Unlike pragmatists, deep ecologists see agriculture as interfering with the natural world and I think most deep ecologists (but not pragmatists) would question Sukovaty's idea that his multispecies grazing rotation system is an ecosystem in the first place. Pragmatists would have to assess particular farming systems in their place and time, but deep ecologists would see all farming as a disturbance that can only be justified in order to meet some vital need.

The next question is whether meat is a vital need. Food is. Even if one doesn't eat meat, the system at the Crown S makes the produce, hay, and grains possible (and better) through the presence of the various animal beings. The animals provide fertilizer, insect control, and soil aeration, though many also require the inputs of hay and grain. The Crown S now grows its own organic hay and grain—hay to feed the ruminants and grain for the poultry and pigs. Since this land could grow food to feed humans more directly, it is not clear that its meat would qualify as a vital need. But without animal inputs it would become increasingly difficult to grow produce without turning to industrial fertilizers, herbicides, and pesticides, so the livestock animals are an important part of produce production at the Crown S.

On this view, raising some amount of livestock is necessary to raise food in general. However, even if there is a way to raise animals for food that respects the environment and the lives of other animal beings, there is a clear need for a deeper examination of our cultural habits of eating meat and the ways in which we raise the animal beings whose bodies we consume and whose manure we use. It also seems that in order to create any change in action, an examination of the underlying beliefs of the actors is necessary. Without discussion of these framing beliefs it is easy to find oneself acting in ways that turn out to betray beliefs and commitments one holds dear. On the other hand, it is also possible for someone to change her or his beliefs about something but not change the practice related to those beliefs. Common examples of this include having the belief that smoking and junk food are not good for human health and should be eliminated from one's lifestyle, or at least severely restricted, while at the same time continuing to indulge in smoking and eating junk food—or believing it is important to eat food that is free from antibiotics and hormones but not going to the effort to find that food. One may also believe animal welfare matters but not be willing to pay the price for meat from animals raised well. An important concern of the people trying to farm in ecologically responsible ways, or ways that respect animal welfare, is whether or not consumers share their beliefs and are willing and able to act in ways consistent with those beliefs. If the metaphysical assumptions of the consumers do not change, along with those of the farmers, there will be a lack of desire or motivation to support a change in practice. Given the difficulty of changing beliefs, and of changing practices, taking an anthropocentric approach might make sense—especially if one wants to stay in business.

The Crown S motto is "Better for the Animal. Better for the Environment. Better for You." This motto makes room for those who have beliefs that lead them to care about the intrinsic value of the other animal beings (including livestock) and the environment generally, but it also works for those thoroughly rooted in the more dominant, anthropocentric view that humans are the center of concern. Does it matter that the primary motivations at the Crown S seem to be that humans have a right to food free from various chemicals, hormones, and diseases? Or that they believe humans have a right to know what is in their food and to see where it comes from? At least in the case of this farm, these motivations have had the secondary effect of providing the livestock animals with lives in which their natural behaviors and physical needs are respected and met. This is not always the case, though. I think human beings need to think carefully about how they understand their relationship with the rest of nature—animal and nonanimal—and remember that this includes the relationships with those parts of nature that humans tend to eat.

No matter one's commitments, though, the discussion of Thundering Hooves and the Crown S demonstrates that it is hard to effect change in the world if one cannot financially sustain desired practices. Profit, however, is not usually the main motive for alternative meat production. The quality of life is at least equally important. Greg Newhall of the Windy N Ranch outside of Ellensburg, Washington, said, "There isn't any reason to feel bad about what one does—the money isn't worth it." Newhall and his business partner, Gary Jones, made a living as developers. They bought the fourteen hundred acres as part of a development company and are building houses on some pieces of the land. The rest is to ranch, and "that is about happiness." Newhall said it's important to make it a home for all—his family and the families of his employees, the dogs, the livestock, and the plants in the garden. Johnson grew up in Cashmere, Washington, and so came from a rural background. Newhall fell in love with the idea of farming from his experience visiting his uncle in Montana when he was young. When we visited we met with Newhall. He said he does this work because of his love of, and for, the land. His love of the land includes an appreciation of its beauty and complexity. His love for the land is manifested in caring for it and the life it sustains. These two kinds of love are intertwined in how he farms. He especially noted the vibrant interaction with the varied cycles of life that come with the different plants and animals. He loves observing, and working with, these interactions.

At the time of our visit (in 2010) they grew hay and raised cattle, sheep, pigs, turkeys, and chickens. Their Wagyu/Angus herd is now over four hundred. Newhall and Johnson do not use artificial insemination for breeding and "try to mirror the birthing cycle of our local deer and elk. It's better weather for the calves." Newhall said most ranchers try to have all their calves born in February so that they are big when they are sent to the feedlot in the fall, but since they are not participating in the feedlot industry, they aim for April births. They use no growth hormones, steroids, stimulants, ionophores, or antibiotics. Once in a while a cow will get an infection from something like cheat grass and then antibiotic treatment is used for the sake of the animal, who is "removed from production." Vaccinations are kept to a minimum because the herd is closed except when they purchase a breeding bull. They feed the cattle a mineral salt mixed with garlic and apple cider vinegar that helps with flies, ticks, and worms. Newhall said, "If you don't work with nature, things get messy. It's better if it's a cooperative effort." Windy N is committed to treating the animals as well as possible if they are going to be killed for subsistence. That includes having the mobile slaughter truck come to the farm so that the cattle don't experience the stress of travel.

The Windy N grows alfalfa and orchard grass hay (organic since 2013). They use fish fertilizer, granulated crab and shrimp shell, and chicken manure. While the cattle are fed off their land, they have to buy feed for the pigs, chickens, turkeys, ducks, and pheasants. They are getting away from having soy in the food, but it's hard to find soy-free food. The pigs are in a pasture, which allows them to have some "greens." There is water so that they can make wallows to cool off and prevent sunburn. Solar panels (and some plug-in fencing) power the electric fence that forms their enclosure. The pigs are very smart, though, and know when it is off. Their personalities and intelligence make it harder to kill the pigs than it is the other animals they raise. Newhall said, "You do wonder how much they know." "But," he continued, "it's part of the cycle of life." They "harvest" them at about six months of age, when they are between 220 and 240 pounds.

Easier to kill are the turkeys and chickens. While they have some tame wild turkeys wandering freely around the barns, Newhall said, they are just "eye candy," like the peacocks. They are safe from slaughter, he said, "and they know it." They are called "non-eaters," and "they are worth a few bags of feed."

The turkeys, chickens, and pheasants meant for eating are out on pasture with shelter and a night enclosure. They tried "chicken tractors" but were not happy with the confinement. Now chicks stay inside for two to four weeks and then go out on the grass. At the time of our visit they had Cornish cross (like Thundering Hooves) and freedom ranger chickens. They have since converted entirely to the freedom ranger birds as "they are a normal bird." Newhall said the Cornish cross "just doesn't feel right. They are a mish mash just designed to grow fast." On the other hand, the freedom ranger website claims they "are a great alternative to fast-growing white broiler chicks or slow-growing heritage breeds." Unlike industrial birds, "Freedom Ranger chicks grow at a moderate rate, reaching their peak weight of 5–6 lbs in 9 to 11 weeks. These active, robust chicks are suitable for free range, foraging and pasture environments and produce tender, succulent meat with more yellow omega 3 fat and less saturated fat than fast growing breeds" ("Freedom Ranger Chickens"). Newhall and Johnson raise black freedom rangers, who mature at fourteen weeks of age. They think this is a better match for their practices. Windy N has been working with WSDA for their organic and AWA certification. Since one of AWA requirements is selecting the right breed of animal to match one's farming practices and environment, the change to freedom rangers was an important step. They also made changes in their laying hens and now use Plymouth barred rocks, black australorps, and Rhode Island reds, who produce no more than 280 eggs a year. Windy N doesn't debeak chickens and would not keep chickens if that were necessary. When the laying hens are old Newhall and Johnson use them in stew. Newhall said, "there is no profitable market for the spent hens, but they can bring one more form of happiness to humans in their death."

At the time of our visit Newhall wanted to achieve the AWA certification for the ranch's chickens. They are now the first ranch to achieve the AWA certification for eight different species: meat chickens, laying hens, laying ducks, beef cattle, pigs, meat sheep, meat goats, and turkeys ("Our Heroes"). Additionally they have achieved AWA's Grassfed certification for their sheep, goats, and beef cattle. They also achieved their organic certification in 2013 and have one of the few organic-certified facilities for butchering chicken, turkeys, and pheasants. They process up to four hundred birds at a time and close the cycle of life by putting the poultry parts in their compost.

Wildlife is an important part of what Newhall and Johnson like about this land and their lifestyle. Part of the land is left wild for deer and other wildlife and they do not allow hunting. Newhall said the wild animals know they're safe, which means there are lots of coyotes too. They lost forty laying chickens to coyotes one year, but the addition of Anatolian/Great Pyrenees dogs brought that down to zero. Newhall said, "The cycles of life you see here, you just can't see anywhere else." Neither Newhall nor Johnson hunts, but they did when they were young. Newhall said most of his family are hunters, but "hunting just doesn't feel fair—especially with long distance weapons. With domesticated animals you can give them a good life and an easy death. It feels better." They are not completely against hunting, though, and think it can be used to keep numbers in balance. Newhall said they try to do things in a way that makes them feel good—"as good as one can feel when killing things." In a letter following our visit Newhall wrote, "Birth, growth, life and dying on a meat producing ranch is a reflection of what we all experience in our own lives and I think it helps us see where we might fit into nature. I don't see humans as dominating and subduing our animal charges as much as treating them fairly while exploiting their natural tendencies to our benefit." Newhall said that humans need to eat protein and livestock are good sources of protein. He went on to say, "If we are going to consume them, though, it is our responsibility to treat them with respect and make the whole lifecycle pleasant. Ask yourself how you would want to be treated if you were an animal." He did note that since he is eating his own meat, he eats less of it. He thought part of the reason for that is that it is dry-aged (versus commercial wet-aged) and so more flavorful and therefore he needs less of it to be satisfied.

At the time of our visit Windy N sold mutton but not lamb, though now their website features organic grass-fed lamb. Other products include organic American Kobe/Angus beef, organic pig, organic grass-fed goat, organic pastured turkey, organic pheasant, and pastured chicken. They also feature pastured chicken and duck eggs. One thing that is interesting about this list is that, except for the beef, the animals are named. It says pig instead of pork. This goes against a common practice that Carol Adams refers to as using a mass term to create an absent referent. What she means by this is that when you use a term like *beef*, the individual cattle are made invisible—they are absent from our thought. But they must be there, or there would be no meat. Such terms also serve to lump all the cattle together and remove any sense of individuality. She thinks terms like *meat, beef*, and *pork* are false mass terms because they hide the truth that when one eats meat, beef, or pork one is really eating individual animals. She believes we use terms like this because we are uncomfortable with the reality of eating individual animal beings—beings who had distinctive personalities, preferences, and life experiences.

Windy N is not hiding the reality and this often is another aspect of buying animal products from such ranches. They make it clear that they kill animals and often are proud of how they kill the animals, as these practices usually differ from those of the highly automated slaughterhouses used by the mainstream industry. They are also proud that they, and often their customers, can get to know the animals individually as well. One should be able and willing to know the animals they eat. Windy N encourages people to come tour the ranch. Education is part of their mission, and they provide a list of articles, books, and videos about food production in the United States.

This ranch is about a way of life, a way of eating, fair treatment for animals, and a family environment. Newhall said the Windy N was "always going to be a small, hands-on farm," but things have grown since our visit. The land that makes up the ranch has decreased, but the number of animals has grown. They have about 450 cattle, 75 goats, 100 sheep, under 100 pigs, 500 hens, and 100 ducks for eggs. While this ranch raises a number of different species, each kind of animal is raised in its own way and in its own area. The Windy N is not an integrated operation like the Crown S. This is interesting, as several of the items on the reading list on the Windy N website are by Joel Salatin. Salatin promotes the integrated raising of multiple species of livestock and their feed much as we saw on the Crown S. He was made famous by Michael Pollan's discussion of his Polyface farm in *The Omnivore's Dilemma* and his interview featured in the movie *Food, Inc.* (both of which also appear on the Windy N list of resources).

In essence, Salatin's system means the animals grow their own food as their manure fertilizes the fields in which they graze and the rotation of different species disrupts parasite cycles. He does raise animal species that require grain, and they receive locally grown non-GMO grain to supplement their grazing, browsing, and rooting. He is able to slaughter chickens on-site but has been frustrated in finding acceptable places to slaughter and process the rest of his meat animals. Salatin sees the more segmented approach of industrialized animal agriculture as an expression of a "disconnected, Greco-Roman, western egocentric, compartmentalized, reductionist, fragmented, linear thought process" (3–4). This kind of segmentation, he believes, results in problems that need not exist: "I am constantly angered at the time and energy devoted to solving problems that should never exist" (134). He thinks humans would be better off if we returned to grass-fed, pastured meat that is slaughtered and processed in decentralized, community-based slaughterhouses. Focusing on the rotation of crops and various animals, he promotes operating without hormones, antibiotics, pesticides, and chemical fertilizers. His view entails the end of CAFOs and the national tracking of animals and meat that goes with this kind of centralized system (270–98).

Unlike Greg Newhall, who allows no hunting on the Windy N, Salatin argues that killing predators is one of the responsibilities that falls to humans involved in raising livestock in a respectful and responsible way. Salatin specifically notes a tension found in the position that chickens should be raised on pastures rather than in confinement. Consumers who support pastured poultry also often argue against shooting hawks or coyotes. Similarly many who are attached to dogs and cats as pets fail to acknowledge the damage those animals do to wildlife and wilderness but object to grazing cattle or allowing pigs to root in the forest. A "forest farm" is one way humans can live with and off of nature, but we've protected the forest and like to think it can and should be separated from agriculture. Salatin says, "You can't take humans out of the landscape. We are part of it, like it or not, and have been for a long, long time. This notion that humans are inherently damaging to the landscape is simply an over reaction to the damage inflicted by humans" (163). Salatin dismisses the views of those who choose to opt out of eating meat. He finds the position of those who will eat eggs and milk but not meat particularly problematic as he thinks that they don't understand the life cycles of the animals who are involved. He finds vegans to be more consistent, he says, but according to him no one can be healthy on a vegan diet (a highly disputed claim). Nevertheless, he understands why the animal welfare movement arose: "Had farm animals never been cramped into CAFOs, the inhumane description would never have seen the light of day.... Industrial farmers don't seem to have a clue that for all their platitudes about efficiency and feeding the world, they can never gain the high ground morally for a production model that despicably abuses animals" (32). Salatin does promote the importance of respecting the animals raised for food but stresses that they are not human and not persons. Ironically, his insistence on this point—his support for a hierarchy of life with humans at the top—is rooted in the same "disconnected, Greco-Roman, western egocentric, compartmentalized, reductionist, fragmented, linear thought process" (3–4) that he critiques. Nonetheless, his approach offers an alternative to industrial agriculture that many think we should follow.

If it is the case that grass-fed cattle are better for humans to eat, and that cattle raised in this way have better lives than those in CAFOs, could we simply move cattle production back to smaller-scale, grass-fed operations? If grazing cattle can be done in a way that improves the health of the land and so also improves the living conditions of various forms of wildlife, why don't we do it? Some reasons seem to be time and cost. It takes longer to raise grass-fed cattle. The time needed could be shortened to some extent with changes in breeding practices (as Swanson noted), but this would result in less meat per animal and thus in a higher price per pound. Another reason seems to be taste. People in the United States, and increasingly across the globe, are used to the taste and texture of grain-fed beef. In fact, the Windy N website lists sources for learning how to cook with grass-fed beef, because it is different. In addition to changing how people are accustomed to cooking meat, a substantial societal switch to grass-fed beef would also require people to consume substantially less beef. Since subsequent chapters will show that there are problems and costs with raising other species of livestock—probably more problems than with cattle—this would mean people would need to consume substantially less meat overall.

Some, like Salatin and Pollan, contest this conclusion. They think we can supply as much meat as we currently do, but in a way that is better for human health, better for the health of the land, and better for wildlife. They argue that when the land that is used to grow the soy and corn that are fed to cattle is factored into what is required for feedlot cattle, grass-fed cattle end up needing less land than feedlot cattle. While it is the case that there is land that is more suitable for grazing than for other kinds of farming, not that all farmland can easily be converted to grazing. To begin with beef cattle, grazing has impacts on the land, and throughout the history of the United States much of this impact has been negative.

The history of grazing on public land is complicated and ongoing. Access to such land during the time of homesteading allowed many to amass wealth and power. Even today's grazing permits are tied to owning specific land that comes with preference for access to public lands—a result of deals that were worked out during the "settling" of the West. The desire to settle the land, combined with a lack of understanding of the western climate, resulted in overstocking and overgrazing. As mentioned in chapter 3, the government responded to this with the 1934 Taylor Grazing Act. Grazing is now managed with leases, with the Bureau of Land Management (BLM) in charge of these leases and responsible for managing the land so that it can support a variety of wildlife as well. The BLM manages 18,000 permits that allow grazing on 155 million of the 245 million acres under their management. Here is how the BLM understands their charge:

> In managing livestock grazing on public rangelands, the BLM's overall objective is to ensure the long-term health and productivity of these lands and to create multiple environmental benefits that result from healthy watersheds. The Bureau administers public land ranching in accordance with the Taylor Grazing Act of 1934, and in so doing provides livestock-based economic opportunities in rural communities while contributing to the West's, and America's, social fabric and identity. Together, public lands and the adjacent private ranches maintain open spaces in the fast-growing West, provide habitat for wildlife, offer a myriad of recreational opportunities for public land users, and help preserve the character of the rural West. (Gorey)

Range management is understood by most to be about protecting and enhancing the soil and maintaining and improving the "output of consumable range products" such as red meat, fiber, wood, water, and wildlife. Rangeland is seen as land that can supply humans with food and fiber by using ruminants to harvest the energy stored in the plants that grow there. Rangeland in the western states supports about 20 percent of the cattle in the United States and 50 percent of the sheep (Holechek et al. 336). These grasslands evolved with the presence of grazers like the bison in numbers equal to those of the livestock that would eventually replace them. But by the late 1800s problems with the uncontrolled grazing of livestock were observed, including decreased grazing capacity, the increase of unpalatable plants, compacted soil, decreased soil fertility and absorption capacity, loss of soil, and increased prairie dog and jackrabbit populations (47). Recommendations to limit the numbers of livestock, control brush, and rest and seed land soon followed. The debates and disagreements about recommendations continue to this day.

There was real growth in livestock after the Civil War, and the government began to try to manage the situation. Further complicating matters, horse breeding often occurred through a process wherein a purebred stallion was purchased and then turned out on the range, with the offspring being later gathered and sold (de Steiguer 133–34). Then the Panic of 1893 hit the cattle industry hard and had an impact on the demand for horses. The mechanization of farm equipment and cars soon after further depressed the market for horses (137–38). But nothing stopped the horses from breeding. The range horses, along with the sheep and cattle, put real pressure on the land, and the government acted, but these actions were often at cross-purposes. The 1862 Homestead Act gave people 160 acres of free land after five years in residence, and the 1909 Enlarged Homestead Act gave away larger tracts of land (320 acres) if some of it was cultivated (which degraded the soil as it was not suited for crops). In 1916 the Stockraising Homestead Act granted 640 acres of land if fifty cattle were raised on it. (This often exceeded the carrying capacity of the land and resulted in range damage). The 1862 Transcontinental Railroad Act increased access to the land and increased pressure to "remove" bison and American Indians. Land had already been set aside for timber and grazing with the 1891 Forest Reserves Act. By the time the 1934 Taylor Grazing Act tried to address range damage by allocating grazing privileges and the 1935 Soil Erosion Act tried to address soil erosion, much damage had been done (Holechek et al. 52).

The "solutions" of the Taylor Grazing and Soil Erosion Acts were attempts to mitigate this damage, but they were far from perfect. Grazing districts were established and divided into allotments that were licensed to livestock ranchers for ten-year periods. These were not to function as property rights but they effectively did as the rights to lease the public land were transferred with the sale of particular ranches. As stocking rates were created the range horses came to be seen as a pest to be removed. One of the first solutions was to use the horses in wars. Later, funneling the horses into the dog food industry became a way to relieve the perceived pressure the horses put on the land. De

Steiguer writes, "In 1935, the United States counted some two hundred firms producing pet food from slaughtered horses, most of which were wild mustangs" (140).

This is an example of the intertwined fate of livestock and pets. The inhumane methods of rounding up, handling, and slaughtering these horses eventually resulted in moral outrage and the passage of the 1971 Wild Free-Roaming Horses and Burros Act. Prior to that, however, government sharpshooters were paid to kill wild mustangs, and the U.S. Forest Service paid hunters to kill twenty-two hundred mustangs in Nevada in the 1920s. The Nevada legislature passed laws in 1897 and 1914 encouraging ranchers to "kill free-roaming horses" (146). After World War II, the settling of suburbia resulted in a rise in the number of pets and another increase in the slaughter of wild horses for pet food. In *Wild Horses of the West*, Edward de Steiguer writes that "in response to the increased demand for horsemeat, the Bureau of Land Management (BLM) in Nevada alone had allowed the removal of some one hundred thousand wild horses from federal rangelands within a mere four years following the end of the war" (153). "Wild Horse Annie" famously publicized the cruelty of such "removals" and worked to protect the wild horses. Cattle ranchers and hunters were her main opposition as horses were seen as competing for grass with cattle and wild game. Since any grazing animal counted in the allotments permitted by the Taylor Grazing Act, the ranchers wanted no horses on "their" land (155).

Other pressures emerged with the passing of the Multiple Use Act in 1960. This required the Forest Service to manage the land for the benefit of grazing, wildlife, timber, and recreation. The Federal Lands Policy and Management Act of 1976 tried to set up guidelines for this multiple use, and the Rangeland Improvement Act of 1978 was passed in order to use a portion of the grazing fees to improve these lands. As a part of this effort the number of livestock and horses on federal lands was decreased between 1960 to 1993 (Holechek et al. 54–55). In the midst of these actions the National Environmental Policy Act passed in 1969 and the Endangered Species Act passed in 1973. These required Environmental Impact Statements for any actions that affected federal lands and protection for listed wildlife species (52). One of those competing interests was, again, the population of wild horses and burros.

In the West there is still evident tension between advocates for the range horses and those who rely on the range to graze their animals. One issue is the relative cheapness of leasing public rangeland for grazing and a history of less-than-stellar enforcement of rules and fee collections. The standoff between Cliven Bundy (who had grazed cattle without a permit and without paying fees for twenty some years) and BLM officials in Nevada in 2014 is one example. More recently in 2016 the Bundys and others participated in the occupation of the Malheur National Wildlife Refuge in Oregon to protest the sentencing of ranchers to five years in prison for unauthorized burning of rangeland on which they grazed cattle. Many ranchers argue that they are the best stewards of these lands, since their livelihood depends on the health of the land. Most follow rules, pay fees, and make improvements on the land that benefit wildlife as well as cattle—augmenting watering holes and improving grass. At the same time, however, most ranchers kill (or seek to eliminate) predator species. Ecosystem health depends on a number of factors, including the presence of predator species. Much of this predator control is carried out by federal employees, sparing the rancher the cost. Federal agencies also remove grazing competitors such as the wild horses and burros. Given that the cost of grazing on these lands is substantially less than buying private forage, many see this kind of access to public lands as a government subsidy for the livestock industry.

The fees charged for using these lands to graze livestock do not equal government appropriations for managing and improving these lands, so it is not the case that the grazing fees pay for other users of the land. It is not clear that these fees even cover the full costs of grazing the livestock. A study that examined the years 2002–2014 found that "the direct federal subsidy of the BLM and USFS livestock grazing programs exceeded $120 million every year for the past 12 years" (Glaser et al.). Since the fee system is constrained by the market price of the meat, it is almost assured to operate as a subsidy to ranchers rather than as a system that pays for use, reclamation, and improvement of the land. This is an important issue, and one that must be dealt with in order to create and sustain ecosystem biodiversity and health. But while these issues gain much public visibility, those who benefit from this arrangement represent less than 3 percent of the livestock industry. Grazing livestock, on public or private lands, raises environmental concerns, but there is less ability to monitor and address the damage done on private lands. There are a number of competing grazing theories: deferment systems that delay grazing until grass maturity is established, rest systems that require a retirement from use for at least a full year, and rotation systems that involve a variety of approaches to moving stock among grazing areas. Continuous grazing is also supported by many but requires lighter stocking rates than other systems (Holechek et al. 228–29). What there is agreement on is that some amount of grazing is probably better for the land than no grazing at all. After that things get less clear.

Much work has been done to identify and understand the interrelatedness of various aspects of the range ecosystems. The cycles are complicated and are impacted by variations in climate. The hope is that these lands can be managed in ways to promote more diverse and productive ecosystems. Fire and grazing are seen as important for maintaining many forest and grassland ecosystems, but this entails getting the stocking rates right to allow recovery and maintain productivity (Holechek et al. 130, 145, 190). The problem is that what might be best for a particular grassland at a particular time might not coincide with the grazing pattern that will optimize weight gain in the grazing animals. Popular now is the idea of pulse grazing, also referred to as mob grazing, controlled overgrazing, or short-duration grazing. Many of the farmers with whom we talked tried some version of this on their land. The idea is to graze cattle and sheep in ways that mimic the natural grazers with whom the grasses coevolved. In the United States, that includes bison, and it is thought that the Blackfeet Nation (who again raise bison today) moved the bison around in much the same way. On this view, there are not too many animals but too few, and these few are mismanaged (Fairlie 191–93). Nicolette Hahn Niman also promotes this idea in her book *Defending Beef: The Case for Sustainable Meat Production.*

Niman brings together much of the research that supports the idea that since millions of caribou, elk, deer, and bison grazed much of the U.S. territory in the past, the key to restoring and maintaining healthy ecosystems now "lies in making herds of domesticated animals function more like the wild herds of herbivores with which the ecosystems evolved" (14, 37). Since grasslands coevolved with grazing animals, healthy grasses require such grazing to remain healthy. Niman advocates mob grazing in order to stimulate "biological activity in the soil." The cattle manure "adds fertility"; their "hooves break the soil surface and press in seed, and push down dead plant matter so it can be acted upon by soil microorganisms." The overall effect is greater water retention and increased biodiversity (39). On this view, overgrazing is not the problem, but rather poorly managed grazing.

This is important not just for those who wish to raise cattle but also for those who want to grow crops as well. With the advent of monoculture agriculture, which relies on plows, pesticides, and fertilizer, the quality of the soil available for crop farming has deteriorated. The United States has lost 30 percent of its topsoil over the last couple of hundred years. The soil has also suffered from degraded water retention and filtration. Niman writes, "Regularly rotating cropland into pastures—especially of mixed grasses and clover—reverses much of the damage done by row crop cultivation. Thus . . . such meadows not only fed grazing animals, but were also fundamental to creating a permanent farming system that could produce food sustainably over the generations" (63). Niman argues that this would also greatly reduce (if not eliminate) the water waste and pollution that results from current agricultural practices.

The Environmental Protection Agency (EPA) attributes 60 percent of river and lake pollution to agriculture—the increased presence and runoff of chemicals, nutrients, pathogens, and sediments being their main focus (69). Intensive animal agriculture is a primary culprit. In her work as an environmental lawyer Niman worked to enforce water pollution laws that CAFOs ignored. Speaking specifically about her work with the hog industry in North Carolina and Missouri she writes, "I met people who'd lived in the same home their whole lives yet could no longer sit on their front porches or hang their laundry outside due to the stenches. I saw cold, lifeless facilities with metal walls and concrete floors holding thousands of sentient creatures. And I saw, and *smelled*, giant festering ponds of liquefied manure behind every cluster of buildings. Manure was leaking and spilling into local streams and rivers, now choked with algae, and periodically filled with dead and diseased fish" (71). The polluted waste stream from the animal operations is only one part of the problem. Over 50 percent of U.S. grain goes to industrial animal agriculture. Raising corn and soy is energy-intensive, soil-depleting, water-hungry, and water-polluting (75).

Niman argues that sustainable agriculture requires that water and soil be protected by an increased focus on rotating grass and crop production, using cover crops to restore soil balance, and *turning animals back out into the pastures*. She says, "All farm animals, but especially cattle and other grazing animals, should be moved out of buildings and feedlots and reared on grass instead, on meadows, rangelands, or as part of mixed-crop rotations" (67–68). While pigs, chickens, and turkeys cannot live on grass alone it is much better if they spend "their days on grass, foraging and grazing, and are given some feeds and crop residues, along with surplus and leftover human foods. Such an approach will lead to reduced pollution from feed production, prevent antibiotic overuse, and allow animals to live healthier better lives." Even more environmental improvements result from turning cattle back out onto grass: "Feed production—with all its attendant problems of fossil fuel consumption, soil erosion, greenhouse gases, and chemical pollution—can be avoided altogether" (79). She notes that such a shift would entail the United States raising fewer livestock animals than it does now and employing more labor in animal care and rotations (68). This would probably result in more expensive meat and dairy products.

Another benefit, however, would be increased biodiversity in the pasture and range ecosystems. First, if the land is being grazed it's not being converted to cropland and plowed and covered in chemicals. Second, many studies have found that grasslands that are not grazed have less plant diversity and more nonnative grasses than grazed land (96). Third, grazed land provides better habitat for many birds and butterflies as well as for foxes and bears. Very importantly, it provides valuable space for pollinators such as bees. This, in turn, is important for the future production of many crops. Niman's point is that if it is done well, grazing cattle is good for the land, the climate, and biodiversity. However, using lands in a way that is compatible with the increased biodiversity of wildlife means predation of livestock will be a reality. Wolves, coyotes, bears, and big cats are all potential predators. If, as Leopold suggests, such predators are important for the maintenance of healthy ecosystems, then ranchers will need to find ways to coexist. Several of the farms we visited used guard dogs and llamas to protect their sheep and goats. Many raising cattle focused on breeding cattle who are capable of protecting their own young. If there is a serious commitment to the flourishing of wildlife, then in addition to a changed mindset about predators, there will also need to be a re-visioning of what is now seen as competition from animals such as wild horses, elk, deer, and moose.

Interestingly, there is no room for the ideas Niman presents in a deep ecology framework, even though the approach she describes could do much to achieve some of the goals of deep ecology. The focus on ecosystems and understanding the systems as a whole would work for deep ecologists, as would the promotion of species diversity. The inclusion of livestock animals, though, has no place in deep ecology except as an unnatural disturbance. I believe this is rooted in an untenable metaphysical view that sees humans as being outside of nature, even as deep ecology calls on humans to see themselves as part of nature. Bringing pragmatism into the conversation is an important corrective as pragmatism more fully integrates humans, and the modifications to the environment that humans make, into the rest of nature. That doesn't mean all human impacts are good or unproblematic. But rather than try to avoid problems by pulling humans out of nature, pragmatism requires that humans wrestle with the long and complex history of human agriculture and face the moral questions that accompany living with livestock.

CHAPTER FIVE

Ruminating with Ruminants

RODEOS, RIGHTS, AND RESPECTFUL USE

In the book so far I have presented an approach that a pragmatist philosophy of animal well-being, augmented by specific insights from ecofeminism, might take when considering the current conditions of fish and cattle. I have also presented some history regarding the introduction of livestock to the United States, with a particular focus on cattle, to illuminate the complex interactions livestock have with humans and with physical environments. I have described mainstream industrial fish and cattle operations and discussed specific examples of farmers who challenge the industrial approach in one or more ways. I have presented several mainstream environmental philosophies, critiqued them from a pragmatist ecofeminist perspective, and used them to examine the practices and beliefs of those who raise livestock and those who consume livestock.

The previous chapter suggests that from a pragmatist perspective some amount of grass-fed cattle is compatible with conservation efforts, the flourishing of wildlife, the health of humans, and the well-being of the cattle themselves. That exact amount of cattle that is sustainable in these ways is not clear, but it is clear that it is not enough to satisfy the current appetite for beef. Human "predation" of cattle (and other livestock) would have to decrease. What about other human appetites? Cattle have been used for entertainment and ritual purposes throughout history as well. I have already mentioned cattle shows. These can be stressful for the animals because they require traveling and being on display. The risk of disease transfer increases as well. While many ranchers are moving to closed herds to limit disease exposure, shows have the opposite effect. But breeders participate in shows to promote their breeding lines. There are numerous state cattle expos where breeding (called seed stock) and feeder cattle are sold. The Fort Worth Livestock Expo and Rodeo is a famous example of this kind of event. While it has showing and education opportunities related to all kinds of livestock and to horses, there is a strong presence of cattle. This event builds on the relationship of cattle and horses to the myth of the cowboy and the West, as the livestock show is combined with a rodeo. Rodeos are sporting events many animal welfare and animal rights groups consider to be cruel, and not without reason.

Several events at rodeos include the use of cattle. Some of these come from early competitions to demonstrate skill at calf-roping, steer-roping, steer-wrestling, cutting, and penning. As with all competitions there are concerns about the stress caused by traveling and competing—especially for the calves. There are concerns of injury occurring during roping and wrestling. Some of the injuries that the cattle can suffer include torn tendons and ligaments, rope burns, dislocated and broken bones, and death from a broken neck. The Professional Rodeo Cowboy Association (PRCA) devotes a section of its website to animal welfare rules, including the humane transport of injured animals from the arena. There is some attempt to prevent injury with fines for pulling a calf over backwards, being unnecessarily rough, or using electric prods when not needed. Cutting and penning have also become specialized aspects of horse competitions, and cattle are shipped around the country so that horses can compete. There is an irony in the fact that specialized horses are bred to work the cattle who pushed their free-roaming relatives off the range and into pens themselves.

To get a sense of the attitude about many of the animals at a rodeo it can be instructive to look at the wild horse race events. Staged to draw a crowd, in this event, a team of three people hold, saddle, and ride an "unhandled" horse. Horses and humans regularly get hurt in these events. When two horses had to be euthanized after colliding head on at full speed at a rodeo in St. Paul, Oregon, the organizers reluctantly canceled future races. Complaining about the cancellation, one person commented, "It's the way you used to break horses in the old days," he said. "Nowadays, they do it kind of different" (Cheesman). There is a nostalgic tone to his remark. Even in races that don't result in injury or death, the event is incredibly stressful for the horses and clearly an animal welfare concern. The person here expresses no concern for the horses, though, and horses are prized animals in U.S. culture. Given this, it is hard to expect real concern for the cattle used in most rodeos. They are generally seen as disposable and replaceable. The one possible exception is the bulls used in bull-riding.

The rodeo event of bull-riding has become its own touring and televised event. It is interesting to note that this world replicates the sexism seen in meat (especially beef) advertisements discussed in chapter 3. For example, the commercial for the Professional Bull Riders (PBR) finals in Las Vegas in 2014 featured the famous bull Bushwacker as "one of the cowboys" trying to get into a party with bikini-clad women. An ESPN article about Bushwacker describes him as seeing bulls as "those he wants to brawl" and cows as "those he wants to bang" (Wright).

Riders in the PBR compete in big-money, televised events, as do the bulls. Both the bulls and the riders are called athletes and both are scored in competition. Being a bucking bull breeder can be quite lucrative, and being a bull on the professional circuit is probably not too bad—travel, eat, buck. Given the money invested in them, bulls are given good veterinary care and time off. Those on more local and amateur circuits, though, often have problematic lives. While their owners may care for them (since they are an investment of money), they are often handled and ridden by less-experienced people. At such events it is not uncommon to see unnecessary reliance on electric prods and hitting as well as lame animals competing. Because rodeos are exempt from the kinds of regulation that accompany other shows, there is little to no oversight. While the large professional rodeos have some self-regulation and enforcement of rules, the same cannot be said for the more local and amateur rodeos and bull-riding events. The lives of the females to whom these bulls are bred vary greatly depending on who owns them and are entirely unregulated.

As mentioned in chapter 3, two of the farmers in this study—Lee and Joe Markholt—were both bull riders. Both thought the bulls and horses involved in most rodeos were well treated. Lee and Joe thought that since the cattle and horses are a financial investment for their owners, they are usually cared for, even if they are sometimes seen as disposable once their competing days are at an end. (This was something they also noticed with some people involved in quarter horse racing, but they did not treat their own race horses this way.) Joe did have concerns about the ways some bull riders, and some who rode horses in rodeo events, thought and talked about the animals. While some expressed an attitude of domination, Joe never talked this way himself, and he did not condone it. I witnessed such talk (and action), though, at a bull-riding event I attended. Some of the riders talked about the bulls in derogatory ways, several taunted the bulls when they were in their pens, and one owner expressed disgust about the "uselessness" of his bulls when they didn't perform as expected. There are clearly concerns about animal welfare at such events, and there is the problem of perpetuating a relationship between humans and cattle based on domination and disregard. But this is not something that has to be the case—Joe being one notable exception to the common trend.

We also visited and interviewed Mike Warford and Tanja Oliver of Way

Out West Bucking Bulls. Mike was a bull rider who rode professionally for ten years. Looking for a way to stay involved as age and injuries took their toll, he and Tanja decided to raise and compete their own bulls. They established Way Out West Bucking Bulls in 2010, and Mike hauls bulls to competitions and works as a handler. A state-of-the-art trailer for the bulls ensures they arrive at competitions in good shape and well rested. Good quality forage and feed give the bulls energy to do their job, and the bulls had shelter and a misting system to keep them cool in the heat. During our visit Mike talked about the different personalities of the bulls he's known and handled and their intelligence. He said, "The bulls get to know the cowboys' styles just as the cowboys learn about the bulls' techniques." When we went out to visit the bulls they were curious about us and several came up to the fence to have their heads scratched. Without any cows around the bulls lived peacefully together and seemed to form friendships with each other. The only thing they lacked was a pasture on which to graze. After a very successful 2015 season Mike and Tanja decided to sell their bulls to another contractor and now the bulls have pasture as well.

Bulls are glorified in contemporary U.S. culture, much as they have long been admired and worshiped. Early cave drawings of powerful aurochs speak to their size and power and there is evidence of bull worship around the world. They have also been used as sacrificial animals. Bullfighting is thought to have its roots in the worship and sacrifice of bulls, but in many cultures it is the nurturing qualities of the cow that are lauded and worshiped. Providing milk, blood, and manure, cows are seen as life-giving and life-sustaining forces. Cattle have been used as a measure of wealth and prestige. Many cultures and religions have had (and some still do have) taboos against eating beef and severe restrictions on killing cattle. The value of the cattle and their integral role in the society often resulted in their protection. One possible motivation for domestication could be the ritual significance of cattle. If one needs to have an animal for a sacrifice at a particular point in time, hunting is not a reliable method of procural (Marshall 104).

Scientists think that cattle were the last of the three common ruminants to be domesticated—around eleven thousand years ago. This may be because they rely on grass and water more than the more hardy and adaptable sheep and goats do and so were harder to keep. It may also have something to do with their size and power. Today's cattle are thought to be descendants of aurochs who were domesticated in Asia in at least two separate domestication events. One resulted in the *B. taurus* group and one in the *B. indicus* or zebu (humped) group. As the domesticated cattle moved with human migration they had opportunities to continue mating with wild aurochs. Some studies of mitochondrial genomes show that such mixing continued well after the original domestication events. Others challenge this interpretation, insisting that such crosses would have been too hard to handle. Ancient Greek and Roman writers described aurochs as very aggressive, and Julius Caesar wrote, "These are a little below the elephant in size, and of the appearance, color, and shape of a bull. Their strength and speed are extraordinary; they spare neither man nor wild beast which they have espied" (Caesar 6.28).

Wild aurochs were regularly hunted and required a fair amount of range. As domesticated cattle and other livestock competed for this range, the aurochs moved toward extinction. They were rare by the thirteenth century, and the last known aurochs died in Poland in 1627 (Achilli). Aurochs are thought to have lived in herds of females and calves with a few adult males. Most males lived either solitary lives or in bachelor groups (Russell et al. 103). This means their lives were not unlike those of domestic cattle prior to the advent of industrial farming—or those of many rodeo bulls today.

In order to fully examine the human relationship with cattle it is important to understand the history of their domestication, their social patterns, and their interactions with their environments. That story continues to evolve as archaeology is supplemented with genetic evidence, but it is clear that there were multiple domestication events from wild aurochs and that modern cattle still retain the same social structure as their wild ancestors. So, it is not unnatural to keep bulls together in social groups separate from cows. It is not unnatural to have herds composed of cows and their offspring. Keeping a bull on his own is natural as well (though this may not suit a particular individual). These are important considerations to keep in mind. So too are the intelligence and social lives of cattle.

While many people are fascinated with accounts of the intelligence and emotional lives of apes, elephants, whales, and dolphins, there is still general disbelief when it comes to accounts of the intelligence and emotions of livestock animals. Jeffrey Masson's book *The Pig Who Sang to the Moon: The Emotional World of Farm Animals* points out, however, that there is no large physiological or evolutionary break between livestock and their wild ancestors or cousins. The only break is in our attitudes. The philosophy behind his main argument has a lot in common with pragmatism, with its focus on embodied, evolutionary processes. He argues that wild animals have intelligence and emotions (which is supported by their physiology and how they survive), that domesticated livestock are not far removed from their wild ancestors in terms of their physiology, and therefore that domesticated livestock also have intelligence and emotions. He goes on to critique how we breed, raise, and slaughter these same creatures—practices carried out with close to total disregard for their intelligence and emotional lives. For example, he writes, "To the extent that you prevent an animal from living the way he or she evolved to

RUMINATING WITH RUMINANTS

live, you are creating unhappiness for that animal. All farm animals, it turns out, from chickens to cows, have evolved to have offspring and guide them through their infancy" (2–3). This is not a practice allowed in contemporary CAFOs. Using Mark Johnson's view (discussed in chapter 2), I would say this is a failure of morality from a pragmatist perspective. It is a failure of humans to acknowledge the moral impulses of the livestock animals themselves and it is a failure of humans to fully embrace their own embodied and interconnected moral status.

What's most interesting here is that the characteristics that make an animal a candidate for domestication are the very characteristics that might make one ascribe intelligence, emotion, communication, and consciousness to those animals. Domestication was and is the result of the similarity and compatibility of these other animal beings with human beings. But they mainly live in circumstances that deny or frustrate these very characteristics. It is also interesting that these are the very characteristics being used to argue for personhood for certain other, nondomesticated animal beings, such as apes. Cows, sheep, goats, chickens, pigs, and fish also share in recognizable emotions and intelligence.

In 2012 a prominent group of scientists signed the Cambridge Declaration on Consciousness. This Declaration states, "Convergent evidence indicates that non-human animals have the neuroanatomical, neurochemical, and neurophysiological substrates of conscious states along with the capacity to exhibit intentional behaviors. Consequently, the weight of evidence indicates that humans are not unique in possessing the neurological substrates that generate consciousness. Non-human animals, including all mammals and birds, and many other creatures . . . possess these neurological substrates." Research documenting empathetic responses in chickens supports the conclusion of these scientists, as does research documenting pleasure in cows who are learning a task, anticipation of pain and stress in pigs, and joy and depression in fish. All these animals have signals and forms of communication that allow them to navigate their social settings and they all have behaviors that are frustrated by the current practices of industrialized farming. While many people see domesticated animal beings as somehow less than their "wild" counterparts—less intelligent, less flexible, less emotionally complex—this view does not accord with the facts. While pragmatist philosophers (especially Peirce and, eventually, Dewey) were clear that such animals were beings with unique personalities, emotions, and intelligence, there is a long history, especially in philosophy, of denying intelligence and emotions to those animals who have long been used for meat and milk. That denial has no basis in reality.

The recognition that livestock animals have personalities, emotions, and intelligence is nothing new. It is what allowed for domestication in the first place, and for the long-standing and mutually transformative relationships between humans and livestock discussed in chapter 1. This recognition has always given some people pause about the condition and uses of livestock (and other) animals, and throughout human history there have been calls to improve animal welfare or to end the human use of other animal beings. While one can reduce the amount of death entailed in the support of one's life, such death cannot be eliminated altogether. As discussed, even vegan diets involve the death of many beings. In some cases the raising and slaughtering of a cow may sustain more life, with less death, than does the production of a soy burger. That said, increasing recognition of, and insight into, the personalities, emotions, and intelligence of cattle and other livestock should give us pause and impress upon us the gravity of raising and killing animals for food and fiber when we realize they can also be friends. As already discussed, many of the farmers we interviewed ate less meat after they started to raise and kill the animals themselves. The recognition of the complex lives of livestock animals results in increased respect and responsibility. This seems more existentially in tune with the reality of human interdependence with the rest of nature than do moves to grant some (but not all) animals rights that require humans to not use them—and especially to not kill them.

That is not to say that nothing can be gained from discussion and debate from a rights perspective. Ecofeminist theorist A. Breeze Harper argues that exploring the connections between the rights of women and minorities in the United States points to a need to change our relationships with other animal beings. She is joined in this call by others, such as Delicia Dunham, who notes that "many of us black female vegans realize that much of how non-human animals are treated in the USA frighteningly parallels the way black females were treated during chattel slavery." Dunham supports this comparison with the observation that the animals "are given no choice of mate; they are forced to engage in sexual activity with one another while their 'master' watches, to live in separate quarters from loved ones and to give birth to beings who are promptly taken away and sold to other plantations. They are forced to suckle beings not their own for the benefit of others" (44). Harper argues that making this comparison diminishes black people only for those with speciesist views that rest on the idea that animals don't matter. Harper experiences the same moral outrage about human slavery as about nonhuman slavery and argues that unmindful eating perpetuates injustice and ecological harm. Harper holds that in order to overcome sexism, heterosexism, classism, racism, and speciesism, people must think carefully about what we consume and "must extend our antiracist and antipoverty belief to all people, nonhuman animals, and Mother Gaia" ("Social Justice" 29). Such an extension, however, need not entail legal rights similar to those attributed to most humans. It is possible to respect the lives, needs, and desires of various livestock animals and still engage in some types of farming. Breeding can occur more freely and offspring can be left with their mothers in many versions of nonindustrialized farming.

In her book *Governing Animals*, Kimberly K. Smith argues that the concepts of personhood and rights do not offer the best approach to improving human relationships with other animals. While she thinks it's important to promote animal welfare and humane stewardship as a way to combat the increasing commodification and exploitation of other animals, she doesn't think person-hood status is necessary or a good idea. In her view such beings lack auton-omy and so are not persons; they do, however, have some natural rights that deserve to be respected since the animals have minds and life plans (what Dewey described as "careers" unique to an individuality—discussed in chap-ter 1). All that is needed by her account is to include other animal beings in the moral community—something she thinks has increasingly happened.

She argues that there is an emerging sense that other animal beings de-serve protection from neglect, abuse, and cruelty but that to define neglect, abuse, and cruelty in such ways as would suit the drafting of enforceable laws would actually be counterproductive and probably not improve the lives of those harmed: "I claim here only that there is sufficient consensus to claim the existence of a public philosophy concerning animals: Viewing (some) an-imals as members of the social contract is consistent with and makes sense of most of our laws, our widespread social practices, our typical ways of talking about animals in public discourse, and well-documented measures of public opinion" (49). This is most clearly true, she argues, for those animals with whom humans have relationships. These are the animals deserving of governmental protection. For her this includes all domesticated animals as they are interdependent with humans but unequal. This makes them vul-nerable and at risk of subordination (53). She lists pets, birds at a feeder, zoo animals, and some wild animals as meeting the criteria for such protection. She also includes livestock in the social contract: "They live with us in close relations of interdependence and mutuality, and . . . have historically received the highest level of government protection. But many will find this position counterintuitive. After all, we often keep livestock in crowded, unhealthy con-ditions where they cannot develop physically or socially in their character-istic way. And then we slaughter them and eat them. It seems inapt to call them members of the social contract, in the same way that it seemed inapt, to nineteenth-century Americans, to consider slaves members of the social contract" (63). The difference Smith sees is that while slaves needed reforms that resulted in political autonomy and legal equality, livestock do not need these things to flourish—"indeed they can't flourish without our care" (64). In her view, livestock's natural liberties are best respected by humans practicing good animal husbandry. She asserts that most large-scale animal agriculture fails to do this and does treat animals as slaves or mere resources. On her account, these are bad farmers, but not all farming is bad.

On the question of whether killing an animal for food violates the social contract, Smith says that most farmers see killing and use as part of the contract. From the farmers' point of view, the animals get a "comfortable and happy life until they are slaughtered." On this view death is not a harm; "it is the inevitable price of living. What matters is the quality of one's life, which for livestock can be quite good" (64). There is a mutual dependence and reciprocity. Given the hard work and low profits of good husbandry, Smith argues there is real affection in these relations and this position should be respected. What about respecting those who see death as a harm and find this position to be self-serving justification on the part of the farmers? Smith makes an interesting move here. She says:

> People who raise livestock in this intimate, responsible, and humane manner commit themselves to a difficult and demanding job, and they make very little money from it. . . . They choose this work and this diet because they like to raise animals. By contrast, the opposing view—that we must end livestock production altogether—does sound rather self-serving to me. Instead of preserving an ancient social practice that brings us into a deeply meaningful and demanding relationship with animals, these advocates want to get rid of that relationship *and the animals that are part of it. True, we may be suspicious of farmers who insist that their animals are getting a fair bargain. But we should also be suspicious of people who want to avoid ethically and emotionally demanding relationships by eliminating the creatures on the other end of those relationships.* (65, italics added)

Smith sees those who want to eliminate livestock (and other domesticated animals) as involved in a kind of moral evasion. Since living out the complex relationships between humans and other animal beings is morally hard, some try to avoid the relationships altogether. I think there is some truth to her charge. Further, the call to eliminate domesticated animals is, in my view, another instance of human exceptionalism and reinforces the very hierarchy most animal advocates say they seek to dismantle. It is a way of denying the coevolution of humans and other animal beings. Further, those opposing the farming of animals often have little or no experience with those animals. They often have little contact with actual farmers as well. This limits their understanding of what might constitute a "good life" and a "good death" for these animals and they fall back on the extreme position of elimination.

Smith goes on to point out that much about current farming would need to change if human and other animal beings are to establish (or reestablish) re-

spectful relationships of use: "Fulfilling the conditions of a reasonable domesticated animal contract asks a great deal more from us than simply ceasing to
eat meat. We would have to radically reform the way we raise livestock. As citizens we would have to take a great deal more care to find out how livestock
are raised and slaughtered, to agitate for their protection, and to support
farmers so that they can fulfill their obligations to their animals." For Smith
this would entail economic support for the "good" farmers by buying their
animal-based products. This rules out being vegan or vegetarian on her account. Further, she says, "we would have to see livestock as animals to whom
the political community as a whole has a particularly broad and compelling
set of obligations. This, I think, is the harder ethical choice. In my view, it is
the more admirable one" (65–66). While I agree that such a diet is one possible ethical option, I do not see the need to preclude the choice to be vegan
or vegetarian. However, veganism and vegetarianism do need to be informed
choices. People should also realize that such diets come with a host of ethical
issues of their own—labor issues, environmental issues, class issues.

Paul B. Thompson makes a claim similar to Smith's in *From Field to Fork*
when he argues that ethical vegetarians are actually morally irresponsible.
His argument is that there are three important questions regarding animal
agriculture: "Is it ethically acceptable to eat animal flesh, or to raise and
slaughter animals for food? Are current farming practices acceptable? How
should current practices be reformed or modified to improve animal welfare?" (134). He says ethical vegetarians answer no to question one and then
fail to be involved in addressing questions two and three—and since we will
not be a vegetarian society anytime soon (if ever), everyone is obligated to
be involved in addressing questions two and three. I agree that everyone, no
matter their personal dietary choices, needs to address current farming practices and animal welfare concerns, but I am suspicious of the view of ethical
vegetarians as generally not involved in critiquing and trying to improve the
lives of livestock animals. While many may focus on getting people to stop
eating meat, this usually entails discussion of why the current living conditions are not acceptable. For some there will be no acceptable conditions, but
more promote the consumption of more humanely and sustainably raised animals even if they themselves do not choose to consume animals. Nicolette
Niman (author of *Defending Beef*) and Wayne Pacelle (president of the HSUS)
are good examples. While I understand Thompson's and Smith's point that
those who are committed to such changes need to provide economic support
to the farmers trying to do things more humanely, I do not think economic
support is the only effective option available. I do think Thompson and Smith
are correct to worry about vegans/vegetarians who do not make any real distinctions among the different ways farmers approach the lives and deaths of

the animals they raise and slaughter, lumping small farms in with CAFOs as if there are no relevant differences. But the same needs to be said for people who eat animal products as well. Many (some willfully) keep the image of the small farm in mind as they buy cheap industrially raised meat. Given the diversity of farming practices we need more nuanced discussions than extreme or uninformed views can allow.

Given that Smith is aiming at a public philosophy that can gain widespread support and lead to reform of the livestock industry, she concludes:

> I don't think it is deeply inappropriate or counterintuitive to consider livestock members of the social contract. On the contrary, if we are going to raise animals for food, we *must* consider them members and accept all the responsibilities that entails. Granted, many people will find my reasoning unpersuasive and conclude that vegetarianism is the only ethically defensible choice. This is reasonable as a matter of personal ethics. . . . But here we are concerned with fashioning a public philosophy, one that can find support broad and deep enough to justify extensive government regulation of the livestock industry. (66)

The current industrial livestock industry sees these animal beings purely as commodities—as economic resources. Given the property rights of those who own the livestock, and their economic goals, many practices that do not support the animal's well-being come to be justified and are now common practice. While many think we need to replace animals' property status with personhood, this is not the best option according to Smith. She agrees that not all things or beings should be treated as commodities, but she thinks some things and beings can, *in part*, be treated as commodities. She thinks that animals should never be reduced to commodities. However, she thinks that the value of the animal as property can be used to give the guardian of the animal rights that can be used to respect it. (This same argument is made by the Cat Fanciers Association in response to animal rights activists who resist the idea of owning pets.)

Interestingly, Smith rejects a future with lab-grown "in vitro" meat, which some animal advocates support on the grounds that it would end the suffering and deaths (and lives) of live animals. Instead she hopes for a future with "small-scale, sustainable operations that respect the cultural meaning of livestock and maintain, in improved form, traditional practices of animal husbandry. Grass-fed bison ranches, urban livestock production, or even hunting could also figure in a defensible vision of a better, more fully realized animal welfare society" (126). Rather than seek rights for animal beings and use coercion to change practices, she hopes to achieve this future by continuing to improve our understanding of animal psychology and physiology. She thinks this has already done much to improve the lives of livestock and argues for continued improvement (138). The focus should be on protecting the vulnerable and helping them flourish. Since we are ecologically and socially interdependent beings, better stewardship is what is needed (166). That entails treating animals not as mere things, nor as persons, but as *"fellow creatures*, co-inhabitants of our ecological and social spaces. They form a wildly diverse set, differing among themselves in terms of physical, emotional, intellectual, social, and, accordingly, moral characteristics. Our laws and practices must attend to those differences, as well as their similarities to and differences from humans" (xiv).

Smith's approach has much in common with a pragmatist approach as it is rooted in an understanding of the natural and developmental histories of the animals, demonstrates a respect for the animals' emotions and intelligence, and seeks to ameliorate their lives and their complex relationships with humans. Her reliance on social contract theory, however, presents some problems. Interestingly these are problems shared by the calls for personhood as well. One concern with these debates about personhood and the social contract is that they rest on a model of humans as rational autonomous beings with a free will that is guided by conscious and deliberate choices. As Mark Johnson has argued, however, this is not an accurate picture of human beings. So, concepts of personhood that rest on demonstrating some specific degree of reason or autonomy are flawed approaches. Since social contract theory generally rests on this view of persons, it too is a flawed approach.

Pragmatists and feminists alike have critiqued social contract theory for relying on a notion of a rational, autonomous, atomistic individual in competition with others. The story of the "contract" is that such individuals, using rational self-interest, agree to be governed (give up some freedoms) in return for protection of their life and property (security). Women and non-Europeans were not considered fully rational, and so they were not parties to this "contract" but were rather part of the property that was to be protected—as were animals. It doesn't work to just add them in as full citizens since the theory relies on their being less than full citizens. Carol Pateman's *The Sexual Contract* and Charles Mills's *The Racial Contract* provide excellent discussions of these issues and point to some serious flaws that should give one pause when appealing to social contract theory today. Most pragmatists and ecofeminists agree that the exclusion of groups of humans is a serious flaw in social contract theory, as is the description of the individual on which the theory relies. Pragmatists and ecofeminists generally understand the individual to be social, interdependent, and emotional as well as rational. What is important here is to realize that humans fail to be persons on most accounts of what personhood entails for such theories because we are not fully rational or autonomous. Given this, social contract theory and its underlying concept of the individual are not the best ideas to use to argue for respectful treatment of human or other animal beings. Further, the expansion of consideration on this model still tends to privilege those beings who are seen as like humans in having some particular kind of rational capacity or intelligence—for instance, apes, elephants, and dolphins. Pigs might make the list, but probably not sheep, cattle, chickens, or fish. Further, as Val Plumwood notes, such approaches privilege animals generally and make no room for various forms of vegetation. For these reasons, though I see some insights coming from wrestling with views like those of Harper and Smith, I do not take the approach of arguing for rights or personhood here, nor do I argue for including livestock (or other animal beings) in some version of a social contract.

Instead, I suggest that humans spend more time coming to understand livestock animals in a more fully developed way *in their own right* and as *interdependent* with human beings. This entails understanding the lives of the wild ancestors of these animals as well as the processes of domestication and the mutually transformative nature of those various histories (and ongoing stories) of domestication. It also means facing problems that emerge for human and other animal beings (given our shared vulnerabilities) as our relationships change over time. As Mark Johnson's Deweyan-inspired approach to morality suggests, "Refusal to examine our changing situation is a form of self-inflicted moral blindness" (212). Today human relationships with livestock animals are not good. As discussed in previous chapters, they are not good for most livestock animals, who cannot live a full life or have a good death. They are not good for many of the humans who make a living by working in slaughterhouses, feedlots, or production facilities. They are not good for consumers or for the environment. It is also the case that relationships between the animal-production industry (it is really not agriculture at this point) and those who critique the practices of this industry are not good. In many cases we have two entrenched camps fighting for the mind, heart, and stomach of the consumer.

For example, the Animal Agriculture Alliance say they seek to help inform the public about the importance of animal agriculture and the steps being taken to ensure that animal products are safe and produced in a humane manner. They also seek to combat animal rights efforts: "Radical activist organizations are leading the fight to grant animals the same legal rights as humans and eliminate the consumption of food and all other products derived from animals. The ideology of the animal rights movement—that animals are not ours to own, enjoy, or use in any way—is a direct assault on farmers and pet owners. Activists often hide their true agenda in order to gain the support of unknowing pet lovers." There is a clear tone of suspicion and antagonism in this statement. They go on to say that they provide "current updates from the world of animal rights. The Alliance monitors the activities of these activist groups and seeks to proactively engage in the same areas they target to correct misinformation and tell the true story of agriculture. The 2015 Animal Rights Conference Report can be found in our resource library as a members-only document." Despite what they say, their list includes many groups that do not endorse the rights-based (personhood-based) approach but rather focus on a set of welfare and environmental concerns. That the Alliance monitors such groups and writes secret reports about their work speaks volumes to the current inability of most to engage in the kind of inquiry Dewey's approach to ethics requires. The recent efforts to pass "ag gag" laws to criminalize attempts to document and make public some of the conditions in which these animals live and die further limits the possibility of productive conversation and critique. On the other side, some of the animal advocacy groups also dig into extreme positions that take the worst actions of the industry as the norm.

While generally disregarded as one of those "useless" college majors, the discipline of philosophy has been particularly active and effective with regard to animal and environmental concerns. Professional philosophers have taken up these issues in their work, and animal and environmental activists have used philosophers' writing to support their own positions and actions. Unfortunately, much of this philosophical work has been done within a framework of moral theory in which some kind of universal moral principle can be consulted to guide actions. This moral examination occurs primarily through the use of reason to arrive at context-free, absolute, and universal positions. It should not be surprising, then, that those involved in animal issues tend to endorse some kind of absolutistic thinking that does not make room for nuance and situational factors.

In his book *Dewey*, Steven Fesmire shows the need for a Deweyan ethic rooted in imagination, empathy, and thoughtful inquiry. But most ethical theory has accepted the idea that there is one "fundamentally right way to organize moral reflection" (119). This has resulted in competing theories such as rights-based ethics, utilitarian ethics, and virtue ethics, but they all share the commitment that there is one theory that can cover the range and complexity of moral issues. Dewey, as a pluralist, sees important insights in all of these approaches but thinks no one alone can grapple with the complexity of lived moral experiences and choices. He holds that such theories are important tools that can "have practical value for streamlining moral deliberations" (122) but that we should be careful not to fall prey to their desire for one foundational, certain, and absolute moral principle or their desire for one certain and absolute moral decision in the face of life's complexity.

Fesmire gives a nice example of the problem when he discusses the moral stance of Joel Salatin's view (discussed in chapter 4) and that of veganism. Salatin challenges industrial agriculture by calling for rotational grazing of animals, while vegans challenge industrial agriculture by calling for the end of all animal agriculture. These two approaches share a common focus but different solutions. Fesmire argues that they also share a common problematic attitude—that they both are absolutist approaches that fail to take note of the complexity and pluralism the world presents. Fesmire writes, "Salatin is no pragmatist in his ethics. He wields the sword of righteousness. For example, he argues that the 'right' diet must be based on grass-fed animal husbandry if it is to mimic perennial natural cycles, so it must include meat" (138). Salatin fails to be pragmatist because he sees only one right way to think and reason about the issues, and only one right answer. In comparison, Fesmire says, "Ironically, vegan abolitionists share the same assumption when they argue that 'meat is murder' and that all animal agriculture is slavery that violates animal rights" (139). While both food choices are possible outcomes of particular moral inquiry, the problem here is that the attitude of absolutism cuts off inquiry rather than encourages it. The problem Fesmire presents is that "moral zealots are often fearful of ambiguity and so cling desperately to settled codes as fixed compass points" (148). While moral theories (and political theories such as social contract theory) generally seek to unsettle such zealotry they often replicate it with a focus on a single moral principle. Dewey's pluralistic approach disrupts this tendency and calls on people to "become more imaginative and responsible" as they wrestle with complex and changing problems (145).

The pragmatist approach to ethics sketched here, and in chapters 1 and 2, challenges the paradigm of universal moral theories and absolutist positions. I believe this approach is a better fit for the lived experience of humans. I also believe it is an approach that is particularly helpful in situations where groups have become entrenched in opposed positions. To support this claim I will begin an examination of some of the issues already raised concerning cattle.

Discussions of cattle are complicated and emotionally laden from the start. As already noted, cattle, and the horses and cowboys associated with them, make up a large part of the "myth of America." The story behind the myth is more complicated, however. Cattle not only have provided material support for life, but they also have been used as political weapons in fights over land (e.g., fights between colonists and Native peoples, fights between cattle ranchers and sheep ranchers, and fights between ranchers and wild horse advocates). Cattle have been demonized as causing climate change and lauded as one of the most environmentally friendly sources of food. Cattle are seen as competing with wildlife and as promoting biodiversity. I could go on.

The point is that when there are this many conflicting positions, and people who passionately land on one side of the issue or the other, we have a "problem" in the Deweyan sense. Society is at a juncture when old habits are being unsettled and new habits have not solidified.

As Johnson points out much of the work regarding what we should and shouldn't do needs to take place in understanding "the problem." People tend to think they have the right take on "the problem," and so the solution they support is obviously correct. Here enter moral absolutes and entrenched, "sedimented" positions. Rather than feeling compelled to take a particular stance on the issues presented above, people should see such complex situatedness as an invitation to inquiry. This inquiry is likely to reveal that there is some "truth" in most of the positions. Now what?

Taking the issue of cattle's impact on wildlife, it is probably the case that grazing cattle in some places, in some particular well-managed ways, can increase the health of the soil, grasses, and the various life-forms who depend on these. We saw this with many of the farms we visited. At the same time, even in these places with these practices, it is likely there will emerge tensions between the lives of the cattle and the lives of plants and other animals who share the land. Finding ways to promote productive coexistence and the flourishing of multiple kinds of beings is an end-in-view that could work (and has worked in some cases) to get ranchers and environmentalists to work together to find ways to balance these interests. Getting rid of the cattle might be less environmentally helpful than having some cattle, but killing predators might harm the ecosystem (not to mention those animals). Killing wolves, for example, often devastates the social structure of particular packs, increasing predation as those wolves who remain try to survive. Without the education and guidance of the pack, individuals who are young, desperate, or both will often turn to livestock as easy prey. So it can be in the interests of wolves, cattle, cattle ranchers, environmentalists, and animal advocates to find ways to support intact wolf packs.

This can only work, however, if ranchers, environmentalists, and animal advocates can talk with each other. That requires an openness to other people's perspectives, a willingness to acknowledge that one doesn't have all the information or answers, a sense that situations and positions can change (and so habits need to change), and the ability to be flexible and experiment with different approaches. In this experimentation many views such as the land ethic, deep ecology, ecofeminism, a care ethic, and an agrarian ethic (and more) will be valuable resources—not in terms of giving answers but in terms of raising issues and pushing conversations. This is an ongoing process, not something to be fixed and finished.

Nor is any one perspective universalizable. The approaches that work in one time and place will probably not work in another. We must ask not only what works but also for whom it works. Cattle grazing that "worked" for the U.S. government did not "work" for Native Americans; what "works" for industrial agriculture does not "work" for cattle or many consumers. With added human population, changing weather patterns, and competing land use claims, there can be no simple return to some past practice (even if that were desirable). What works in the mountains of Wyoming won't work on the plains of Nebraska or the plateaus of New Mexico. These "solutions" are shaped by places, histories, politics, and specific circumstances. There is no one-size-fits-all. Aldo Leopold noted this when he complained about government officials in Washington, DC, trying to set policies for wildlife conservation and land use that fit the whole nation. Leopold thought that people needed to be invested in local land in order to effectively change their habits and attitudes from a use perspective to an interdependence and respect perspective. He said, "This face-about in land philosophy cannot be imposed on landowners from without, either by authority or by pressure groups. It can develop only from within, by self-persuasion, and by disillusionment with previous concepts." In other words you can't force people to change their habits. He also thought there can't be general solutions to particular problems. Particular ecosystems have particular and changing needs that a national policy cannot take into account. He wrote, "A wildlife plan is a constantly shifting array of small moves, infinitely repeated, to give wildlife due representation in shaping the future minds and future landscapes of America" (Leopold and Schwartz 198). This requires ongoing conversation and experimentation in order to make things better.

The same kind of analysis applies to how the cattle themselves are born, live, and die. Before humans could provide sophisticated nutritional and medical interventions in the lives of cattle, the only way to successfully raise them was to house and care for them in ways that promoted their capacity to give birth independently, protect their offspring, resist parasites and disease, and put on weight. This meant leaving calves with cows, providing enough room to graze so that manure (and parasites) did not become concentrated, and giving them time (years) to grow. This respected their intelligence and emotional connections too. While the cattle industry in the United States moved to an early division of the calf/cow operations and the feeding operations, the cattle still had to be kept in health-promoting ways until close to the end of their lives. This can be contrasted with today's quick-finishing cattle who don't live long enough to create the need to raise them in healthful ways. The breeding cows (and bulls) are a more long-term investment and these are the cattle more commonly living lives that fit their physical and social needs.

It is not hard to get those cattle ranchers who specialize in calf/cow operations to find some common ground with animal advocates. They have long-term relationships with the cattle and are invested (financially and emotionally) in their welfare. Those who focus on feeding operations (and sometimes supply "the genetics" to promote fast growth) see welfare in a more limited way—are the cattle well enough to gain weight? Those who slaughter and process cattle are more focused on the carcass size and quality. For them, as welfare issues can impact size and quality they do get some consideration—mostly, however, they address welfare concerns in order to avoid bad press or fines. With the life of the cattle divided up in these ways it is difficult to get any consensus on how the lives of cattle could be improved, much less a willingness to invest in changes that would improve their lives.

One way to start reintegrating the lives of cattle, though, might be to link the interests (financial and moral) of the various aspects of the industry. This is what Niman tries to do in *Defending Beef.* She realizes that the market for their grass-fed beef is limited by the public's concerns with the beef industry as a whole. While lack of public confidence in feedlot production gave rise to the market for grass-fed operations, it also causes people who aren't clear about these distinctions to lump all beef in the same basket and see beef as bad. She thinks the beef industry as a whole needs to work together and make changes that address the public's concerns about animal welfare and the environment. Such changes would probably entail longer lives on pastures and quicker, healthier, more sustainable finishing operations. This would require ongoing discussion among all those in the industry and then between those in the industry and the industry's critics.

The process of slaughtering and processing would also need to be addressed. One advantage of some feeding operations is that they are next to the slaughtering facility. This decreases the stress involved in transporting the cattle. If these facilities are well designed, the cattle can be kept calm until stunned. If stunned properly, the slaughter can be painless. But none of this can be done at the scale and speeds of today's slaughter lines. There would also need to be a willingness to reexamine the move to more centralized slaughter facilities that are owned by the same companies that own the finished cattle. These issues, however, are "problems" for all the meat industries and will be examined in subsequent chapters, especially chapter 10.

To further consider a pragmatist ecofeminist approach to living with livestock I will now turn to the lives and deaths of other livestock animals. The "problems" presented by cattle may seem much easier to address than the problems with pigs and poultry. Among the most common livestock, cattle and other ruminants usually have better lives than do pigs and poultry. By "better" I mean lives that more fully support the needs and desires of the particular species, breeds, and individuals and acknowledge the animals as distinct social individuals. This allows for a more nuanced approach to their care and potentially a more respectful approach to their death and use. This is what is necessary for any meaningful amelioration of the lives (and deaths) of livestock.

CHAPTER SIX

Sheep and Goats

AN ECOFEMINIST CRITIQUE OF
WENDELL BERRY AND BARBARA KINGSOLVER

Current evidence suggests that the first animal domesticated by humans is the dog, and that this relationship is thus the longest relationship between humans and a domesticated animal. It took longer to domesticate sheep and goats, the ruminants those dogs help herd and protect. And now llamas, like dogs, have become commonly used to protect herds of sheep. Domesticated about six thousand years ago, llamas and alpacas are members of the camelid family native to the Americas. Found in the Andes, they reside in Peru, Bolivia, Argentina, Chile, Colombia, and Ecuador. The llama was domesticated from the guanaco and the alpaca from the vicuna. Valued as pack animals and for their wool, meat, and manure, these animals were well cared for and revered until the arrival of the Spaniards in the 1500s disrupted these relationships and the llamas and alpacas were replaced with sheep. At the same time, the wild guanaco and vicuna were hunted for their pelts and to remove them in order to make room for the sheep ("Llama History"). Interest in the alpaca's wool and the llama's ability as a guard animal resulted in their importation to the United States. For the most part, however, they remain a hobby animal here. Sheep and goats, however, have been used as sources of food and fiber since the first Europeans arrived in North America and are on their way to facing the same kind of industrial farming methods that most other livestock in the United States experience.

Sheep and goats were domesticated in the Fertile Crescent about thirteen thousand years ago (11,000 BCE; DeMello 86). Early domestication was more on the herding than on the farming model. The process of domestication

PHOTO 3. Guard llama at 90 Farms. Photo by Danielle Palmer.

would have covered some range of decades, with kept goats and sheep still interbreeding with wild goats and sheep. While it can be difficult to disentangle the competing methods and assessments of their evolutionary past, scientists posit at least three separate domestication events, followed by various migrations with humans. Hunting of wild goats and sheep was one early source of meat, and hunting continued for some time after domestication. People hunted primarily in the winter when the domesticated herds birthed young. Given uncertainty about how many of these domesticated kids and lambs would survive, it was wiser to hunt the wild goats and sheep that came down from the hills as the snows arrived (G. Stein).

Wild goats tend to be social in the winter and more solitary in the summer. Goat herds are controlled by a dominant female except during mating season; males live in bachelor bands except when they join the females for mating. The general grazing range of a goat is fourteen square miles. In addition to grazing and browsing, they take time to dust bathe and bed down at night. They generally live nine to twelve years, reaching sexual maturity around two and a half years old. Goats are more independent than sheep, who prefer to herd together (Bradford). Nonetheless the physical and social nature of wild sheep is similar to that of the goats. Their lifespan is typically thirteen to fifteen years and they reach sexual maturity between two and four years of age. The males and females live separately except during breeding season in the fall. They will browse like the goats but prefer to graze when grass is available. The males establish a hierarchy through their displays during the rut. The females establish their own hierarchy as well and ewes form groups to protect the lambs, whistling at predators.

Sheep and goats are hardy and can graze and browse on plants not generally eaten by humans. Valued mostly for their milk, blood, wool, and dung, ruminants were one important source of food in areas where the climate did not support farming. In farming communities, these same animals could glean the fields after harvest and supply manure to renew those same fields. They were highly valued and used as money and a status symbol (DeMello 88). Humans began spinning wool around 3500 BCE, increasing the value of sheep and goats. Many of the first sheep to arrive in North America were used for both wool and meat, and by 1664 there were ten thousand sheep in the colonies, with laws requiring teaching children to spin and weave ("Sheep in History"). When England objected to the colonies exporting wool and restricted the raising of sheep, raising sheep and producing wool became revolutionary acts, and the export of breeding sheep was prohibited. In addition to creating political upheaval, these animals had a big impact on the ecosystems into which they were introduced. For instance, from the beginning wolves were seen as dangerous predators that needed to be eradicated in order to protect sheep. Rather than enclose and protect sheep, the idea was to make "the wild" safe for the sheep. Goats, too, largely roamed the woods and fields—damaging apple trees as their numbers grew (Anderson 101, 109, 147–48). First introduced to North America by the Spanish colonists in the sixteenth century, goats became another important source of meat and milk for early settlers. Many also became feral.

Mohair fiber from Angora goats makes up the bulk of fiber from goats, with cashmere being important as well ("National Animal Health"). The Wool Act of 1954 provided subsidies for mohair production, but those payments were phased out between 1993 and 1996, and Angora numbers dropped by two-thirds between 1997 and 2002. A study of small producers (those with 500 or fewer goats) in the United States found that only 1.5 percent of farms are primarily focused on fiber, with another 1.5 percent harvesting some wool despite a primary focus on meat or dairy. Of U.S. Angora goats, 76 percent are in Texas, where herds average 250 goats; Arizona is second for Angora production, with herds of 500 on average. Angora goats are usually shorn twice a year—the younger the goat, the finer the hair. Unlike mohair, cashmere does not come from a specific breed of goat, but from the soft underdown of the hair that some goats produce. This can be harvested as the goat naturally sheds, but larger producers shear the goats. Limited processing capacity in the United States constrains this market and it is hard to know how many goats are kept for this purpose, as these goats fit the milk and meat categories as well.

While goat milk is a growing market, the primary market is for meat. Of U.S. goats, 60 percent are meat goats, and 36 percent are milk goats ("Goats"). The meat industry grew from 600,000 in 1992 to about 2.5 million in 2014. Texas, Tennessee, and California are the top goat meat–producing states, while California leads the way in dairy goats. The average herd size of meat goats is between twenty-eight and thirty goats. There are at least eleven recognized breeds of goats raised for meat in the United States; Boers, Kikos, and the Spanish goat are the most numerous. While goats have remained largely unspecialized producers of wool, milk, and meat, some breeders are now focusing on the Boer to increase meat production (Animal and Plant Health Inspection Service). Some goats are used to graze unwanted weeds and vegetation. This not only provides "weed control" but also supplies the farmers with income before the goats reach slaughter weight. Alternative work includes using them as pack animals and in research. Their small size and gentle nature make them desirable for research and the teaching of surgery and other procedures. They are used in research on rheumatoid arthritis, HIV, myotonia, and immunology (Fulton et al. 21). While their commercial and biomedical use is growing, goats seem to have remained mostly an animal kept for personal use—for milk and meat.

Sheep, however, took on commercial value for both their wool and their meat early on and competed with cattle for grazing space. California, Colorado, and Wyoming are the top wool-producing states, but the United States produces less than 1 percent of the world's wool. Direct marketing of wool to spinners is the best way for U.S. producers to make money. Some of the contemporary concerns with wool production include the methods of shearing the sheep, mulesing, tail-docking, and castration. Castration and tail-docking are welfare concerns connected to most sheep farming and will be discussed later in the context of specific farms. Shearing and mulesing are specific to wool production. Concerns about shearing involve the speed of the process. When shearers go fast to get through a whole herd, the sheep are often handled roughly and cut. They also may not be offered sufficient shelter or a blanket after they are sheared. Skilled shearers and ranchers can avoid these problems. Mulesing involves removing skin from the hindquarters of sheep in an effort to prevent flystrike. This is when flies lay their eggs around the buttocks of the sheep and the larvae burrow into the sheep—causing death.

The mulesing procedure is most commonly performed on the now popular Moreno sheep, who have deeper folds in the skin on their hindquarters, and it is done without numbing or pain relief. Breeding sheep with less wrinkled skin is an alternative many are now pursuing, thanks to public concern about mulesing.

While sheep and goats are a dominant meat animal on the world market, in the United States they represent a smaller niche market. But it is a growing market. Some of my earliest experiences with livestock were with sheep. As mentioned in chapter 1, my oldest sister had sheep as part of a 4-H project and I often fed these sheep. I wouldn't say I formed any particular relationships with them, but when the butcher arrived I tried to save two of them. Ten years later my parents bought two sheep to feed and slaughter. They were kept in the horse barn and became a "chore" for me. When they were slaughtered I felt some relief at getting my barn back. Once they were gone, however, I missed them. In my family a signature meal was leg of lamb with "crispy potatoes" that cooked under the meat and were covered in the drippings. I *loved* the potatoes and I ate some of the lamb.

Many in the United States do not eat lamb, though. Changing demographics provide the USDA with hope for growing the market and suggest to farmers that they focus on various ethnic markets and specific religious holidays. Given the small size of the market, meat sheep have been raised on a small scale. Much like grass-fed cattle operations, sheep farmers graze small flocks and time breeding so that slaughter can take place around holidays like Easter. While many still have this picture of sheep farming in mind when they choose to purchase lamb for themselves or their dogs, lamb is increasingly coming from commercial feeding operations that copy the system in place for industrial cattle. Schoenian writes, "In some parts of the US, lamb feeding is a seasonal enterprise, occurring primarily in the fall and winter, after pastures have stopped growing and crop residues are available for grazing. In other areas (e.g. Texas, Colorado, and the Corn Belt), lamb feedlots operate year-round." While there is increasing segmentation of breeding and feeding, many farmers still raise and feed their own lambs. Those who operate primarily as feeders must be able to cover the purchase price of the lambs as well as the feed. While grain is a common way to finish lambs, it is not the only method. They can also be finished on crop aftermaths, pelleted rations, and by-product feeds. The versatility of the sheep makes their feeding affordable and can limit their environmental impact. When they eat by-products they help eliminate the "waste" involved in other crop and meat production. This is one reason the first partnerships between these ruminants and humans began.

Given their long partnership, sheep, goats, and humans share a number of diseases. Q-fever is caused by bacteria present in the milk, feces, and placenta of infected goats and can infect humans who inhale contaminated dust. Toxo-plasmosis is caused by a parasite transmitted by cats that causes abortions in goats, sheep, and humans. According to the CDC, toxoplasmosis is a major cause of deaths attributed to foodborne illness. Sore mouth is a common skin disease in sheep and goats that is caused by a pox family virus—highly con-tagious for humans. Brucella bacteria cause brucellosis in pigs, cattle, bison, sheep, goat, dogs, and humans. Pinkeye covers a number of contagious infec-tions that spread between domesticated animals (sheep, goats, cattle, horses, and dogs) and humans. Unpasteurized milk products are the most common way for humans to be affected, and this will be discussed in the next chapter, on dairies.

We were able to visit several farms that focused on raising sheep. Fido's Farm, as the name implies, is primarily a place for dogs—herding dogs. Chris Soderstrom has just over two hundred sheep (and a few ducks) on one hun-dred acres near Yelm, Washington. This land was originally part of a two-hundred-acre, seventy-five-cow dairy. When Soderstrom was looking for land she wanted dairy land because "dairy land would have good grass." She con-tinues to support the grass, and the bedding from the sheep's winter barn is composted and used on the hay-producing fields. In this way the sheep help "grow their own food." This is important to Soderstrom as "hay robs the land, while grazing adds to the soil."

The sheep are Coopworth and North Country Cheviot. They are wool sheep, but Soderstrom said there is no profitable market for the wool: "It takes too much time to shear, sort, pack, and transport." She breeds these sheep pri-marily because they make good mothers. She said, "They are good at convert-ing grass to milk. They can give birth (even to triplets) on their own, outside, and keep the babies safe." The ewes teach the lambs how to shelter during bad weather and how best to graze a pasture. The rams (who are generally desirable for fiber farming) "move on" so that new blood can be introduced to the breeding program. For the rest, Soderstrom selects some for the herding program. Those who make it earn their living giving herding lessons and in sheepdog trials. Lesson sheep get used regularly. Some secure a long life by being good at starting young dogs. The sheep used for trials are used more sparingly for lessons and, while they do have the added stress of traveling to trials, at a trial the length and number of runs on any given day is monitored and minimum rest periods enforced. Those who aren't selected for the herd-ing program are sold for meat.

Soderstrom slaughters about one hundred lambs a year at twelve to eigh-teen months of age. Fido's Farm has worked to develop a market for older lamb, which is called hogget. As with many of the cattle operations we vis-ited, Soderstrom often sells lambs while alive and there is joint ownership until slaughter. The farm owns shares in the USDA slaughter truck run by the Puget Sound Meat Producers Cooperative. While this would make on-farm slaughter a possibility, they don't slaughter on the farm. They take lambs to the slaughter truck when it is on the other side of Yelm—the nearest town. Soderstrom said that the herding customers "don't want to watch." Ironically, dog food companies are the main market for this meat and the bulk of the lambs go to a USDA processing plant for this purpose.

Sheep at Fido's Farm have their tails docked and the male sheep are castrated. Soderstrom said that they used to castrate the males between two and four weeks of age. The idea was to let them get a bit stronger before stressing them. But she looked into the standards for Animal Welfare Approved (AWA) and now castrates within the first three days. While they are not AWA certified, they want to use the best practices. Soderstrom said they "had good results with less stress for the animals." They don't use painkillers, as this would introduce a toxic chemical into the sheep's system, and Soderstrom said it wasn't necessary because "[they] just cut off the circulation. You don't use a knife like you do with pigs." As mentioned, they do dock tails, though Soderstrom would like to move away from that practice. The main reasons for docking are to cut down on flies bothering the sheep and so the sheep are cleaner at the time of slaughter, but there is little research to support the practice. Soderstrom said the European Union had moved away from docking tails since "whether the tails are docked or not they still clean under belly and rear before slaughter." The USDA reports that about 80 percent of lambs have their tails docked. For the tails and the castration Soderstrom uses an elastration band that cuts the blood supply to the tail or testicles, which then die and slough off. There is debate about whether this is a humane procedure. Research *does* show that the lambs feel pain, mostly at the time the band is applied, and this could be addressed with anesthesia at the time of application.

At Fido Farm they crutch the sheep—that is, remove the wool around the tail and between the rear legs—in September or October. They shear sheep in March. Soderstrom was in a quandary when we visited, as the man who did the shearing had just decided to quit the business. He came from Wales to shear sheep and could do the whole flock in a day and half. Castration, tail-docking, and shearing are the most stressful events faced by the sheep at Fido's Farm. Otherwise they are in social groups out on pasture for most of the year. There is a barn for shelter when the weather is bad, and they are fed hay as needed. When sheep give birth, they are kept in quieter parts of the farm. Dogs and people work to monitor any potential predators (some sheep are lost to coyotes, but the worst loss was to a neighbor's dog).

While this is a farm that raises sheep, the main focus is dogs. Soderstrom said, "All the dogs are working dogs. They are seen as partners; they are part of a team that must work together. It's like a dance." In the end, though, the various aspects of Fido's Farm can't be separated. Soderstrom served as an organic inspector, and this impacts how she farms. She has a degree in animal husbandry and livestock experience. Her father was a poultry farmer and she used to run a goat dairy during "the goat cheese craze." She was interested in pig and cattle farming, but it is difficult to farm pigs on the West Coast. The costs of bringing in feed and of shipping the pigs to the slaughterhouse are prohibitive. She said she's glad she got out of the dairy and never started with the pigs: "The welfare of pigs in our current industry is unconscionable and inhumane. The livestock industry, given its large scale, has become horrible. Humane farming can only be done on a small scale. You can't expect to make small farm practices work on a large scale. Livestock are humans' partners, just like the dogs, and deserve the same respect."

Here, I would argue, Soderstrom represents some of the key aspects of the pragmatist ethic sketched earlier. She has identified what she finds to be problematic with industrial agriculture and approaches farming in a different way. But her own practices are also evolving as she experiments with different approaches that might improve the lives of the animals and the land. Fido Farm is an intertwined whole made up of pieces that impact and support each other. Soderstrom is unwilling to participate in livestock production that reduces animal beings to mere things to be grown quickly and slaughtered efficiently. She sees this as violating the nature and needs of the animals, harming the land and wildlife, and "transforming the human from skilled stockperson to wage worker" (reminiscent of Sukovaty at the Crown S). Instead, she has found a way to respect and improve the land by respecting and meeting the needs of the sheep and dogs. She is also increasing communication between humans and the animals. While it might seem that the well-being of the dogs is prioritized, I don't think this is so. Sheep can be stressed or harmed when used in herding. The first thing Soderstrom teaches her students is how to "read the sheep" so that they can ensure the sheep's well-being. She said, "Sheep deserve to feel safe and at peace during herding. We need to make sure the dogs understand what the sheep are feeling. Ultimately our job is to tell the dogs what to do based on what we observe about both the dog and the sheep." Under these conditions the sheep are not harmed and actually benefit from the physical and mental exercise. The sheep learn and often outsmart the humans and their dogs. While comfort and protection are an important obligation of humans with regard to domesticated animals, the well-being of these same animals sometimes is improved by physical and mental stress. This can boost their immune systems, solidify social bonds, and promote learning and flexible problem solving for the sheep, dogs, and humans involved. The activities at the farm also increase the health of the land, water, and wildlife. To be sure, some aspects can still be improved, and Soderstrom continues to experiment and change. All the animals involved (sheep, dogs, and humans) are seen as valuing creatures deserving of respect, and Soderstrom works to make sure such respect is central to the practices of Fido's Farm.

One thing that might be critiqued from the pragmatist perspective is the slaughter of the sheep. On-farm slaughter would decrease the risk of injury and stress in transport and reduce the use of fossil fuels. The sheep are transported to the slaughter truck to spare the humans the sight, sound, and smell of their death. This allows the humans to evade this reality and their responsibility in the deaths of the sheep and promotes the illusion that humans are not enmeshed in the full cycle of life and death. If the humans involved don't eat such animals, their dogs almost certainly do. Further, the activity of herding relies on the use and death of sheep, and not facing that reality is a kind of moral evasion. It is like thinking that milk and egg products don't involve the death of animals (a fact that is discussed later). The same is true for having healthy land. The land thrives with some amount of grazing and manure. Several of the farms already discussed composted the by-products of slaughter to use to increase the fertility of land or to feed wildlife. The processes feed each other and sustain life.

While it was her ability to work with the dogs that "drug me back into livestock," Soderstrom says, she primarily sees herself as a grass farmer. "Sheep didn't evolve to eat grains. They eat a mix of greens." Because of their diet, they depend on healthy pastures. At the time of our visit in 2014, the largest field was twenty-six acres, with the next-largest being twelve. Electric fencing allows her to section the pastures by soil type and move the fence line when needed to prevent overgrazing. Soderstrom allows overgrazing only when there is a grass type she wants to get rid of quickly. She likes "working with the land she has." For instance, at first she wanted to remove blackberries (blackberries are on the list of noxious weeds and classified as an invasive species in Washington). But sheep like to eat blackberries. So she uses the sheep to manage the blackberries rather than try to remove them. They also like the roses and dandelions.

She's glad she's saved this land from being a housing development. Soderstrom said the farm benefits everyone, as it supplies a source of food, provides activities for dogs and their people, helps filter the water that goes into the groundwater, and supports wildlife. Several bald eagles nest in the area, as well as hawks, ducks, and geese. She leaves the sedge unmowed for the birds and doesn't allow anyone to hunt, though Soderstrom has been seen chasing off coyotes on her ATV. Soderstrom talked about the "good feeling of being on the land and seeing all the biodiversity" (including insects). She said the farm's current setup meets her personal standards for how livestock should be managed, and she likes how they are treating the land.

While Fido's Farm is focused on sheep, Mountain Stream Farm, run by Laura Faley in Mt. Vernon, Washington, is more diverse. During our conversation she also focused on stewardship of the land and the various animals she raises. She said, "The two need to go together because animals provide food and resources to enrich our lives; the soil and plants are the substrate for the health of the whole. Humans must take responsibility for caring for these interrelated systems." But she does not "just let nature do as it wants." She said they worked hard to manage the forest, keep the streams flowing, cut through the blackberries, and weed the garden. "Invasive species of vegetation need to be controlled." She thinks that with domesticated animals there is an added level of responsibility. Echoing Kimberley Smith (chapter 5), she said, "Domesticated animals do better in captivity. They rely on us for food and care." At the time of our visit she had ninety sheep and sixteen horses on forty acres of leased land near her house. Up the hill at her house she had pigs, turkeys, ducks, chickens (for meat and eggs), and a few more horses. She had rabbits too but said they were just for "the petting zone," as she can't yet use them for meat until she finds someone to process them. Most of the animals she raises for meat or eggs are heritage breeds that have been (or will be) discussed elsewhere. Here I briefly discuss the sheep.

The sheep are Suffolk X, bred to finish on grass. Faley feeds some grain so that they finish a little faster. Suffolks are black-faced sheep known for their meat and wool. They are naturally polled (so no need to dehorn) and have no wool on their head and legs (so no need to crutch). They are known to be good mothers, capable of birthing on their own. These characteristics make them easy to keep in an outdoor flock. Like Soderstrom, Faley docks their tails by applying an elastic band when they are just a few days old. Unlike Soderstrom, Faley slaughters and butchers on-site. They also shear the sheep, sell the wool, and host their own fiber sale. Her sheep farming is part of her stewardship of the land and the animals. According to Faley "stewardship requires animals to fulfill a telos, or purpose." The gene pool, the food chain, and the companionship of the creatures are all related and included in her sense of "stewardship." The gene pool is important practically and aesthetically. Practically, it is important to have diversity in the gene pool in order for a species to survive various health and environmental pressures and crises. As industrial agriculture has progressed, it has focused money and research on a more and more limited gene pool. Heritage breeds have survived on small farms that work to help preserve the desired variety. Aesthetically many of the heritage breeds are prettier. (Her sheep are very cute!) Aesthetics of taste relate to stewardship of the food chain as well. Many of the heritage breeds taste different from animals raised on industrial farms. Faley told us about some-one who bought her meat chickens and finally could make chicken soup that tasted like her grandmother's. The same recipe had not yielded the same taste until she had a chicken more like the chicken that the recipe had been built around. Preserving these tastes and connections is important to Faley. In fact, the farm website states, "We enjoy gourmet cooking and gourmet foods. We are convinced that the best tasting food begins with the best ingredients we can find. It is our goal to raise the best-tasting meat you have had. We believe the best-tasting meat comes from happy, contented, well-fed animals." In addition to valuing the taste of these animals' meat, though, Faley values these animals for companionship. Heritage breeds are known for their physical hardiness and their intelligence. She said, "They have not lost the ability to think for themselves and adapt to changing conditions." While this can present challenges to farmers who want them to "just be eating machines," she said, "the strong personalities and intelligence often make these breeds fun and interesting companions."

The land is also included in Faley's idea of stewardship: "The soil and the plants are the substrate for the health of the whole system." She talked about the cycles of the land: the sun helps the grass grow, as does the soil; the grass helps feed the soil, as does the manure from the animals; the soil, fertilized by the animals' manure, grows the grass to feed the animals, and so on. She doesn't use chemicals on her soil or plants. Her land also includes some forested areas. When we asked how the forest fit into these farm-focused cycles, Faley said, "The world should be enjoyed; so we cut paths for hiking and hope to maintain the streams. Management and care are of great import." The birches and alders growing on the ranch are managed and cut. She saw what she was doing with her land as very different from what was happening at a development site nearby. Faley told us that the "developer" had built a detention pond that flooded a house below. The salmon stream was also disrupted and diverted. She did not see this kind of development as any form of responsible stewardship but rather as something that put profit ahead of healthy productivity and long-term care. She told us has she had a list of fifteen priorities inside her house and the "money priority" is close to last on the list.

Yet while Faley may be preserving the land as grass and forest (and keeping it from becoming more houses), she turns animals into products and sells them for profit. Death is something that is regularly experienced here. It is the ultimate fate even of the animals who are productive, and if an animal is not productive then death is the more immediate result. Faley said that all the animals on the ranch do some work. Most are there to produce eggs and meat. The dogs are work dogs; there were three shepherd dogs and one coon dog at the time of our visit. She has since added Turkish Kangal dogs—livestock guardian dogs—to keep her sheep safe. The horses were a bit different. They don't really earn their keep, but she did use them in a natural horsemanship program that teaches people a different way of relating to animals. The idea is to work *with* the nature of the horse in a clear and kind way. Building communication that goes both ways is important. While the horses gain the benefit of being cared for into their old age (something denied most of the other animals living—and dying—at the farm), this focus on building bonds, meaningful communication, and kindness *does* apply to all the animals there. This is why she keeps the rabbits and some Silkie chickens as part of the petting zone. She said, "It's important for children to experience this kind of connection."

In the United States today it is unusual to find people who seek connection with the animals they eat. As we saw at Fido Farm, many find it troubling to connect their eating (or their dog's) with the death of particular knowable animals. Even as some want to escape industrial animal agriculture, most still do not want to know the particular individuals they will be eating while they are alive. Faley's approach provides an interesting counterexample to this tendency and so to Carol Adams's notion of the absent referent and mass terms (discussed in chapter 4). In short, when using mass terms like sheep or chicken the animals involved are abstract and not individualized. Adams says, "Behind every meal of meat is an absence: the death of the animal whose place the meat takes. This is the 'absent referent.' The absent referent functions to cloak the violence inherent to meat-eating, to protect the conscience of the meat eater and render the idea of individual animals as immaterial to anyone's selfish desires. It is that which separates the meat eater from the animal and the animal from the end product." The individual animals are the "absent referent" as they are made invisible by the mass term to make it easier for people to consume them. Adams writes, "The function of the absent referent is to keep our 'meat' separated from any idea that she or he was once an animal, to keep something from being seen as having been someone, to allow for the moral abandonment of another being" (Adams, "Sexual Politics of Meat"). While Adams calls for veganism (for reasons discussed in chapter 9), Faley calls for people to deepen their connection with the very animal beings they consume. She is also encouraging people to more fully understand what is necessary to provide food (animal and plant) in a sustainable way. She shares the commitment to help do so with Linda Neunzig at 90 Farms.

Not far from Mountain Stream Farm, in Arlington, Washington, Neunzig has "had sheep for over twenty years and birthed over two thousand lambs." As the 90 Farms website says, this fifty-two-acre farm seeks to "provide a safe and educational agricultural adventure for children, and to supply healthy, naturally grown foods for families while including our own children in the lifestyle of the sustainable family farm." Neunzig raises purebred Katahdin

PHOTO 4. Sheep at 90 Farms. Photo by Danielle Palmer.

sheep. Unlike Faley, who uses her sheep's wool for fiber, Neunzig likes this breed because of their lack of wool (they have fur instead). She said that "wool costs more to cut than can be earned from its sale." The Katahdin are an intentionally created breed developed in Maine in the 1950s. The desire was to create meat-producing sheep that did not need to be sheared. This fits with the increasing specialization of sheep—to focus on meat or milk or wool. Developed as meat animals, Katahdins are known for their hair coat, meat production, flocking instinct, breeding capacity, and lack of horns. They do well in a variety of weather conditions and can tolerate parasites. The ewes are great mothers and lamb easily. The breed is good out in pastures since they thrive on grass and lambs are born vigorous and alert ("Breeds of Livestock—Katahdin Sheep"). Predation is a concern, so Neunzig keeps llamas with the sheep. The llamas kept their eyes on us while we were there, and when we came near the fence they stomped their feet.

She said the farm and the lambs are not certified organic because she would not make any more money than she does with her current customers. While she has used antibiotics when necessary (on sheep who were attacked by a coyote for instance), she is generally antibiotic- and hormone-free. This seemed to be more a practical position than a principled one. Noting the vulnerability of sheep to attack and disease she said sheep are basically animals "waiting for a place to die. By the time they are sick antibiotics don't usually work." The paperwork and extra costs were also factors she considered when choosing not to get certified as organic. She said, "It's not worth the effort. I have a day job and don't have the time. My customers know how I raise my sheep and do not mind that it's not certified organic." Neunzig has worked hard over the years to establish this sort of relationship with her customers. Along with sheep, she produces "all-natural, ethically raised" veal. She started this about eight years ago. She said she wouldn't eat the veal at restaurants even though she "kills for a living," and so she knows other people don't want it either. She wanted to produce an alternative. Her calves are slaughtered at four to six months of age. This means they are slaughtered before they are weaned and so do not suffer the stress of weaning (very different from the veal calves on industrial dairies discussed in the next chapter).

Neunzig uses a number of dogs to help her move and manage the sheep and cattle. In fact, as with Soderstrom, dogs got her involved with raising sheep. Neunzig breeds corgis and got the sheep to work the dogs. She started breeding sheep because there weren't many around, but there was a demand. Given the rarity of the Katahdin breed on the West Coast she uses artificial insemination to breed her sheep—ordering shipments of frozen semen. This evolved into producing meat herself. Since she knows the owner of the first mobile slaughtering unit in the area she was able to join their rounds, even though she is not within their normal boundaries. She butchers every month, but she doesn't butcher on-site. While meat production is her focus, she still sells the "cream of the crop" sheep as breeding stock. These sheep do make good milking sheep, but she has no desire to attempt milking because she "has enough to do as it is."

She sees humans as facilitating the "circle of life." "We have to be a partner with nature. When farming we need to work with nature rather than against it. This means we must understand the nature of the land and the animals. We must observe natural cycles and attempt to replicate them on the farm. We need to look at how each thing functions in nature and think about how we can help it." For instance, "cows aren't meant to eat grain so don't feed it. Let them eat grass." She said that in nature everything is integrated: the animals' manure, and offal from the slaughter, make compost to nurture the fields on which the animals feed. She encourages the barn swallows to stay and eat bugs and captures and uses the rainwater to water the fields. There have been three severe floods since Neunzig has owned the farm and she has to evacuate every animal during a flood. So she has put fourteen acres in the Conservation Reserve Enhancement Program (discussed in chapter 3) and planted it with about nine hundred native plants and trees in order to restore native habitat and help prevent this kind of flooding in the future. She is trying to work with nature to find ways to mitigate the problems caused by those who don't take an integrated approach.

When talking about what inspired her to take on this life, Neunzig pointed to Wendell Berry. Berry inspired a number of the farmers in this study. He would be pleased with Neunzig's focus on supporting farming in her own county. Berry is a poet, novelist, and environmental author who has done much to call attention to the problems with industrial farming and the promise of alternative approaches. Born in 1934, he grew up in Newcastle, Kentucky, working on his father's tobacco farm. When his life as a professor of writing and literature brought him back to Kentucky, he bought a farm where he writes and farms to this day. His many poems, novels, and essays take on a range of issues from farming to war, soil erosion to globalization, coal to the death penalty.

The most relevant of Berry's work here is *The Unsettling of America: Culture and Agriculture* published in 1977. One of his main points is that humans, plants, and animals are part of one another. He argues for a commitment to a particular place because he sees that "our land passes in and out of our bodies just as our bodies pass in and out of our land." He writes, "As we and our land are part of one another, so all who are living as neighbors here, human and plant and animal, are part of one another, and so cannot possibly flourish alone" (22). While he sees miners as not respecting this and so exploiting the land, he sees farmers as recognizing this interdependency and so as nurturing the land (7). This kind of "kindly use" requires an intimate knowledge of the land and special attention to soil fertility (32–33). He believes this is something that small, local farms can achieve and that large, industrial farms cannot. He notes that the industrial approach to farming is based on separation and specialization—a fragmentary way of thinking rather than one based in seeing unity and interdependence:

> It is within unity that we see the hideousness and destructiveness of the fragmentary—the kind of mind, for example, that can introduce a production machine to increase "efficiency" without troubling about its effect on workers, on the product, and on consumers; that can accept and even applaud the "obsolescence" of the small farm and not hesitate over the possible political and cultural effects; that can recommend continuous tillage of huge monocultures, with massive use of chemicals and no animal manure or humus, and worry not at all about the deterioration or loss of soil. For cultural patterns of responsible cooperation we have substituted this moral ignorance, which is the etiquette of agricultural "progress." (48)

Berry argues that while humans need to live off of the land, plants, and other animals, this should be done in a way that sees and respects our interdependence, or humans risk their own demise. This means, as we heard from several farmers, recognizing that death and decay are as much a part of life as are birth, care, and growth (56).

Berry makes this point when talking about soil. He sees the soil as that which holds communities together. It creates life out of death and decay; it heals and restores: "It is alive itself. It is a grave, too, of course. Or a healthy soil is. It is full of dead animals and plants, bodies that have passed through other bodies.... But no matter how finely the dead are broken down, or how many times they are eaten, they yet give into other life. If a healthy soil is full of death it is also full of life: worms, fungi, microorganisms of all kinds, for which, as for us humans, the dead bodies of the once living are a feast. Eventually this dead matter becomes soluble, available as food for plants, and life begins to rise up again, out of the soil into the light" (86). Berry does not see agribusiness or agriscience respecting this guiding insight of agriculture. His problem with the industrial approach is that it sees soil as a resource to use rather than as a living system that needs care—that it treats soil, plants, animals, and humans as machines and misses the reciprocal supporting relationships that exist among them all. For Berry, humans' illusory sense of autonomy and mastery is problematic (87, 90, 98, 111). He notes that human bodies "are not distinct from the bodies of plants and animals, with which we are involved in the cycles of feeding and in the intricate companionships of ecological systems and of the spirit" (103). This view returns humans to being a part of nature rather than outside or above it: "While we live our bodies are moving particles of the earth, joined inextricably both to the soil and to the bodies of other living creatures. It is hardly surprising, then, that there should be some profound resemblances between our treatment of our bodies and our treatment of the earth" (97).

Berry worries that the industrial mindset treats our bodies and the earth as things to use. We use chemicals for short-term gain, without caring for the long-term health of humans or the earth. This is not a sustainable view. He writes, "The life of one year must not be allowed to diminish the life of the next; nothing must live at the expense of the source. Thus in nature the food species is dependent on its predator, and pests and diseases are agents of health; so populations are controlled and balanced" (93). Failing to recognize this, we produce food "at an incalculable waste of topsoil and of human life and energy, and at the cost of destroying communities and poisoning the land and the streams" (167). According to Berry, part of the reason for this failure to recognize the interdependence of life (and death) is to be found in the separation of the household from the production of food. Food is not grown at home and food is not made from raw ingredients. Rather, the home has become a place where food is consumed with no sense of what was required to produce it (51). Berry believes that this change took place when men were removed from the nurturing work on the land to work in factories. Nurturing came to be seen as belonging only to women. He writes, "Women traditionally have performed the most confining—though not necessarily the least dignified—tasks of nurture: housekeeping, the care of young children, food preparation" (113). As the industrial economy saw the real work as that which earned a wage outside the home, women's status was diminished by this arrangement. Further, her nurturing came to be done by purchasing cleaning and cooking "gadgets" and providing easily prepared meals. This left her time to focus on being "fresh, cheerful, young, shapely, and pretty." Even breastfeeding was removed from women, and formula was purchased (114–15). For Berry, the removal of men from their nurturing roles and connections to the home, along with the debasement of women's contribution to the home, has resulted in the disintegration of marriage as a commitment to communities and places (118).

Berry worries that there can be no healthy love when the partners can't do substantial labor in support of one another. On his account, sexual energy, when divorced from working for and with each other, comes to be both uncontrolled and unsustainable. This is exacerbated, for Berry, by the emergence of birth control. He equates the use of birth control with the use of chemicals on the land to remove pests and weeds. The use of birth control is accompanied by the further use of chemicals to "help" infertile women and infertile fields (132–32). He writes, "By 'freeing' food and sex from worry, we have also set them apart from thought, responsibility, and the issue of quality" (135). For Berry, this is not real freedom, and we need meaningful work in production and reproduction: "We are working well when we use ourselves as the fellow creatures of the plants, animals, materials, and other people we are working with. Such work is unifying, healing. It brings us home from pride and from despair, and places us responsibly within the human estate" (140). Berry's response to this state of affairs is to urge people to grow their own food—if not on a farm, then in a garden. Ideally, this should be done with the respectful use of animal and human labor rather than machines, in order to help maintain (and restore) the health of the soil and reintegrate human and other animal beings into partnerships. Cooking should be done at home, using raw ingredients rather than prepared food.

While I respect this view, and know many who consider themselves part of a local and slow food movement, I do worry about some of the accompanying effects. Women still do more that 80 percent of the household labor in heterosexual partnerships, even if they also work outside the home. The call to add gardening, canning, and cooking from scratch often has the effect of further increasing this workload and adding a dollop of guilt for those who don't manage to do it. For those not living in any kind of partnership, and doing all the household labor on their own, the workload is even higher. Single life doesn't seem to enter into Berry's view at all.

Another person to espouse a similar view is Barbara Kingsolver in her book *Animal, Vegetable, Miracle.* This book relays her family's experience moving to a farm in Virginia, where they began to produce much of their own food and made a commitment to eat in season and as locally as possible for a year. Their property had fruit trees and they planted a garden and raised chickens and turkeys. The turkeys she decided to raise were a heritage breed—Bourbon Reds—and she eventually established a breeding population to help with the recovery of this breed. The only reason she seems to want to do this, though, is because they are a tasty bird with large breasts; she shows little respect for the animals themselves. When the turkeys first try to eat and drink they have to be shown how. "Oh, well, we don't grow them for their brains," she writes (88). She finds their "witlessness lovable" but is happy they won't stay this cute as they are not pets (89). When starting her flock, she sees no issues with sending the chicks through the mail since they don't need to eat for the first forty-eight hours. Later when her turkeys have trouble figuring out how to breed she laments the hatchery system that removes the mother from the equation but doesn't seem to connect this back to how she received her young chickens and turkeys in the first place.

While she rightly notes that many things die in the production of any food and says we need to respect the plant and animal life that dies to feed humans (221), her respect seems limited to me. Turkeys who can forage like the Bourbon Red are not witless. Her lack of knowledge when it comes to their breeding behavior also shows that she didn't feel the need to educate herself about these particular birds. While she has much to say about "vegetarians" who don't know anything about livestock, her situation is not all that different. While she exhorts everyone to raise and cook their own food, she berates vegans and vegetarians for their "moral superiority" and "billowing ignorance" (223). She writes, "The farm-liberation fantasy simply reflects a modern cultural confusion about farm animals. They're human property, not just legally but biologically. Over the millennia of our clever history, we created from wild progenitors whole new classes of beasts whose sole purpose was to feed us. If turned loose in the wild, they would haplessly starve, succumb to predation, and destroy the habitats and lives of most or all natural things" (223). While she's right about the environmental hazards of turning these animals loose (not something generally being proposed) she is not correct that they would all just die. Populations of feral pigs, goats, and chickens attest otherwise. And the mindset that these animals' "sole purpose was to feed us" is far from respectful. At the very least, the animals themselves envision their purpose as living a good life and raising young. While I agree that humans need to remember that animal life and death are necessary to grow plants and trees, this reality should not entail reducing those animals to beings who have no other purpose in order to make humans feel less bad about killing

them. Like Neunzig, Kingsolver is also inspired by Wendell Berry. Berry's work
has, in fact, inspired many people to raise their own food. When this includes
animals, though, lack of knowledge about these animals can result in much
suffering. This is a point to which I will return in the chapter on poultry.

The other danger, I think, is that many inspired by Berry romanticize the
farm life and underestimate the amount of work it takes to raise and prepare
food on a year-round basis. Part of Kingsolver's commitment to her year of
food included cooking from raw ingredients. Kingsolver recognizes that some
people may not be situated in a place where they can grow their own food
(though she thinks most can have some kind of garden), but she thinks everyone can cook their own food. She knows that for many women this is a
touchy subject as the women's movement has worked hard to make it possible for women to work outside the home and not be responsible for all the
work in the home. But she thinks this came with a cost and says, "When my
generation of women walked away from the kitchen we were escorted down
that path by a profiteering industry that knew a tired, vulnerable marketing
target when they saw it. 'Hey, ladies,' it said to us, 'go ahead get liberated. *We'll*
take care of dinner.'" While this sounded good to many, she thinks it is what
allowed the move to industrial agriculture to take such a strong hold in the
United States. She writes, "They threw open the door, and we walked into a
nutritional crisis and genuinely toxic food supply. If you think *toxic* is an exag-
geration, read the package directions for handling raw chicken from a CAFO.
We came a long way, baby, into bad eating habits and collaterally impaired
family dynamics. No matter what else we do or believe, food remains at the
center of every culture. Ours now runs on empty calories" (127). She points
to women in France and Spain who work but still shop on the way home to
cook a meal. She urges women (and men) in the United States to stop seeing
cooking as a chore and instead view it as an outlet for creativity, as one of the
things we do for fun.

From an ecofeminist perspective, I am worried about Berry and Kingsolver
essentially laying the blame for the growing domination of industrial farming
and processed food on the women's movement. I think it is important to note
that Berry's wife works on the farm and types his manuscripts; Kingsolver is
supported in her gardening, farming, and cooking efforts with an income not
available to all, a schedule that is more flexible than many people's jobs allow, and a husband who regularly cooks and bakes bread. She moves beyond
calling on people to prepare meals from raw ingredients to making things
like bread, pickles, tomato sauce, and jam. These are necessary if one plans
to eat locally during the winter. She also says people should make their own
cheese. Ironically, while she is committed to understanding food as a process
and participating in that process, this commitment falls short when it comes

to cheese. While she admits to loving its taste, she is not willing to be tied down to the twice-a-day milking schedule that comes with dairy animals: "I couldn't imagine, myself, having an unbreakable milking date with every five o'clock of this world" (160). But someone has to do that work. The cheese-making endeavor is not only time-consuming—it also takes one into the realm of dairies and the problems with milk. That is the topic of the next chapter.

CHAPTER SEVEN

Dairies

ANIMAL WELFARE AND
VAL PLUMWOOD

Kingsolver's cheesemaking drew her into the world of dairies and the history of humans' consumption of milk and its by-products. She expresses no real direct concern for the dairy animals themselves. Her concern is for human health and desire. As she notes, cheese is a way to store milk by using bacteria to turn the liquid into a solid. Many prefer raw milk for this process, but that can be hard to find given current regulations. Some people end up getting a cow or a goat in order to support their interest in making cheese, but they can't sell the cheese without meeting strict regulations regarding where and how it is pasteurized. While pasteurization is meant to remove pathogens from the milk, it removes good microbes too. Ultra-pasteurized milk will not make cheese. Pasteurization, and the regulations, were not without reason, though. In the 1890s it was not uncommon to have bacteria in milk that could make people sick. As mentioned in the last chapter, unpasteurized milk is a way tuberculosis (and other diseases) can be spread. This was one of the issues that pushed Jane Addams (see chapter 1) to work for women to get the right to vote. She thought women would demand safe milk for their children. Today, bacterial contamination is most likely to occur in large-scale industrial dairies—despite all their precautions and equipment—because of the condition of the cows and how they are kept. But one should also be careful about assuming that all small or private dairy operations know how to keep their milk safe.

Our guts and our food are full of various microorganisms that help us remain healthy. Fearful of some microbes we create systems that seek to eliminate them all, but this goes against our evolutionary history. Kingsolver notes that "many of our most useful foods—yogurt, wine, bread, and cheese—are products of controlled microbe growth. . . . Our own bodies are bacterial condos, with established relationship between the upstairs and downstairs neighbors. Without these regular residents, our guts are easily taken over by less congenial newcomers looking for low-rent space. What keeps us healthy is an informed coexistence with microbes, rather than the micro-genocide that seems to be the rage lately" (135). In fact, many humans have guts that are not able to digest milk after the age of four (when children would be weaned from the breast). Lactose intolerance results when the enzyme that digests milk stops working. Some groups of humans who kept cattle, goats, and sheep developed a genetic mutation that extends the life of the lactose-digesting enzymes. This occurred around ten thousand years ago, when domestication of these animals began (just one more example of how livestock make us who we are). Humans also found ways to make milk more digestible by making it into things like yogurt, kefir, butter, parmesan, and ricotta. Lactose-eating bacteria curdle the milk in these processes. The human history with milk is one that transformed the human body, the possibilities of storing and transporting food, and the lives of the animals from whom we take the milk. (No matter what Kingsolver suggests, the dairy animals do not exist solely to feed humans—their milk is meant for their offspring.) When humans raise animals primarily for milk rather than for meat, the relationships can be very different. While the offspring of the milking animals are often sold or killed and eaten, the milking animals themselves live long enough for the humans to develop relationships with them. While this is more difficult in the modern industrial dairy, where one to five thousand cows or four to seven hundred goats might be milked, it is still more likely to occur than on farms and ranches raising animals primarily for meat. A large sheep dairy would have only about one hundred milking ewes, with the average being closer to fifty. The average goat dairy has around thirty-five goats. In smaller and medium-sized dairies deep relationships commonly develop among the animals in the herd and between the humans and the cows, goats, or sheep.

These relationships often include a very protective element—whether that is primarily about protecting an asset or investment or primarily about protecting a friend, it results in some strained relationships with other animals. An example of this can be found in an email correspondence from M. Clare Paris at Larkhaven Farm—a goat and sheep dairy in Tonasket, Washington, that focused on making farmstead cheeses and meats. The cheeses were made from raw milk from the animals on the farm, and the farmers sold lamb from their own sheep and chevon from their own goats. They also sold whey-fed pork—a longtime natural complement to dairy operations but much harder to find in today's segmented animal agricultural industry. When we contacted the farm in 2010 they were too busy (as many farmers are) for a visit. But here is part of what Paris sent in reply to our two questions:

> We love where we are and the natural world it includes but this place has been a farm a long time. We have a lot of animals (sheep, goats) and also have a bunch of dogs to discourage predators, which they do by barking. We have state land on two sides that hasn't been cattle-grazed for several years. We feel a kind of natural blend of ourselves with the natural world here, but we are pretty dominant. We see deer and game birds. We have a lot of doves right now, they seem to have just arrived for the season. We are wary of owls because they once killed a whole lot of our chickens, but all we do is go yell at them when they hang out in our biggest trees, which makes us feel sort of equal with them. I guess that sort of exemplifies our view of the mix of the natural and human world, that we just feel like part of it and when we change it significantly, we try to do it respectfully. We have both lived more closely in tune with natural rhythms for a long time, for periods without electricity, etc, and all of that informs our systems.

This nicely shows some of the tensions faced by those who farm livestock. It also shows a deep sense of connection with the natural world and the connection of that world to the livestock animals they raise. It is a mixed community that involves respect for animals (domestic and wild) even as some of the wild animals present a threat to the livestock. In addition to the threat of predation, though, Paris discussed the perceived threat that the livestock present for the wild animals:

> Once a young Big Horn sheep ram came and hung around in our sheep flock for three days so I called fish-and-wildlife in case he had lost his way and I'll be damned if they didn't come shoot him because of domestic diseases he might take back to his herd. They did all their consulting with Olympia, not with locals. Since I know sheep farmers who have Big Horns come in and out of their flocks all the time, I knew this was horseshit but what could I do? Except (duh) not call them again. We try to keep our practices very natural and within our fences, although we are certainly an impact and so are the dogs. We feel gratitude toward nature and always that we have been blessed to work in such a beautiful place.

Historically, wild and domesticated sheep, goats, and cattle would mix and interbreed from time to time. This can pose risks for both communities of animals, but rigid demarcating rules are also dangerous (and unpragmatic).

A recent visit to the Larkhaven website shows that they have stopped making cheese. They were raising a few pigs and lambs to sell in 2015. As I discussed earlier, economic viability of farming and ranching is always a con-

PHOTO 5. Danielle Palmer with kid at St. John's Creamery. Photo by Jonathan Stout.

cern. So is the amount of work (physical work) this kind of life entails. Their website says, "Sorry, we stopped making cheese! We worked hard and we had fun" ("Larkhaven Farmstead Meats"). This is the reality behind Kingsolver's more idealized approach. Milking animals require constant care and a regular milking schedule. Their health depends on healthy land that also requires care. Then there is the work of processing the milk and making the cheese.

Another dairy, which has moved into cheesemaking since our visit, is St. John Creamery—a goat dairy in Lake Stevens, Washington. The dairy has 175 Oberhasli goats, some rare heritage-breed chickens who lay eggs and eat bugs, and livestock guardian dogs. At the time of our visit in 2010, the dairy had yet to make a profit. They made money by breeding the dogs and running a housecleaning business. St. John does sell kids, mostly as pets. She can't afford to keep them; they would drink too much milk. She is able to sell her milk for $16 a gallon. She said that in a month she gets about $480 from a milking goat. She can't afford to share her "product" with the kids. She has sold some kids for meat but said that it's hard. She's not opposed to it, but she loves her goats. The reality, though, is that dairies must have a market for at least the male offspring. St. John said, "All the animals have to be useful. The horses are gone since they were free loaders. Everyone has a job. The terriers and cats do pest patrol, the other dogs do predator control, and the chickens do parasite work." She can't keep unneeded male goats.

PHOTO 6. Jonathan Stout with kid at St. John's Creamery. Photo by Danielle Palmer.

This all started for St. John just before 2000 as a hobby. She began keeping goats in response to concerns about Y2K. If systems were going to go down and chaos were to result, she wanted to be self-sustaining. So she started to garden and got two goats. She was living in Seattle at the time, though, and the goats were illegal. After 2000 came and went she moved out to the country and got more goats. She got serious about the business and started the dairy in 2007. This required culling the herd and focusing on breeding to improve milk production. She said, "It's hard work, but fun." Milking seventy to eighty goats a day, delivering milk, working on fences, and composting manure (and the list goes on), she often works close to eighteen hours a day. While the hours are probably similar to what many who raise livestock experience, the schedule at a dairy is often more exacting. The goats (or cows or sheep) need to be milked twice a day at regular intervals. If this doesn't happen, problems such as mastitis can arise.

St. John is very concerned with the health of her goats. The dairy is not organic since she uses penicillin when needed (she doesn't want the goats to suffer). When the goats are three months of age she trims their hooves and burns off their horns (called debudding). She doesn't like this practice, so she tries to get naturally polled goats with her breeding. Otherwise, she is "rabidly organic" and won't even use flea medicine on the dogs. For sick goats she uses CEG (cayenne, echinacea, and garlic), something she got from the veterinarian who consults for Organic Valley dairies (see chapter 3). "But the real key to healthy animals," she said, "is healthy land. In New Zealand, dairymen consider themselves primarily grass farmers" (as does Soderstrom—see chapter 6). To help keep the pastures and the goats healthy St. John regularly rotates the goats among the pastures to cut the parasite life cycle. Ideally pastures rest for forty-two days, but when that's not possible, a rest period of at least twenty-one days cuts coccidian—a parasite that causes diarrhea in young goats. If necessary she uses a sulfa drug to deworm. St. John said she can tell when that is needed because the goats get anemic and she can see it in their eyes. Free-roaming chickens help with parasites as well. The chickens eat bugs and spread the manure with their scratching, exposing everything to the sun. This had worked so well that St. John was expanding the chicken side of the farm. There were sixty-five chicks inside when we visited, and eighty more on the way. The plan was to put chicken tractors in the pastures and close them in at night.

As with many of the farmers we talked with, St. John's goal is to try to replicate natural cycles as much as possible in order to produce healthy animals with the least amount of intervention. She sees her relationship with the land and the animals as a form of stewardship. Her job is to provide what the plants need and work from there. To improve the health of the land they are able to use most of the animal waste products on-site. St. John said, "I pay for the herbs and minerals I feed them, and they poop it out. Why not put it back in the grass?" She planned to plant an herbal berm that would be fed directly to goats. It will contain things like mulberries, comfrey, and wormwood. St. John said, "Ideal pastures would have fifty different plants for the goats to eat. Now my pastures have about ten different plants." Her goats who are being milked also eat kelp, keifer, an assortment of herbs, and a little grain. St. John was proud that she had been able to cut the ration of grain in half and hoped that when her pastures were in good enough shape, and the parasites under control, the goats would be off grain completely.

Healthy goats help make for healthy milk as well. St. John is passionate about raw milk. She said, "Raw milk is better because it is alive. When you pasteurize milk the fat molecules break down and can get into the blood stream, as does disease." She believes that when people pasteurize milk, they don't bother getting clean milk in the first place—she uses at least eight cloth surfaces, with iodine, to clean the does' udders. "But," she said, "my milk lasts fourteen days, while most milk lasts seven. I've had it last as long as twenty-two days." She thinks it's important to provide an alternative to the dominant cow milk; she discussed studies that indicate there might be a link between the milk from Holstein cows (who dominate industrial dairies) and autism and diseases like diabetes. She also sells cheese and a line of goat milk for pets. Her raw milk and cheese products contain live enzymes, and St. John emphasizes the health benefits these provide. Her concerns envelope the land, wildlife, livestock, pets, and humans—no sharp lines separate these communities for her.

Given the regulations involved with selling milk and cheese, though, many goat dairies focus on soap. I visited one such farm in southern Illinois—Bearden's Back Acre Farms. I met Jennifer Bearden when she was selling some of her MommaBear's Goat Milk Soap at a farmer's market. When I visited her farm, Bearden had about thirty-five goats and milked about eight at a time. She now has fifty goats, leaves the kids on the does, and partially milks them at night. This supplies her with more than enough milk and allows the does to teach their young what to eat and how to behave. While Bearden comes from a farming background (her family farmed wheat in Idaho), raising animals was new to her. She started raising dairy goats when she found that her daughter was allergic to cow's milk. She has also raised chickens for some time and now raises pastured poultry on a separate farm along with some meat rabbits. The goats are protected by Great Pyrenees dogs, as are the chickens and turkeys who are under the care of her son. The farm with the goats was more recently purchased and was chosen because the land fit the family's plans for farming. Rather than change the land to do what they wanted, they looked for land that was already good for the animals they planned to raise. This land has lots of ravines and woods, providing space for the goats to browse and providing good land for pigs. They have added two pigs, who are happily eating extra milk and cheese by-products. The pigs supply meat and lard for the soapmaking.

Most of Bearden's goats are Nubian/Alpine crosses. She is quite proud of the changes she has seen in the quality of her goats and had recently added a purebred Nubian buck and a purebred Alpine buck. She sells and trades goats to keep the herd diverse and has added two Boer bucks to "take advantage of the growing demand for chevon." While Bearden has killed and butchered goats herself she is happy that her son has taken over the work of killing them. She said that even though you raise them knowing they are "going to freezer camp," it's still hard when the time comes. Early on her daughter had insisted on naming all the animals, hoping that if they had names they wouldn't be killed and eaten. All the animals still have names, and they are loved and respected, but that doesn't alter their fate. Dairy operations of all kinds are tied to meat production, but not all take on this aspect of the work themselves as Bearden's family does. (For instance St. John sells off the male goats she can't keep.)

According to the USDA there has been growth in the goat dairy industry since 2005 and there are over 360,000 dairy goats in the United States. Wisconsin, California, and Minnesota have the most, but numbers are rising in Iowa and Texas (National Agricultural Statistics Service, *Sheep and Goats* 16). Most of these goats are Alpine, LaMancha, Nubian, Oberhasli, Saanen, and Toggenburg as these breeds can produce two thousand pounds of milk a year during their 285 days of lactation ("Dairy Goats"). Goat milk is valued for making cheese and soap and because it's easier to digest than cow's milk. But cow's milk still accounted for 95 percent of the milk consumed in 2014, with a cow producing about twenty thousand more pounds of milk a year than a goat. Many choose to buy goat milk products since goats are less likely to be in an industrial-style dairy than are cows. The average goatherd size in California is 29 and in Wisconsin it is 39. In contrast to the increasing use of commercial production for meat goats, most of the dairies remain small. Industry analysis notes that "the dairy industry seems to have retained many small farms where the products are used either for home consumption or in the production of dairy products on a small scale. There are, of course, notable exceptions of large dairy herds supplying processors or producing milk on a large scale for commercial goat cheese production" (Animal and Plant Health Inspection Service). Since the USDA literature provides guidelines and costs for a 500-goat dairy, the move to larger goat dairies may not be such an exception for long.

My sister and brother-in-law, Megan and Don Greve, helped run such an industrial dairy. Galaxy Dairy was a family business located in Turlock, California, that operated for thirty years (1964–1994). They had 700 goats in the herd, milking 400 at any given time. It took approximately eight hours to milk 400 goats using milking machines (four hours in the morning and four in the evening). Plans for further growth (to 1,200 goats) were discussed before the decision to sell was made. While they drank the milk raw on the ranch, they produced 20 percent of the milk going to two plants that produced powdered and condensed milk for Meyenberg Goat Products. The Greves did raise and eat sheep and beef from time to time, but generally they did not eat their own goats.

In response to our questions about their view of nature the answers were mixed. On the one hand we were told "the dairy animals are a business" and "nature relates to the parts of the environment which can be used for recreation (hiking and camping)." The family altered nature when they cut down trees to build on their sixty-acre dairy, put in irrigation pipelines, and killed magpies (until they saw their usefulness for eating bugs). On the other hand, the business of a dairy is affected by the weather and the seasons, requiring one to understand and pay attention to "nature." Don said, "It affects how you grow crops and how you raise and care for animals." They grew close to 50 percent of their feed, but given the prices it was usually cheaper to buy corn than to grow it. Growing feed required summer irrigation. Following the cycles of the goats, kidding took place between March and May, and the goats were dry during December and January. Many dairies use controlled lighting to get twelve months of milking, but they did not. The two months of rest were seen as important for humans and goats alike.

The kids were taken immediately and bottle-fed until they went to auction at four days old to be sold to meat ranchers. It is now harder for goat dairies to get money this way, as the meat producers prefer the Boer goats (like those being added to the Bearden farm). The goats were bred when they were a year old. Don said that in the 1960s the productive life of a dairy goat was ten to twelve years, producing one to two quarts of milk a day. By 1984 the productive life span had been reduced to six to seven years, but they produced two to eight quarts a day. While less extreme, this transformation mirrors changes in dairy cow productivity. Breeding for productivity was an important aspect of running the dairy, and Megan said they kept careful records. Most of the goats were registered. While most of the goats were not named, top breeders like Samson and Sally Ann were. Goats were purchased at the start of the dairy and again in 1980 during an expansion. Other than that they bred their own and managed a closed herd. This was important for keeping out disease. One of their early purchases of goats brought in lice, pink eye, and mastitis, which required a lot of care. The Greves were determined to produce a clean product, which meant starting with healthy goats. As part of record-keeping each goat had an ear tag, and to ease handling they had each goat wear a chain around her neck. Horns become a problem when the goats play or fight, so debudding is seen as important by most people who keep goats. This process involves applying a heated rod or caustic chemicals to the horn nub of very young kids. At Galaxy Dairy they cut tails and burned off the horns. Don said he hated dehorning the babies and that his mother did a lot of that work.

Both Don and Megan grew up loving animals. In addition to the goats there were dogs and lots of cats. As with many dairies, the cats did important work by hunting, but between people dropping cats off on the road and natural reproduction, the cat population could get out of hand. To keep numbers down they didn't feed the cats and only a few of the cats were named. The dogs were generally named but didn't live in the house. Don said that part of loving animals is to help them with their death—they should not suffer. Some animals would be shot on the farm, but others were sent to the auction. If an animal was being shot, it was not a healthy animal. While it was hard to do, and hard not to cry, he felt it was the right thing to do. Megan and Don later ran a horse boarding and training facility (The Triangle G Ranch) and Don did note it was harder to kill or send a horse to auction (which was more personal) than it was to send a goat (which was business): "With the horses you spend time working with the individual animal. When you have over 700 animals (goats) it changes the relationship."

They did show some of their goats. Showing is popular among dairy goat producers, and the United States maintains its own set of breed standards. Breed differences are evident in appearance and behavior. Nubian goats are the most numerous dairy goat even though they are not the highest producer. The high fat content of their milk and their appearance (long, floppy ears) account for their popularity. Alpines, the second most numerous dairy goat, produce a lot of milk and are known to be bossy. The Saanen, second only to the Alpine for milk production, is usually described as gentle. LaMancha goats, another gentle goat, have no external ears. Toggenburgs are the oldest breed of dairy goat and are popular for their fawn-like appearance—brown with white spots. Known for their deep red color, Oberhasli goats are not particularly high producers, but breeding is changing that. Nigerian Dwarf goats are good milkers whose size makes them popular as pets and as 4-H projects. The Pygmy goat is another small milker whose heavy muscling also makes for good meat. An article in *Mother Earth* put it this way: "We have found that our Nubian Goats are the divas of the bunch. They are very loving and loyal and incredibly demanding. If a Nubian goat does not want to go on a milking stand, then there is no way of making her, short of picking her up. No small feat at an average of 200 pounds, and she will remember this 'humiliation' and get even at some point. Our LaManchas are sweet and hardworking and easy to train. Our Saanens are the clowns of the dairy and always ready for mischief" (Shewchuck). There is a great deal of diversity among goats, and their individual personalities need to be respected.

Goats are friendly and want to play, but they maintain hierarchies. Bucks can kill each other. Don said that goats are harder to handle than sheep and are smarter than cows. Goats don't herd the way sheep do and will eat most plants they can find—including some prized gardens! Goats are very active and can climb. This means some find sheep easier to keep, but there are fewer than 100 sheep dairies in the United States with about 10,000 ewes being milked. Average flock size is about 150, with half the flocks having fewer than 55. Sheep milk is especially good for making cheese given its higher solids content. They do, however, produce less milk than do goats or cows. East Friesian and Lacaune are the breeds of dairy sheep used in the United States. They can produce between 400 and 1,000 pounds of milk per year. While some farms only milk once a day until the lambs are weaned at from thirty to sixty days, many operations remove lambs within the first twenty-four hours and begin milking twice a day (Schoenian, "Dairy Sheep Basics"; Thomas). Most of these dairy operations keep the sheep grazing on grass, providing shelter as needed and some supplemental feed concentrates. This makes them a desirable alternative to cow dairies for many people concerned about the increasing industrialization of the dairy industry.

Among the animals commonly considered livestock, the ruminants are generally considered to have the best lives. Many of those cattle, sheep, and goats who are raised for meat spend some or most of their time living outside on grass in social groups. While, as already discussed, more and more cattle spend more of their time confined to a feedlot, the smaller scale of goat and sheep meat production means that many of them still live in a fairly "natural" way. The same can be said for those who are raised for wool, though they face issues of shearing and mulesing (discussed in the previous chapter).

Those ruminants raised and used for their milk, however, have a more varied existence. The dairies we visited are not the kinds of operations that supply the bulk of the dairy products in the United States. Many dairy animals spend much of their life in confinement—especially cows and goats. According to F. Bailey Norwood and Jayson L. Lusk in their book *Compassion by the Pound*, over nine million cows are milked each day in the United States. The average size of individual dairies has gone from one hundred or fewer cows to between one thousand and five thousand cows (144–45). Norwood and Lusk report that in the United States 50 percent of the dairies use tie stalls to house the cows but that since larger dairies are less likely to use this method of housing, a smaller percentage of the overall dairy population face this restriction (down from 44 percent to 22 percent between 1996 and 2011). They are still restricted in other ways, though. Norwood and Lusk report that in the United States "19 percent of lactating cows have no outdoor access, 22 percent are provided pasture, and the remainder has access to a concrete pen (17%) or dry lot (49%) in the summer" (147). This access to the outdoors goes down in the winter.

The selective breeding in the dairy industry has resulted in increased milk production. This has come at a cost to the cow, however. Unnaturally large udders make it difficult to walk and result in mastitis (a painfully inflamed udder). The cows are also often lame, as the nutrients in their diet are diverted to milk production rather than healthy bones. Such lameness is made worse by their having to stand on concrete floors and in the mud that develops in the "dry" lots. All of this makes movement difficult, which may be a reason the cows are not out on pasture. It also raises concerns about the milking process itself. Most cattle are moved from their stalls or the lot to a milking barn to be milked. Norwood and Lusk write that the milking itself is pleasurable as "cows experience pain if they are not milked and their udders swell too much. Additionally, forcing the animal to walk from the paddock to the barn provides beneficial exercise" (147–48). That they need to be "forced" to make the walk to the barn indicates a certain unwillingness to move, and the extra-large udders that they "need" to have milked are part of what contributes to this unwillingness. A paradoxical situation to be sure.

Such confinement is a welfare concern, as is the discomfort. So too are the often accompanying practices of dehorning, castration, tail-docking, and early weaning. About one-third of U.S. dairy cows have their tails removed in order to promote cleanliness and to make using the milking machines more convenient. This is done without anesthetic and often when the cow is older and certainly feels pain (148). As already mentioned most dairy goats have their horns removed either by their being burnt off or through the application of caustic chemicals. This is true of dairy cows as well (something Joe Markholt said was more stressful than castration—see chapter 3). Common to all dairy operations is the removal of offspring. Dairy animals must give birth to produce milk. While their milk production can be augmented and extended by the now controversial use of hormones, they must have babies. While some small dairies leave the calves, kids, or lambs on the mother for an extended time and share the milk, commercial dairies remove the offspring almost immediately. This is traumatic for mother and baby, and evidence of stress abounds. Livestock expert Temple Grandin remarks on the sound of bawling calves who have recently been removed from their mothers. Even when this is done at "weaning age" (four to six months) it can be quite traumatic. She said, "I remember one mama who was mooing frantically and trying to jump the fence to get back to her baby. The babies acted really stressed and agitated, too" (*Animals in Translation* 110). When this separation occurs at a few hours (or at most days) old, it is much worse. Further evidence of the stress is found in their increased susceptibility to disease. To limit disease exposure, the female calves who will be retained are housed in individual pens for the first few weeks before being moved to a group pen. This means they are denied not only their mothers but also all physical and social contact with their kind. Most female calves will be raised as replacement animals. This is necessary, as the productive life of the modern dairy cow is now limited to four or five years because her body cannot hold up under the stress of the increased levels of milk production (Norwood and Lusk 148). For goats this is six to seven years and for sheep it is about three years. The male calves, kids, and lambs generally have one fate—meat production.

Some calves join their beef counterparts in feedlots (though the specialized breeding makes them less desirable as beef cattle). The rest (about 30 percent) go to veal calf production. These calves are housed in small individual or group pens that allow little movement and are fed a purely liquid diet that often results in anemia (144). The life of the veal calf is one of the main targets for animal advocacy groups, and consumption of veal has fallen in the United States. For goats and sheep the fate of an early death is the same, but they often have a group life out on pasture up until that point. Feeding operations for sheep and goats may be changing this. Given the amount of death, disease, and dismemberment involved in the dairy industry, many argue that if one is concerned about animal suffering it would be more important to stop consuming dairy (and egg) products than to stop eating meat (though later chapters will show this does not apply to chickens and pigs) (Masson, *Face on Your Plate* 14). Norwood and Lusk try to counter the concern about veal by suggesting that while consuming dairy products does support the veal industry, consuming dairy products does not really implicate one in much suffering and death. They say:

> Two 8 oz servings of milk is only 1 lb of milk, and one cow produces about 19,125 lbs of milk each year. Even if you drank two 8 oz servings of milk each day, you are only consuming 1.9 percent of a cow's annual output of milk. Thus, your milk consumption refers to only a fraction of a cow's output, and the veal produced from 1 lb of milk is tiny, implying your milk consumption is only responsible for a small amount of veal production. Moreover, veal would be produced even without milk production. Milk purchases do subsidize veal production, but only a by [*sic*] tiny amount. If veal production were outlawed the number of dairy cows would barely change, and if milk production were banned veal calves would easily be obtained from beef breeds. All things considered, a vegetarian can consume milk and cheese even if they are opposed to veal production, knowing their action subsidizes veal production only by a miniscule amount. (144–45)

In my opinion, this is more than a little disingenuous. The fact that one is only consuming a tiny amount of a cow's overall production is misleading in a number of ways. First, most people consume much more than the sixteen ounces Norwood and Lusk use in their "calculation." Second, an individual human is consuming only a small fraction of an individual cow's production only because of the unnaturally elevated levels of milk production found in modern dairy cows. Much suffering results from this for the lame cow with an oversized and diseased udder. Further, all offspring are removed from their mothers, not just the veal calves. Norwood and Lusk admit that this causes suffering when they write, "In addition to inducing stress in the calf and mother at the time of separation, the absence of the family bond prohibits the calf from maturing properly. The calf will experience greater stress in new environments, will be less able to solve problems, and will show a reduced motivation to solve problems. The calf never suckles from its mother's teat. . . . Calves have a natural desire to suckle a teat. . . . It is not just the milk the calf wants, but the feel of the teat as it is drinking" (142–43). Since this is denied to all calves on large commercial dairies, it seems odd that Norwood and Lusk would factor in only the suffering of those calves diverted to veal production. While it is true that the veal calf may be the "poster calf" for animal rights and welfare groups, it is far from the only concern with the dairy industry. Many aspects of the lives of animals in industrial dairies violate commonly understood principles of animal welfare.

Norwood and Lusk say that since dairy cows generally get along (even when crowded) and are fed a nutritionally dense diet, access to pasture is not really necessary for the welfare of the dairy cows. This assessment does not match up with emerging understandings of animal needs. One measure of the well-being of various animals that has gained ground (especially in Europe) is the Five Freedoms. These are *freedom from hunger and thirst*, in having ready access to fresh water and food that maintains health and vigor; *freedom from discomfort*, in having an appropriate environment, including shelter and a comfortable resting area; *freedom from pain, injury, and disease*, which is ensured through prevention and, when problems arise, rapid diagnosis and treatment; *freedom to express normal behavior*, in having sufficient space, proper facilities, and company of the animal's own kind; and *freedom from fear and distress*, in having conditions and treatment that do not cause mental suffering. This list of freedoms is important, as it goes beyond the prevention of physical pain and suffering to recognize mental and emotional distress. It also goes beyond the prevention of suffering to insist on the promotion of normal physical and social behaviors as an important aspect of well-being.

The one cow dairy we were set to visit is one that seems to take these five freedoms to heart. We had an appointment to visit the Pride and Joy dairy in Granger, Washington, another promoter of raw milk. When we arrived, though, no one was around to talk with us. We played with the kittens and observed the calves who were housed in small outdoor pens with doghouse-like shelters. These calves are raised either as replacement dairy cows or as grass-fed beef (to accompany Pride and Joy's grass-fed lamb). This farm also has free-range chickens for egg production. The farm is advertised as on organic dairy selling Grade A, grass-fed raw cow's milk from Jersey, Holstein, Ayrshire, Swedish Red, Normandy, and crossbred cows. As with those who run St. John's Dairy and Fido Farm, the Voortmans see themselves primarily as grass farmers. Their pastures have clover, alfalfa, and chicory. Moveable fencing allows the pastures to be adjusted in size and moved as the grass demands (as at Fido Farm). Organic hay is available during the winter, and salt, minerals, and water are readily available in the pastures. Their cows have a productive life span of twelve years—much longer than the industry standard. As the farm website notes, "being 100% grass-fed results in lower production per cow, but improves overall herd health and produces impeccable milk quality" ("The Pasture Grass"). The cows walk over a mile a day while grazing, and their long life span results in stable herd relationships. These farmers are proud of the low stress levels and say there are no sick pens on the dairy, given the health of the cows. If a cow does need antibiotics they are administered for her well-being, and her milk is taken out of production. No hormones are used, and tails are not docked (on cattle or sheep). According to one article they get about five gallons a day from each cow: "The Voortmans note that being 100% grass fed changes the financial picture completely because they are achieving this level of milk output with minimal expense and get a value-added premium. They also have an extremely low involuntary cull rate (3–4% compared to national average of 37% in dairy industry). Due to their low involuntary cull rate, the Voortmans can sell 25–30% of their herd each year. The sale of excess animals represents a large part of the dairy's income" (Donovan). This means that since there is a low mortality rate in the herd they can sell more for breeding or for meat.

These cows enjoy the first four freedoms as they have ready access to food and water; they have pasture and shelter available; they are treated for injury and disease as needed; they get to walk the pasture and graze in a stable herd; and they are generally free from fear and distress. The last freedom is the hardest for any dairy to guarantee as there is always distress at the removal of offspring. However, as cow dairies go, this is about as ideal as it can get.

On purely environmental grounds Nicolette Niman (discussed in chapter 4) argues that confinement mega-dairies are the "most offensive farming system." Denying the nature of cows, she says, "they deprive animals of exercise and grazing, and they channel enormous volumes of manure into festering storage ponds that leach to ground water, can spill to rivers and streams, and emit ungodly odors and pollutants to the air." Further, since the cows aren't eating a natural grass diet their "soy-and grain-based feeding regimens raise the same pollution and resource concerns as pig and poultry facilities. But worst of all, this bundle of problems is being foisted onto the backs of grazing animals—creatures that indisputably belong on grass" (80). The cows themselves suffer from lameness and disease connected to their overproduction of milk; they get little individual attention due to the large number of animals; and the concentration of so many animals greatly increases the environmental risk from their manure.

Niman notes that USDA research found that grass-based dairies are the most ecologically friendly. They protect soil (87 percent less erosion) and water (25 percent less runoff of phosphorus). Carbon sequestration is higher, and greenhouse gas emissions are lower—"methane, nitrous oxide and carbon dioxide were 8 percent lower in the grass system than in the confinement system. Ammonia emissions were lower by about 30 percent" (76). While an ecofeminist like Carol Adams (discussed more in chapter 9) would be pleased that these operations cause less damage to the environment, Adams insists that they mirror and reinforce a logic that sees females as machines to exploit and so are not acceptable. The lactating mother is still separated from her calf and hooked to a machine. This kind of "feminized protein" is connected to the general objectification of the female and so Adams calls on all feminists to be vegans.

While Val Plumwood (discussed in chapter 1) agrees with much of what Adams has to say, she does not agree that one should necessarily adopt a vegan diet. Plumwood does not even argue that we should necessarily adopt a vegetarian diet. Instead, Plumwood argues for contextual eating (more in line with the approach suggested by Niman) as she seeks to identify methods of *respectful use*. For Plumwood, this concept needs to be applied to all our interactions with other animal beings and the rest of nature. Plumwood agrees that meat and dairy animals are now completely commodified. She refers to Adams's concept of the absent referent (discussed in chapters 4 and 6) and agrees that our language covers up our acts of violence and hides the individuality of the animals involved in the production of meat, dairy, and egg products. She agrees that the "ruthless, reductionistic . . . treatment of animals as replaceable and tradeable items of property characteristic of the commodity form and a capitalist economic rationality" are not good. But she disagrees with Adams, who thinks that such treatment is inevitable. Plumwood suggests we find a form of respectful use. To do this we have to reject entire ways of thinking about women and other animal beings. She writes:

> As production moves out of the household at the beginning of the modern era, the role of farm-household animals is transformed in the new separation of public/private in much the same way as the role of women. Both the working farm wife and the working farm animal now become subject to the modernist polarity that construes "rational" economic relationships in alienated, masculinist and narrowly instrumental terms. . . . The "familiar" working animal . . . is replaced by the bourgeois "pet" who, like the bourgeois wife, leads a sheltered life in a protected private household. The hyper-separation between the "pet" animal and the "meat" animal is intensified as the meat animal becomes subject to the rationally intrumentalised mass-production regime of the factory farm or laboratory. The "familiar" animal disappears, and the complementary polarity of the subjectivised and underemployed "pet" animal and the reduced and instrumentalised "meat" animal takes its place. (162)

In other words, some women (the poor) and some animal beings (livestock) are reduced to objects to use, while others lose all use value and become purely decorative (the bourgeois wife and the pet). For Plumwood, these conditions are related to each other and neither condition is good.

However, Plumwood disagrees with Adams's view that ontologizing another living being as edible is always a form of domination. She thinks this move "results in a deep rejection of ecological embodiment for those beings, since all ecologically-embodied beings are food for some other beings" (156). She argues that we need nonreductivist understandings of food and non-reductivist farming practices. She says, "We cannot give up using one another, but we can give up the use/respect dualism, which means working towards ethical, respectful and constrained forms of use" (159). This would mean that the way most livestock are currently raised and used would have to stop, but it would not mean respectful alternatives cannot be found.

Plumwood argues that we need to stop trying to get other animals included in the realm of rights-bearers, as this continues the dualistic mindset ecofeminists seek to challenge (see the discussion of personhood in chapter 5). It pits animals against each other and leaves plants outside the realm of what we need to consider when making choices. Instead she focuses on use and respect. She says it is possible to "respect animals as both individuals and as community members, in terms of respect or reverence for species life" if humans "rethink farming in a non-commodity and species-egalitarian" way. It does not require humans to "completely reject farming and embrace an exclusively plant-based form" (156). It does mean drastically changing, but not ending, the farming of livestock. This would entail context-specific eating that prioritizes the well-being of plants and animals (individuals and communities) used by humans for food. It would entail rejecting absolutist positions (as with pragmatism) and instead focusing on developing caring practices that take the earth and other beings into consideration *from their own point of view* (as much as we can).

To consider the point of view of livestock, it is worth considering a number of different ways to understand and measure animal welfare. While Norwood and Lusk pointed to the Five Freedoms as a way to assess the welfare of dairy cows on industrial dairies, and I used that framework to assess grass-fed dairies, it is only one possible approach. It is an approach that has been taken up by animal welfare advocates and lawmakers, so it is influential, but it is based on a limited number of mostly negative freedoms. Animal welfare scientists continue to refine this approach and to develop other models—all of which should be considered (Mellor). For instance, scientists note that living without any fear or stress at all compromises and weakens immune systems and overall health. Some zoos try to respect animals by creating housing arrangements where prey animals experience some amount of predation threat and predators have a chance to express stalking and hunting behavior. Part of animal enrichment includes animals working for food, competing with each other, and solving problems. Keeping livestock animals can similarly be done in ways that respect their needs and natures. For example, weaning is a stressful but natural event. So weaning young animals, which is part of most

livestock farming, is not inherently bad. But weaning offspring too young (as
is commonly done in dairy operations) is morally problematic and can cause
health problems. Similarly, death is part of life, but being hauled hundreds of
miles in crowded containers (with no attention to social bonds) in hot and
cold weather is not. Living in one's feces is not natural or healthful for livestock animals and forcing them to do so fails to respect what makes life acceptable, much less meaningful, for them.

One farm that tries to see life from the point of view of the animals, and
to embody respectful use, is another supporter of raw milk (goat milk in this
case)—Akyla Farms in Sedro-Woolley, Washington. This farm is much more
than a dairy, but the dairy goats are integral to the whole operation. At the
time of our visit their goat herd was primarily La Mancha and Nubian goats,
but they had plans to transition to Keiko goats since this breed doesn't need
their hooves trimmed. The Ostermans also have laying hens, meat birds, beef
cattle, horses, and pigs. Since it takes a lot of time to keep the animals rotating
through the pastures, and since the daily milking schedule adds to the time
commitment, they said, they "need low maintenance animals." Carol and
Kevin Osterman have more moving parts to their operation than most do, as
they also rent out their goats. The herd is hired out, along with a guard llama,
to eat back blackberries and other invasive vegetation. They advertise this as
a form of noxious weed control that is chemical-free and good for the environment. It also keeps their goats well fed.

Like St. John's Creamery, the Ostermans have a passion for raw milk. They
referred to studies that show that children who drink raw milk have a lower
rate of asthma. It was not just the milk that was important to them, though,
but living with livestock. They brought up Charles Mann's book *1491: New Revelations of the Americas before Columbus*. This book makes the case that living
with livestock gave Europeans immunities not shared by Native Americans.
Managing herds for meat and dairy is part of what allowed the Europeans to
colonize other lands. Not only were they able to take a food source with them,
but they also had an immune system that helped them survive contact with
new places and new diseases. The Ostermans believe these long-standing relationships with livestock have made humans what they are—good and bad.
The main use they see for these animals now is as fertilizer and food. They
said, "We use animals—we are omnivores (see our teeth and gut). Humans
have to eat meat to be healthy. Cows, goats, horses are true herbivores. Dogs
and cats are true carnivores—they must eat flesh." Following Plumwood's
idea that everyone is food for someone else, they said they would probably
eat dog: "It all depends on the purpose the animal is intended for. If it's raised
as a companion that is different than when it's raised to eat. The different intent leads to a different frame of mind. Pigs and chickens are cute at first, but

then transition into something else. You're glad when they're gone. They have no concept of tomorrow, so they are not harmed by death. They have a good life for the time they have." For them, this applies to horses too. While Carol's interest in farm animals and healthy pastures started with her interest in horses, the Ostermans don't romanticize horses. She said, "The horse is still an animal—an animal we can eat." They both said they would eat horsemeat, though their own horse will probably be buried on the farm.

While they provide food for humans and other animals, the livestock also improve the fertility of the land. Kevin said, "Goats—love their job, which is to eat. They eat the woody things, cows eat grasses, sheep eat herbs, birds eat bugs. They all add fertilizer so we get healthy pasture. The healthy pasture gives us good meat and milk. We feed the by-product of the dairy to the pigs and poultry. The poultry really improve the fields; it's very green wherever the poultry pens have been. They help put fertility back in the land." The Ostermans see themselves, and the other animal beings, as part of the land and of nature more generally and like to work with the web of life to keep the soil healthy: "We love the animals, the animals improve the land, good land improves everyone's health." Kevin said, "Nature—we are part of it. Everything we do either benefits it or disrupts it. Chemicals disrupt and damage cycles. There may be an immediate payback from using chemicals, but long term it will cost you and the land." For example they don't use ivermectin for worming. If they did, all the bugs would be affected and this would weaken the animals and the land. They would then need to use the veterinarian more as the animals would be sick. They said, "Parasites don't like a healthy animal." Their goal is to raise healthy animals on healthy land. At the time of our visit in 2010 the motto listed on their website was "You are not what you eat. You are what your food eats." Now their website says, "It's not just what you eat, it's what your food eats."

One reason the Ostermans started farming was to have safe food. Although they were inspired by Joel Salatin (see chapter 4), they also work with the Weston A. Price Foundation (WAPF). Price was a dentist who found good food made a difference in people's health. The foundation "supports . . . organic and biodynamic farming, pasture-feeding of livestock, community-supported farms, honest and informative labeling, prepared parenting and nurturing therapies. Specific goals include establishment of universal access to clean, certified raw milk and a ban on the use of soy formula for infants" (Nienhiser). At Akyla they focus on providing nutritionally dense food (including raw milk) and avoiding GMOs. While their own health was a big motivation for the Ostermans' farming the way they do, so was their love of animals.

Speaking about the animals Kevin said, "We put them in this situation so we owe them good food and care." The goats in the milking herd all have

PHOTO 7. Chickens at Akyla Farm. Photo by Danielle Palmer.

PHOTO 8. Chicken tractors at Akyla Farm. Photo by Danielle Palmer.

names, as do some of the cows. Carol said, "Some of the neighbors love the animals and see them like children. This can be a problem when it's time to slaughter them and they end up in the freezer." When the Ostermans get the animals out of the freezer they talk to them by name: "Hi Ashley. Sorry." This fits with Plumwood's hope to combine use and respect. To make life good for the animals the Ostermans do things differently from how most do. They don't debud the baby goats, since goats need their horns. They said it's harder to care for dehorned goats, as the horn is part of the sinus. For the same reason, they breed naturally polled cattle. They also don't want big-framed animals who need grain; the cattle must do well on pasture, be hardy, and be able to give birth on their own. The Ostermans let the calves wean themselves, and we saw a yearling who was still with his mom. They don't vaccinate the cattle but depend on the general health of the cattle to protect them from disease and parasites. They said, "Health starts with good quality pasture. When a pasture is done, the cows talk and tell you to move them. If they get ill at the drop of a hat, they would never survive in the wild, and we don't want cows like that in the herd." With the goats going out to eat, the Ostermans can't control the cows' or the goats' exposure, so the animals need to be healthy. The laying hens and meat birds also need to be capable of surviving life in the pasture. The Ostermans have about ten different breeds of chickens. They said, "We like the variety as it makes it easier to watch individuals, and we allow the birds to live out their lives with us as we see the older birds as being wiser in that ongoing predator/prey story." The meat birds are also pastured and killed on-site. The Ostermans use Freedom Ranger birds (see chapter 4) because these birds are hardier and actually graze the pasture instead of just eating grain. The Ostermans feed some of the excess goat milk to the birds and to their pigs.

Like the chickens, the pigs are killed and processed on-site, lessening the stress they face during their lives. According to the farm website the pigs "enjoy fresh pasture on a regular basis, depending on how fast they utilize their area. We use portable electrified netting to keep the pigs where we want them and be able to efficiently create new areas for them in the tall grass, Japanese Knotweed and blackberry patches. Along with their pasture and daily ration of organic grain they also receive occasional organic produce, surplus eggs from the laying flock and some milk from our dairy does." This kind of integration of dairy with pigs and chickens used to be common but is much harder to find today. (It is what Bearden has in mind for her farm in Illinois as well.) Pigs have long been an important part of such integration as they can eat "waste" products. Pigs were generally kept on small diversified farms and fed off the scraps from the humans and other livestock. This made them an economical animal to keep. But that kind of life is no longer available to the pigs used for most pork production. While the ruminants have increasingly been confined, many of them live something more like a normal life than do pigs and poultry. The next two chapters will turn to these two most confined and concentrated of the animals found in industrial agriculture. The five freedoms mentioned earlier arose, in large part, in response to pig and poultry operations and remain missing for most pigs and chickens. Here there is only use—no respect.

CHAPTER EIGHT

Pork Production

PIGS AND PRAGMATISM

The human relationship with domesticated pigs goes back nine to eleven thousand years. Domesticated in different parts of the world at different times, pigs continue to be an important part of many cultures. Known domestication events occurred in China, India, and Southeast Asia (Essig 35). There is now evidence suggesting that domesticated pigs were first introduced to Europe from China but then were replaced with pigs domesticated from European boar (Larson et al.). Many believe that humans' increasingly sedentary way of life, along with their accumulated waste, attracted pigs to human settlements and supplied the multiple opportunities for domestication. In *Lesser Beasts: A Snout to Tail History of the Humble Pig*, Mark Essig argues that pigs' similarities with humans may have made this a fairly easy process: "The two species have similar digestive systems, from teeth to stomach to intestines, because they have similar diets. Both are omnivores who thrive on meat, nuts, roots, and seeds. And because pigs and people eat the same foods, they evolved to form a symbiotic connection—a bond so tight that 10,000 years later, it remains unbroken" (17).

This similarity has been a double-edged sword. Humans breed pigs specifically for biomedical purposes such as harvesting organs for transplantation to humans: hearts, lungs, skin. Their similar anatomy and vulnerability to disease make them popular for biomedical research and testing. They too suffer from conditions like arthritis, diabetes, and ulcers. As with humans, stress is a real factor in their well-being, given their social nature and intelligence. Their intelligence, however, raises ethical concerns about using them in this way. It

also raises issues about their much more common use as food. Their popularity as a source of food is rooted in their omnivorous diet. Historically, pigs
could eat human leftovers and so did not require extra effort in farming to
feed them. In addition to removing food waste, pigs can fatten up by eating
human feces—an important service for the newly settled human populations.
They also provided a ready source of manure for emerging agricultural production. Further, pigs could basically be left to their own devices and did not
require humans to build them enclosures. Often in a semi-domesticated state,
pigs retained the ability to return to the "wild" as needed. This remains true
today as feral pigs have established populations in much of the world, including most of the United States.

   There are about five million feral pigs in the United States, most easily
found in Florida, Texas, California, North Carolina, Tennessee, Hawaii, and
Puerto Rico. This distribution results from their introduction by explorers and
early settlers, but pigs came with colonists in New England as well. Logs suggest that 60 pigs arrived in Jamestown in 1585. This number quickly became
600 and then exploded to "infinite hogs all over the woods" by 1614 (Gray 19).
As with cattle, fencing the animals out of one's property was more common
than enclosing them; this practice led to uncontrolled breeding. It was not
until the 1800s that pigs were imported to "improve" domestic stock so that
a two-year-old grass-fed hog would be between 300 and 450 pounds (Bidwell
and Falconer 229). Despite these breeding efforts pigs generally roamed freely.
There was some importation of European boar in the early 1900s in North
Carolina, but most bred with feral domesticated pigs. Since pigs are an ex-
otic species in the United States they are often seen as a threat to the ecosystems in which they live. The rooting of pigs is known to increase the speed
of decomposition, making nutrients available in the soil and promoting the
growth of trees, but there is concern that as a nonnative species pigs may
harm native flora and fauna and carry disease that could impact both wildlife
and livestock. Around the world they are seen as a pest by farmers, as pigs
trample and root out crops. Electric fencing is one way to keep them out, but
hunting is the most common response.

   In the United States there are outfits that specialize in providing the experience of hunting "boar." Others make their living by doing the hunting themselves. Boar meat has become a popular item in some restaurants, so hunting has become more than "pest control." An article in *American Hunter* tries
to both justify such hunting and show that it's profitable: "The availability of
specialized firearms, ammunition, gear and even websites and magazines all
point to the fact that hog hunting is becoming big business. With rambling
hordes of porkers now found in 35 states and with an estimated 2 million in
the South alone, the destruction these heavy critters are wreaking across their

range is extensive. Hogs uproot crop fields and yards and destroy habitat that must be shared with a broad range of other species including wild turkeys and deer" (Howlett). Part of the allure of hunting hogs resides in the challenge they provide. They are secretive and smart; this speaks to their intelligence and ingenuity. Described as smarter than dogs, pigs are used as retrievers, truffle hunters, and service animals. They are quick problem-solvers and engage in cause-and-effect thinking. In testing automated feeding systems that granted access to food by reading electric collars, researchers found that pigs would pick up collars they found on the ground and use them to regain access to food. Pigs have been worshiped for their strength and fertility, as well as for their intelligence. In the United States today, though, they are not worshiped and their intelligence is not respected in industrial hog production.

The USDA report "US Hog Production from 1992 to 2009: Technology, Restructuring, and Productivity Growth" describes current hog production. The title alone makes clear that raising pigs is a technological affair and that growth in productivity is the main goal. The report begins with an error in reasoning. The report says, "US hog farms declined in number by more than 70 percent over the past two decades while hog inventories remained stable. The *result* has been an industry with larger hog enterprises, increased specialization in a single phase of production, greater reliance on purchased feed rather than feed grown on the farm, and an increased reliance on formal contracts—connecting farmers, hog owners, and packers—to coordinate production" (italics added). But this is backward. The industry they accurately describe did not *result* from the decline in the number of farms, but rather the decline in the number of farms occurred as technology enabled hog production to become bigger and more concentrated. The report continues, "This structural change contributed to substantial productivity gains for hog farms, likely benefiting U.S. consumers in terms of lower pork prices and enhancing the competitive position of US producers in international markets—though larger farms may increase environmental risks by concentrating production in areas with limited land available for manure application" (i). The focus of the report, however, is not on such environmental risk (some of which was described in chapter 5) but on examining the slowdown in productivity growth in the industry since 2004. The gains in productivity that came with the major intensification and industrialization of pig production have leveled off, and the USDA report concludes that "the era of dramatic growth in hog production is likely over, absent new technological innovation" (iii). There is no real concern with the environmental issues, and no mention of the possible impacts on the farmers, much less those on the pigs themselves.

The move to partially or totally confined housing of pigs began in the 1970s. This pushed the industry to further specialization and growth in numbers that allowed for a decrease in labor hours (24). This growth in production came as farms went from raising an average of 945 pigs in 1992 to an average of 8,389 in 2009. Increased specialization helped with profit margins, and those farms that bred, birthed, and raised the pigs to slaughter weight have declined in number. These are known as farrow-to-finish operations. Instead, the more dominant model is for some to focus on breeding and birthing while others feed to fatten—the latter known as feeder-to-finish operations, which accounted for 73 percent of "finished hog output" in 2009 (27). Adding to the specialization, some now focus on farrowing (farrow-to-wean) while others focus on raising the weanlings (wean-to-feeder) (5). At the same time, the share of farmers who signed production contracts grew from 5 to 67 percent. This helped promote the growth in the size of the hog operations, as such contracts made possible the investment in the technology (e.g., artificial insemination, confinement housing, manure treatment) needed to more intensively raise hogs. In these specialized operations farmers lose autonomy as they become "growers." The USDA report points out that such contracts specify things like the feed, labor, energy, transport, and veterinary services. This also allows contractors to gain more of the market. The report says, "In 2009 and 2010, the three largest contractors owned about a quarter of the national sow herd. . . . Many of the largest contractors are also pork packers that are vertically integrated, obtaining hogs under production contracts directly with growers" (13). This means they profit from the slaughter and processing as well as from raising (feeding). Interestingly this results in the farmer making less on the hog than do the owner and the processor, who charge the consumer more than they paid the farmer (34).

Another change that resulted from the contracts is that the people who own the hogs are not the same people involved in raising the hogs, and neither of these groups slaughters or processes the hogs. The USDA report describes the relationships as follows: "Under contract production, a hog owner (a contractor) engages a producer (a grower) to take custody of the pigs and care for them in the producer's facilities. The producer is paid a fee for the service provided. Contractors typically furnish inputs for growers, provide technical assistance, and assemble the commodity to pass on for final process or marketing. Contractors often market hogs through marketing contracts or other arrangements with packers or processors. Packers or processors also act as contractors and have production contracts directly with producers" (4). Note that the pigs have become an "assembled commodity" and farmers and packers are paid for services rather than being invested in the "product" themselves. Since the contractors are usually large corporations like Smithfield Foods, it is safe to say that the hogs' owners have no relationship with the porcine beings themselves. This distance can facilitate "improvements" in genetics as artificial insemination, terminal cross-breeding programs, phase feeding, and all-in/all-out management practices increase efficiency and the "performance" of the hogs, whatever they might do to individual pigs. The same applies to the use of antibiotics. Rather than being an important tool for treating sick animals, antibiotics became a way to promote growth. This USDA report does note that "antibiotics may be promoting the development of antimicrobial drug-resistant bacteria, prompting concerns that this resistance can spread to bacteria that infect humans" (19). Consumer and governmental pressure have caused a decline in the use of antibiotics for growth promotion, but use of antibiotics is still a major controversy in livestock production in the United States. In addition, many of the steps taken to lower the risk of disease exposure and so limit the use of antibiotics entail the confinement of pigs indoors, on cement, with nothing to occupy their minds or satisfy their instincts to root, nest, and socialize.

Much of the explosion in U.S. pig productivity occurred when North Carolina became a major hog-producing state, but the North Carolina boom ended in 1997 when the state became concerned about the environmental impact of the industry. This pushed the industry back to its original base in the heartland, where the food is grown—Iowa—and the West, where there is open space—Colorado, Oklahoma, Texas, and Utah. The report notes, "Open space and a relatively low population density in these States provide greater flexibility in managing animal waste" (16). The writers of the report support these changes by appealing to consumers, even while noting some environmental concerns: "The dramatic structural changes in the hog industry . . . have helped lower pork prices for consumers. . . . On the other hand, in some States these changes have concentrated livestock manure in regions with relatively little available cropland for spreading, making it more costly to apply as fertilizer in environmentally benign ways" (33). The larger volumes of manure are an environmental concern, though, as too much manure on the cropland results in runoff that pollutes water: "These runoff contaminants can harm aquatic life and degrade drinking water. In addition, increased concentration of hogs per farm has led to conflicts with nearby residents and communities over odor and air quality" (36). As Nicolette Niman suggests, in this system manure changes from "ecological benefactor to ecological nuisance and from economic asset to economic liability" (74).

The report ends by suggesting that while the increased scale per farm poses environmental risks, the increased efficiency of these large operations may mitigate the damage:

> Higher productivity means that fewer resources—including land, fertilizer, and pesticides—are required to grow the feed required to produce a particular

amount of pork. Depending on how the feed inputs are used, this could result in lower greenhouse gas emissions (e.g. less fertilizer manufacturing and use), reduced water pollution (e.g. from less fertilizer or pesticide over-application), or other environmental benefits. Also, concentrating manure sources in fewer locations potentially affects fewer people and may also make some manure treatment technologies (e.g. energy from bio-waste, or processing into concentrated fertilizer) feasible (36).

These are highly conditional possibilities and are generally focused on anthropocentric concerns. The concentrated confinement of pigs creates environmental concerns, but that same confinement is supposed to mitigate those concerns. Nowhere is the pig (or the farmer) considered. This report represents the mindset that sees pigs simply as a commodity, not as living beings with needs, desires, and personalities of their own.

The farmers we interviewed who raised pigs did see the pigs as a commodity (to make money) and a tool (to improve land), but they also respected their needs, desires, and personalities. Vickie Hinkley runs New Heritage Farms in Toledo, Washington, where she raises Tamworth pigs. When we arrived we were first introduced to the two new "girls" who had just arrived for breeding. They were housed, with the boar, in a front pasture that had comfrey so that the pigs could browse on it as a source of protein; Hinkley said the boar was also good at eating the blackberries. After spending some time scratching and socializing we headed up the hill to help Hinkley with the morning feeding. There were a number of animals to feed: more pigs, turkeys, chickens, Jersey cattle, and Kiser mustangs. Our work was supervised by a beautiful Australian shepherd. During feeding we met Gigi—a six-year-old sow. Breeding sows are generally killed around four years of age because they usually have fused vertebrae and arthritis by this time; Hinkley was watching Gigi closely to monitor her well-being. Gigi was way out in the pasture under some trees when we went in to feed, but she came up to the trough at a pretty good clip and seemed happy to get some attention. While we watched Gigi, Hinkley explained that she doesn't cut her pigs' teeth or tails. These are common practices on industrial pig farms where crowded and bored pigs bite each other and chew on each other's tails. Hinkley said clipping teeth (which is usually done at one to two days old) "is not necessary if the pigs are not raised in overcrowded places. Since you can tell if a pig is sick by how it holds its tail, it's important to keep the tail intact."

Inside the barn we fed Lucky Lucy (Gigi's daughter) and Lucy's eight babies. These piglets were half Tamworth ("for their long lean build which produces good bacon") and half Large Black. Mom and babies were out in the pasture and we went out to meet them. The babies came running up. Hinkley

PHOTO 9. Lucky Lucy and her piglets at New Heritage Farms. Photo by McKenzie Williams.

said they are naturally very curious. They were curious, and a little cautious, but soon we were all sitting in the dirt scratching piglets. Mom made her way up more slowly. While feeding this group, Hinkley told us about a sow she'd had who ate one of her offspring. Hinkley believes she must have done something to the sow's environment or diet that created the conditions that led to this action. For instance, she wasn't sure she had provided an environment where the mom could sit down and not have to constantly be feeding the piglets. Generally Tamworths are strongly attached mothers, but even so, accident prevention remains a main priority. Hinkley said, "They need room to farrow and make a huge nest." Providing ample room is important, as the sows are big animals and the piglets are little. Hinkley rejects the industry's attempts to justify farrowing crates as necessary in order to protect the piglets. As she noted, "wild pigs don't roll over on their offspring and a species that did wouldn't last very long. If there is a problem it is a human problem." Hinkley is constantly evaluating the setup of pastures and pens—on the lookout for sharp corners where a pig could get cut, or water that is deep enough for a piglet to drown. She said that the best, and safest, precaution is to keep them out in the pasture as much as possible.

While commercial producers want the babies off the mother as soon as possible and wean a few days after birth, Hinkley weans at around eight to nine weeks. Before weaning, most male piglets are castrated—usually at around two weeks old. She said, "People don't like the taste of meat from intact males and not too many males are needed for breeding." The vet had been there the day before our visit to castrate the one male in this litter. This is done with an incision between the legs, without sedation or stiches. Hinkley said, "You don't sedate piglets—the weight of pigs is too unpredictable." Interestingly, while Hinkley had invited us to come and view the castration, the veterinarian was not comfortable having us there. He was worried about being attacked by "animal rights types." The veterinarian's concern returns me to a central point of this book. Extreme positions in the debates over animal welfare and animal rights have resulted in a polarized discourse and much secrecy. This makes meaningful change less likely to happen. Hinkley is a good example of someone trying to figure things out without following any dogmas. She is new to farming (raising the pigs had been her late husband's dream) and she admits she has much to learn. She learns by experimentation and she seeks out advice and new information. While she respects all the farmers from whom she's learned, she doesn't like absolutist stances on anything and is open to doing things as naturally as possible.

She called her farm a "naturalized confinement system." Unlike industrialized farming, which she described as "horrible," she focuses on the health of the land and on the quality of life for the animals. She tries to worm and vaccinate as little as possible. She watches the quality of the dirt on the farm, as that is a big source of minerals (iron specifically) for the pigs and decreases her need to supplement their food. She feeds rolled barley since she wants to avoid genetically modified organisms (GMOs) and barley is a grain that is low on the list of organisms that are often genetically modified. The pork pigs get less than seven pounds of grain a day, as compared to industrialized pigs, who eat about ten pounds. She would like to follow the example of Walter Jeffries, whose pigs at Sugar Mountain Farm in Vermont get 80 percent of their diet from pasture forage, hay, and things like pumpkins. This, supplemented with some eggs and dairy, makes a good diet for pigs. Hinkley's pigs do spend most of their time in the pastures and in the woods, living as natural a life as possible. They are ready for slaughter at one year old (as opposed to five or six months for confined pigs). She said it is a constant dilemma—"killing them at twelve months when they could live a longer life." At the same time, however, she does not completely agree with those who focus on animal rights: "I don't abide by any fundamentalism well. I can't agree with PETA on farming since what I do is so different from commercial farming." She said she can support their anti-cruelty stance but doesn't see raising and harvesting livestock as inherently cruel. The absolutism of the position that calls for the end of raising all farm animals does not make sense to her and "gets in the way of the important work of raising such animals respectfully." She has chosen breeds

PHOTO 10. Cow and pigs at New Heritage Farms. Photo by McKenzie Williams.

to match her land and adjusts her husbandry practices to meet the needs and desires of the various animals. Her view shares much in common with both Plumwood's and a pragmatist approach.

She offers pastured pork and woodlot pork from pigs who eat the acorns and apples found in the woods. Much of her attention, however, is on providing stock for others to raise and breed. She is dedicated to Tamworths and can sell breeding stock for from $300 to $600. According to the Livestock Conservancy, "Long, lean, and athletic, the Tamworth is probably the most direct descendant of the native pig stock of northern Europe." First imported to the United States in the 1800s, "Tamworths have an active intelligence, and they are agreeable in disposition." Hinkley loves their personalities as the many pictures and videos on her website attest. If young pigs get sick she takes them into her house to care for them. She's had good luck nursing them back to health and becomes very bonded to them. These particular pigs, however, are pretty hardy: "The characteristics of the Tamworth reflect the breed's centuries of selection for an outdoor life. Pigs of this breed were expected to find their own food, especially mast (or acorns) of oak and beech forests. Long heads and impressive snouts enable these pigs to be efficient foragers. Long, strong legs and sound feet give Tamworth pigs the ability to walk for considerable distances. Ginger red coats make the pigs adaptable to a variety of cli-

mates and protect them from sunburn. . . . Sows are prolific, able to produce
and care for large litters. The piglets are vigorous and often have 100% surviv-
ability" ("Tamworth Pig").

Heritage breeds may take longer "to grow" than do breeds developed
for industrial farming, but they are hardier. We went to a second sixty-acre
property, where Hinkley kept the pigs and cattle who were "destined for the
freezer." Here the pigs and cattle shared the land and, while Hinkley fed them
in separate feeders, they also shared each other's grain. While we were feeding
the pigs and cattle some apples, Hinkley told us that she views the animals
as people and cares about their quality of life. She finds veal disturbing and
won't sell suckling pigs. She likes that her animals gain weight more slowly
than those bred for industrial production, as this allows them to develop
more muscle. She said, "Meat from animals who grow fast is soft." She hates
the word "slaughter" and won't sell her older animals for meat. "I'm not a financially smart farmer," she said. Although she is raising animals destined to
die, she doesn't agree with hunting: "We raise enough animals. We consume
and kill enough already. We've already skewed the natural balance; we don't
need to add to it." She also said she feels guilty (morally and existentially)
when she makes mistakes that negatively impact the lives of her animals.

As I've said, she views her approach to farming as a "natural confinement
system." She said she feels bad because it's an artificial life we have created for
these animal beings but does think "they have a good quality of life considering." She sees her animals as being a part of nature. She also said that "people
eating animals is natural." Given that, she does not see predation as an unnatural event: "Once every few years there will be an attack on the turkeys
and chickens by raccoons, weasels, or opossum. People who grew up farming
assume they need protection against predators." Hinkley sees it more as part
of nature. She takes steps to keep her animals safe and mourns any loss, but
ultimately, she says, "most of her animals will be food for someone." To keep
it as natural as possible, she thinks, it is important to bring together species
of animals who can function in symbiotic ways. For instance, she noted that
the pigs love to eat the turkey manure. The chickens and the turkeys keep the
bugs down on the farm and pick out parasites from pig, cattle, and horse manure. The chicken eggs make a nice snack for the pigs and the dogs. It is also
important to choose breeds that are hardy and can thrive on the pasture conditions she is providing. As mentioned, Tamworths fit the bill as they are good
foragers with a good disposition who procreate readily. Hinkley's husband,
John, had milked cows and chose the Jersey, which is typically known as a
dairy breed. The Jersey has a smaller frame and is lighter on the land. Hinkley
doesn't milk them now but uses them for companionship (they are friends)
and for beef. She has crossed them with red Angus to get finely grained beef

with marbling and a "sweet" flavor. She doesn't slaughter them until they are almost three, and then they are "still on the small side." The turkeys are primarily Narragansetts, along with one bourbon red from Kentucky and some blue slate and Spanish black. Hinkley doesn't clip their wings. She said, "It might not be torture, but still it's not necessary." Most of the turkeys were in a small pasture in the middle of her circle driveway. They had a variety of shelters, brush, and trees. Several had chosen to come over the fence, though, and wandered around the barnyard with the chickens, and a few had joined the horses in their paddock.

She kills her own chickens and turkeys on-site with the help of friends and uses a mobile slaughter truck for the cows and pigs. The animals "don't have to leave their familiar surroundings." She could make more money if she sent the birds to a USDA-approved slaughterhouse, but she doesn't want to enter that system. Transporting the birds adds a lot of stress to their lives. She noted that pigs aren't prey animals, so she doesn't think they are really afraid of transport; they are naturally curious animals. Hinkley said it takes just five minutes "when it's time to load up breeding pigs on their way to a new home." She sees her job as giving each animal the best life and death she can. She said that with her way of farming "you won't get a twenty pound turkey at Thanksgiving but you get better tasting meat, pest control, and a lot of enjoyment from having them around. The same goes for the pigs—they have a good life and bring a lot of joy." Friendship is as important on this farm as food.

This description of New Heritage should remind the reader of the pragmatist approach sketched earlier. Hinkley understands the evolutionary history of the various animals she raises and thinks about the ways humans and these other animals have influenced and transformed each other (naturalism). She is open to seeing the world from the perspectives of all the animal beings (pluralism) with whom she lives and works to develop mutually satisfactory relationships. She understands that these relationships are always in process, as is the nature of both the human and other animal beings (developmentalism). She sees the need to experiment (experimentalism) with new and different ways to sustain and to improve (ameliorate) the relationships, and she is willing to admit when she makes mistakes (fallibilism). She recognizes the other animals (domesticated and wild) as valued and valuing beings in their own right (as did Dewey) with whom she must live in dynamic interaction.

This interconnection ties her own flourishing to the flourishing of the land and of the other animals. While the various animals need appropriate food and climate, clean air and water, care, nurturance, and protection (from predators and disease), they also need interpersonal relations. While some industrial farming can supply some versions of the first seven things on this list, industrial farming of pigs fails on the last. To review from chapter 2, sociality is an evolutionary aspect of most life, and is a necessity for mammalian life. The physical, psychological, emotional, and social well-being of mammals requires attention to this aspect of life, since their very existence relies on extended care, nurturance, and learning from others (Johnson 56–57). The neuronal organization of mammals and social birds promotes bonding, causes distress upon separation, and prompts nurturing behaviors directed at others, even others beyond kin (59). Hinkley embodies Mark Johnson's understanding that "the care that is necessary for survival and flourishing is for the most part predicated on the possibility of empathy, which is our capacity to experience the situation of another person—an ability to feel with and for them" (60). We come to be, and to understand ourselves, through and with others in our environments. Interactive social creatures find value in things that help with cooperation, cohesion, and harmony.

Pigs provide an interesting case for the pragmatist approach given the intimate relations between people and pigs. Not only do pigs form social relationships with each other, but because through history they have lived in close and intimate proximity with humans, they also form such relationships with humans as well. These connections have often complicated the process of slaughtering pigs but have also highlighted the many interdependencies between the species. Pigs provide food, fiber, and friendship. In addition to the already-mentioned cycle of waste removal and fertilization, pig fat (lard) has been (and still is) an important food ingredient for humans. It could be procured in climates where olive trees could not grow and cows were not available for the production of butter (Essig 87). This fat was also used to lubricate gears and machines as the industrial era emerged (it was later replaced with petroleum products). Meat from pigs was easier to preserve in the time before refrigeration and so was an important source of preserved foods. As Essig notes, another term for pantry is "larder," and "scraping the bottom of the barrel" gets its meaning from coming to the end of one's food stores as the bottom of the pork barrel is reached (85, 178).

In the Americas, pigs became a tool of colonization as well. This pattern follows the story told in the earlier chapters about cattle and sheep. Imported pigs brought disease that decimated native peoples and impacted local wildlife; their foraging changed the ecological landscape. Pigs were turned loose along the European routes of trade and colonization so that they could breed and be available as a future food source. Ironically, as the pigs' presence helped destroy the roots, trees, shellfish, and deer cultivated by the Indians, Essig notes, some tribes turned to raising pigs as a replacement for these lost resources: "Indians boiled hog carcasses to render fat just as they had once done with bears, and they used lard in place of bear grease to oil their hair and skin. When deerskins for making moccasins were in short supply, pig hides sufficed" (140–41). Another set of complex relationships involving pigs concerns class and race in the United States. Free-roaming pigs who require little labor and few resources were ideal sources of meat for the poor. As middle- and upper-class (majority-white) populations turned to beef and chicken with the advent of refrigeration, not only did the meat one ate become a marker of class, but the practice of keeping pigs came under attack. While pigs had roamed towns and cities eating garbage and other waste products, on occasion they harmed some human and other animal beings. They also deposited their manure in city streets. Under the guise of sanitation and safety, laws emerged that restricted the ability of the poor to keep pigs and identified those who ate pork as lower-class (if not less human). Eating an animal who ate waste marked one as lesser in a number of ways. Ironically, those same animals are now kept in sanitized environments to be used in biomedical research and procedures—valued for their similarity to humans.

There is no one set of relationships between humans and pigs but rather a varied and complex set of evolving relationships. That means the "absolute prohibitions, commandments, and catechisms of customary morality" will not work (Fesmire 126). As discussed earlier in chapter 5, Steven Fesmire's book *Dewey* shows the need for a Deweyan ethic rooted in imagination, empathy, and thoughtful inquiry. He gives the example of the complexity of drinking a cup of coffee while watching the birds out of his window on a New England morning. This act involves complex relations among peoples, species, and the land: "Many migratory songbirds I enjoy in summer while drinking a morning cup of coffee are declining in numbers, in part because trees in their winter nesting grounds in Central America have been bulldozed to plant coffee plantations. Awareness of these relationships amplifies the meaning of my cup of coffee as new connections are identified and discriminated, and employed" (135). He notes that one can respond by drinking shade-grown coffee, donating to wildlife conservation groups, supporting habitat protection, or putting it out of one's mind. While none of these options is perfect, and all present a host of other problems, he says, realizing these complex relationships is an important step in promoting "inclusive interaction." He writes, "Ideally, this amplification of meaning operates as a means to intelligent and inclusive foresight of the consequences of alternative choices and policies" (135). Vicky Hinkley is someone who has come to recognize the complex relationships among humans and other animal beings. She eschews the "absolute prohibitions, commandments, and catechisms of customary morality," of other farmers, and of PETA, to instead use "intelligent and inclusive foresight" to think through these relationships for herself. This kind of approach helps to challenge and reshape individual and social habits. Fesmire says that for Dewey the main role of philosophy "is the interpretation, evaluation, criticism, and redirection of culture" (146). Such philosophy is at work at New Heritage Farms. But life at New Heritage (and Sugar Mountain) Farms is a far cry from what the majority of pigs face.

This chapter began with some description of the industrial system. As with the development of the farming of chickens (which will be discussed in the next chapter), the increasing confinement of pigs took place over time and for ostensibly good reasons. Pigs tended to live near the farmhouse—waiting for food scraps—and ranged widely (foraging in fields and forests). Diseases and parasites that affect the pigs themselves, and the humans who eat them, could be better controlled by getting pigs out of the dirt and mud. By 1913 farmers were experimenting with concrete floors and closed pens, and by the 1950s most pigs were inside on concrete. In *Pig Tales: An Omnivores Quest for Sustainable Meat*, Barry Estabrook writes, "Evolution has equipped sows with an overpowering urge to gather brush, grass, and leaves together to make nests for their young" but industrial pigs are on concrete without nesting materials. They become frustrated, bored, and lame. "Since their feet are designed for walking through the soft ground of forests and wetlands, it's little wonder that more than three-quarters of confined sows develop hoof injuries. Being unable to move freely causes the animals' muscles and bones to weaken, making sows lame and susceptible to sprains, twists, and breaks" (222). While pigs were long part of the corn belt system of fattening animals for slaughter, new feeds and drugs allowed the pigs to be raised entirely inside, and this added more control and resulted in faster growth. By 1934 a pig had about thirty-two square feet in which to live; this is now between six and eight square feet. As this confinement proceeded, though, increased fighting resulted in the practice of clipping their teeth and tails. Sows without room and material to make nests sometimes crushed or ate the piglets. They were deemed "bad mothers" and further confined in gestation and farrowing crates to address this "problematic" behavior. There is still a reported 25 percent mortality rate with the farrowing crates. Crates were further justified by the pigs being "aggressive" over feed (Norwood and Lusk 134–36). While these crates decreased the need for human labor, they increased lameness issues and the boredom and distress of the pigs. The confinement—though it brings on increased aggression and makes natural behavior hard to manage—is never seen as part of the problem. Such aggressive behavior in pigs often results in abusive handling practices by humans; pigs are hit, cut, dragged, and have their eyes gouged in efforts to get them to move (Genoways 124). This clearly causes physical and emotional distress.

Pigs are actually quite social and share much in common with humans (and dogs). In *The Pig Who Sang to the Moon*, Jeffrey Masson notes, "Like us, pigs dream and can see in color. Also like us, and like dogs and wolves, pigs are sociable. (On warm summer nights pigs snuggle up close to one another and for some unexplained reason like to sleep nose to nose.) The females form stable families led by a matriarch and her children and female relatives. Piglets are particularly fond of play" (19–20). This is not surprising given that wild pigs are social, coming together for warmth and protection. A study of standard commercial pigs living in a research park (not in confinement) found they spent six to eight hours foraging and rooting. They spent time eating, nuzzling, making nests, and marking trees. According to the study, "the pigs also formed complex social bonds: females from the same litter tended to stick together long after weaning, and piglets maintained bonds with their mother even after she'd given birth to her next litter" (Essig 238). Complex communal nests, as well as individual farrowing nests, are an important element of the pigs' social life. This sociality, complete with greetings and affection, can result in cliques that are hard for newcomers to enter, and this needs to be taken into account in any social housing system.

Several states and companies have now called for phasing out gestation and farrowing crates. However, if nothing more is done than removing the crates, this might not actually improve the welfare of the pigs, as the pigs would still be overcrowded and bored. As the public has begun to object to such conditions, pastured pigs have grown in popularity. On a small scale, pigs have become integrated into the farm ecosystem at Zestful Gardens, a CSA in Puyallup, Washington. Committed to the principles of biodynamic farming, Holly Foster and her mother, Valerie, have converted this farmland to organic production and run a successful CSA focused on produce and eggs. Chicken, turkey, lamb, and pork are also sometimes available. The animals are there primarily to provide the manure to help fertilize the fields that grow the wide variety of produce. Over the years I have seen the impact the chicken manure has had on the soil—shoveling some of it myself. Now there is less need for shoveling chicken manure as the chickens move around the fields themselves. So, instead of shoveling chicken manure, on my last visit my students and I were cleaning out the pig house and taking the straw and manure to the compost pile. In addition to providing fertilizer, the pigs have helped clear out the brush and berries from the orchard. One sow is there as a breeder; the babies are for meat. There was a litter there as we worked, and they loved playing in the fresh straw. The two older pigs, who were "awaiting slaughter," went outside while we worked and joined the one cow on the farm. The chickens were out in the field in the mobile shelter enclosed with a moveable fence. Predation is a risk for those birds as part of the farm is left in forest and is home to a number of species of local wildlife. Because of this, the chickens who needed a little extra care (one was blind, and one had a foot injury) were around the barn.

Holly mentioned that the sow with the litter had just recently returned to the farm. She had loaned the sow to a neighbor to have a litter for him. The sow had lost a lot of weight while off the farm, though, and Holly didn't think she'd be doing that again. This experience revealed how pigs are prone to being considered as purely utilitarian—they are tools and commodities. Holly's concern for the pig, though, wasn't just about wear and tear on an asset. As a mother of two herself, she showed real empathy for this sow having had litters so close together while not being properly fed. (There are obvious connections here to ecofeminist concerns, taken up in the next chapter.) Holly regularly mentions the time in her life when she was a vegetarian. But now she eats the meat from the animals she raises. She likes feeling part of a holistic system that puts nutrients and energy back into the land rather than simply extracting them. Cover crops can help maintain soil health, but animal manure makes an important contribution to her produce production. She buys organic grain for the animals and says that the idea that it is wasteful to feed grain to an animal in order to feed that animal to a human rests on a limited understanding of what that animal provides. When you include the value of the manure you get back, as well as the meat, she's not sure it's wasteful at all. She does acknowledge that the need to supply grain for these animals is something that keeps the farm from being more self-sufficient, though. This is one reason she will never raise meat animals on a large scale. They, and the meat they produce, "need to stay in balance with the land."

Zestful Gardens is an example of a farm that has grown slowly and by experimentation. Holly and Valerie do their research, get training, and always start a new venture on a small scale. I saw the plastic that was used on the land to suppress weeds disappear as the land regained its health and the cover crops and animals did their work. I saw the orchard emerge from the tangle of berries and brush as the sheep, goats, and pigs did their work. This is a farm always in some kind of transformation—physically on the land and in the thinking and approach of the farmers. Not all small-scale farms are this committed to the process of critical inquiry, though, and the inquiry is not always as successful.

"Soft Farm" (a pseudonym) was a farm in Sedro-Woolley, Washington. It has recently been sold to a hardwood company, and the family who ran the farm is done with the farming venture. When the farm was in business, its website described the farm as "an organic farmstead . . . offering grass-fed lamb, pastured pork, poultry-to-order and more. We are committed to practicing sustainable agriculture techniques and humane animal treatment. Our animals are heritage breeds and are out on our certified organic pasture every day." The family lived on the land and wanted a beautiful place to live. They left the creek on the land as wild as they could and had herons, wood ducks, and owls; they got rid of any lawn, using pigs to dig it up, and turned it into meadow. This family did not have previous farming experience, but they had become concerned about food production in the United States, especially animal agriculture, and wanted to join the growing movement to grow food locally and more sustainably. A few years after our visit, this farm had shifted focus. Their revised website described the farm as being committed to biomimicry and permaculture. They sold hay but were no longer producing eggs or meat. Their focus was on raising nursery plants and offering educational tours of the land and its wildlife. They still had some livestock to supply manure and graze the fields.

This experiment started because the daughter, who had been working in finance in Seattle, was increasingly unhappy with that work. When we visited in 2010 the family had been running the farm for about six years. They had ducks, turkeys, laying hens, goats, pigs, Jacob sheep, and one donkey, named Precious. The focus was on rare and threatened species and the priority was being compassionate to animals while being as organic and natural as possible. The pigs were a favorite—Tamworth pigs (originally bought from Hinkley at New Heritage), sought out by the family for their personality. The pigs were in a good-sized pasture with shelter, mud puddles, and grass, and they were moved around the field every ten days. They came right up to the fence to greet us and get scratches. They crowded around to each get their share of at-

PHOTO 11. Pigs at "Soft Farm." Photo by Danielle Palmer.

tention. The family likes the personality of these pigs and clearly spends time with them. But they tried not to get too attached; none of the pigs had names. The pigs were especially hard for this family to slaughter as "they are naturally smart and long lived." But they felt it balanced out if the pigs had a good life first. They said, "Those who are kept for breeding have a good life and those who go for meat do too." Interestingly, once they started running the farm they ate less meat. They said they had more respect for the work that goes into producing good meat, and more respect for the sacrifice of the animals involved: "We are more thoughtful and thankful when eating meat instead of taking it for granted."

To be profitable, they also raised poultry. Their heritage turkeys were so popular that they were usually sold out. At the time of our visit they had 210 laying hens out in big pastures with egg-mobiles. They also raised organic meat chickens and turkeys. The major issue was the cost of feed. They said, "We are three years into the business and still working out the costs and pricing. We are still in the experimental phase—trying out a few different things." They said the sheep were working out; they ate grass and hay raised on the farm. But the pigs and poultry required feed brought in from off the farm. Like Holly and Valerie, they tried to calculate how this balanced with the manure these animals provided but said it wasn't clear how it all worked out. Much like Hinkley, though, they reported that the pigs brought a certain joy (though mixed with some sadness) that made the pigs' lives worth more than the balance sheet alone indicated.

In addition to trying to get a handle on the costs, they were still learning how to care for the animals they were raising. One issue with people entering into farming without experience is the harm they can inadvertently do. As discussed above with Hinkley, mistakes will happen, and Hinkley agonizes over any errors on her part that result in harm to the animals in her care. In the case of "Soft Farm," they had incorrectly fed some of the turkeys chick starter feed. The insufficient protein in those early days had resulted in leg issues in the turkeys. We saw some who were unable to walk and were covered with sores from being attacked by other birds—something we witnessed. The daughter felt bad about this and wanted to slaughter the suffering turkeys immediately. Her parents, however, wanted them to "live out their lives." Since each turkey chick had cost eight dollars, and they had already invested a fair amount of feed in them, they wanted them to live long enough to profit from their slaughter. Here the balance sheet won out.

They had about sixty Standard Bronze turkeys. Bronze turkeys have long been the most popular commercial breed of turkey. They come from crossing the turkeys brought by colonists to North America with the wild turkeys found here. This resulted in large, tame birds. In the early 1900s these were crossed with larger-breasted birds and the Broad Breasted Bronze became the main commercial bird. As the Livestock Conservancy notes, "Further selection improved meat production, especially that of breast meat, growth rate, and other performance qualities. At the same time, changes in conformation (especially the shortening of the legs and the keel) nearly eliminated their ability to mate naturally. For this reason, most Broad Breasted Bronze turkeys have been artificially inseminated since the 1960s" ("Standard Bronze"). In the 1960s these were replaced by the Broad Breasted White turkey as commercial growers further focused on increased breast meat. Heritage breeders, however, have retained an interest in the Bronze turkeys. The Conservancy notes, "Naturally mating, long-lived, slow growing strains of Bronze turkeys, known as the Standard Bronze, have been left even further behind by the turkey industry. A few tenacious breeders maintained small flocks, participating in poultry shows, and raising a few for family and friends" ("Standard Bronze"). While I admire the efforts of many small farmers to raise and protect a variety of heritage breeds—be they turkeys, chickens, sheep, or pigs—sometimes good intentions are not enough. Many of the turkeys we saw that day were clearly suffering.

In addition to heeding the impetus to save heritage breeds, many of these "amateur" farmers are responding to the local food movement. Many people have decided it is important to eat more locally, and so they raise poultry in their backyard. With the farmers not having much knowledge, many of these chickens are fed improperly and fall to predation from neighborhood cats and dogs. On a larger scale, many have been inspired to start a farm—usually after reading the likes of Wendell Berry, Joel Salatin, Barbara Kingsolver, and Michael Pollan. Like Kingsolver, many don't really consult those who have been farming for generations as they think either that it can't be hard or that they can do it better. Still others read Berry and have no idea how much work farming really is. The current climate has everyone believing that as long as a farm is relatively small and local it is a better place from which to buy produce, eggs, and meat. To be sure, there are many fewer animals on these farms than in industrial farming. But the suffering is often as bad or worse as the farmers often don't understand the nature and needs of the animals they try to raise (the next chapter will discuss this more). The turkeys on "Soft Farm" provide a clear example of this. Nonetheless, the family was considering increasing their poultry production to one thousand animals a year as there was plenty of demand for "the product." There was also unmet demand for the pork. But the pigs raised on this farm also highlight my concerns. The boar died from parasites, which indicates a lack of knowledge and proper husbandry. The family acknowledged this, saying, "We want this to be a home and a business. We need to keep the scale manageable, but make a profit. Our desire for a 'simple life' pretty quickly got complicated. We are focused on humane farming, yet we've made mistakes that hurt the turkeys and the chickens."

But animal welfare wasn't their only, or even their primary, concern. They were inspired by David C. Korten's book *Agenda for a New Economy*, in which Korten presents an argument for abandoning what he considers the fake and unproductive economy of Wall Street for a more locally owned, community-oriented economic structure that seeks to have a positive impact on people and the environment. He writes, "Millions of people the world over are joining together to rebuild their local economies and communities. They are supporting locally owned human-scale businesses and family farms, developing local financial institutions, reclaiming farm and forest lands, changing land use policies to concentrate population in compact communities that reduce automobile dependence, retrofitting their buildings for energy conservation, and otherwise working toward local self reliance in food, energy, and other basic essentials." By taking control of their lives, and building resilient local economies that use local resources and employ local people to meet local needs under local control, they are declaring their independence from the colonial domination of Wall Street corporations (Korten, *New Economy*).

These are concerns we heard from many farmers in one way or another. While some, like Joe Markholt (chapter 3), voiced it in terms of consumers having choices, others, like Carrie Little (chapter 9) and Linda Neunzig (chapter 6), talked about the importance of local food and local control in order to sustain the land and provide food security. Sukovaty (chapter 4) and Foster (this chapter) talked about the importance of CSAs as a way to reconnect people, not only with their food but also with real, local farmers. For the family at "Soft Farm," helping the daughter get out of her career in finance to find more meaningful work that connected her with people and the land was very important. They had love, respect, and compassion for animals, but the animals were not the primary focus. Feeding people healthy food and developing an alternative to the more corporate and industrial economy seemed to be the primary focus. There is an irony here. Both "Soft Farm" and industrial agriculture are shaped and directed by "absolute prohibitions, commandments, and catechisms of customary morality." To be sure, they each have a different focus, but they both let some set of central commitments direct their actions with little attention to context or collateral damage. While industrial agriculture tends to focus on providing a ready supply of cheap and consistent meat products, the collateral damage to consumers, farmers, the environment, and the livestock animals themselves does not really get counted. In a similar move, the commitment of "Soft Farm" to "the local" also made them inattentive to context and collateral damage. The turkeys and pigs suffered, but since they were the most profitable meat animals in the "local economy," the family

PHOTO 12. Pig at "Soft Farm." Photo by Danielle Palmer.

planned to expand their production. As mentioned in the discussion of New Heritage Farms, while no particular option is perfect, and each option presents a host of other problems, realizing the complexity of relationships is an important step in promoting "inclusive interaction." Unlike Hinkley, however, this family did not fully use "intelligent and inclusive foresight of the consequences of alternative choices and policies" (Fesmire 135). They remained committed to the overarching goal of "local" at the expense of the pigs and turkeys.

This is an important caution for consumers as well. Commitment to any particular diet, held in an absolutist and universalizing fashion, overlooks changing contexts and competing needs. As Fesmire notes, "despite faddish proliferation of books and blogs proposing the correct, best, or 'natural' diet, Dewey's ethics provides no basis for assuming that such a thing can be determined in advance of the situations that require us to make dietary choices. There are multiple ways to pursue better lives in relation to food, and no diet exhaustively deals with all of the often incompatible exigencies inherent in agriculture and eating" (138). Holly Foster demonstrates this as she has altered her diet in ways consistent with the needs she sees on her land. This does not mean anything goes and no criticism of various farming and eating practices is possible. Fesmire continues, "Dietary choices are not arbitrary. We do not need an absolute dietary compass to perceive that many choices and policies do little to move us toward a more humane, just, healthy and sustainable food system. Nor do we need such a compass to infer and test ways forward—such as the hypotheses of perennial polyculture and veganism—to judge by their consequences the extent to which these hypotheses are well grounded or groundless" (138). What is needed is informed and intelligent deliberation about food that is sensitive to the actual but sometimes changing needs and desires of the land and animals involved.

CHAPTER NINE

Poultry Production

CHICKENS, "CHICKS,"
AND CAROL ADAMS

Pig production in the United States has copied many aspects of industrial chicken production. It is ironic that pigs and poultry, who historically both shared greater proximity to humans by virtue of living in the backyard, are now the most industrialized livestock animals. While some are disturbed by this development when it comes to pigs (given their intelligence), few share the same level of concern for poultry, as they are considered stupid, or "bird-brained." The long and complex relations between people and poultry (domesticated about eight thousand years ago), however, belie this description and call for changing the current lives of most chickens, turkeys, geese, and ducks.

As mentioned in chapter 3, chicken meat is now the most consumed meat in the United States. Direct egg consumption has declined from a little over one egg a day in 1945 to just over half an egg a day in 2013 (Ferdman). But this does not account for all the eggs in processed and baked foods. Egg demand supports 277 million laying hens with every 100 hens producing over 75 eggs a day ("Industry Overview"). In the past the same breeds of chickens were used to produce eggs as were used to produce meat. The move to specialize in either meat or egg production did increase the rate of production and lower the cost to the consumer, but it came at a cost to the chickens. Since the laying chickens have no real value as meat, the males are sorted and killed—often ground up while alive. The females are of value only as long as they are laying, so there is no regard for their long-term health. They are housed in conditions that allow manure to accumulate, and the resulting pollutants burn their skin and lungs. Even those who are labeled organic, cage-free, or free-range are usually housed in barns with ten thousand or more hens and may never step outside. The industry focused on producing hens that could "lay an egg a day." This requires the artificial manipulation of light, and so confinement is necessary. Forced molting can also prolong egg production, but this requires withholding food and water from the birds.

The life of broilers is also highly confined. Housed in barns with twenty-five thousand or more birds, even those who are labeled organic, cage-free, or free-range may never step outside. No longer worried about their egg-laying capacity, the meat industry focused on breeding chickens for specific purposes. For example, the Cobb Sasso 150 is for the free-range, organic producers; the Cobb Avian 48 is for live-bird markets; and the Cobb 700 produces a greater-than-average amount of breast meat. The Cobb 500, however, is one of the most popular varieties of meat chickens. It grows faster on less food. They grow so fast that they suffer from severe leg deformities and chronic pain. But their life is short—they reach the slaughter weight of five pounds at just six weeks of age (Herzog 167). Even at this young age, they suffer from blisters on their hocks and sores on their feet because they are too heavy to stand and spend much of their time lying in their own feces. The accumulated manure also pollutes the air with ammonia, and this burns their lungs and eyes. The process of catching the chickens for slaughter is very stressful for them, and many end up with broken bones as they are snatched by catchers (four or five in a hand at a time) and stuffed into small boxes. A mechanical "harvester" has been developed that lowers the injury rate and the stress for the birds, but it is not yet commonly used. Once they arrive at the processing plant, chickens are hung upside down on a conveyer line while still alive. They are sent through an electrified bath to stun them before their throat is slit. If they are not the standard size, then they are not properly stunned and the knife misses their throat. This means some birds are still alive at the third stage of the process when they are dunked in scalding water (Herzog 168–69).

The production of chicken meat and eggs was the first form of animal agriculture to become highly industrialized. In *Compassion by the Pound*, economists Norwood and Lusk provide an account of how egg production moved inside and got big. One hundred years ago chickens lived outside and foraged for bugs to supplement the grain they were fed. They were free to roam and could lay eggs in nests built in shelters. But these chickens fell prey to weather and to predators, so some farmers moved the hens inside to keep them safe. Since buildings are expensive, they needed to put a lot of birds in one building to keep it affordable. When put in cramped conditions, chickens fight. As Norwood and Lusk point out, "chickens can only remember the pecking order of a flock of up to 30 birds. In larger flocks, there are continual fights. Birds injure one another, and even cannibalism can occur. Fighting chickens are bad for business and bad for the animals" (47). To help stop the fighting, farmers put the chickens in cages in groups of about five. The cage system allows farmers to use a conveyer belt to catch and move the eggs so that the eggs aren't contaminated with feces. Housing chickens on slanted wire floors with no bedding did not impact egg production and made life easier for farmers. Consumers buy more of these eggs; they are clean and cheap. Farmers who didn't adopt this system couldn't and didn't compete (46–47).

Technology also contributed to the changes in the lives of hens. Before feeds could be supplemented with vitamins and minerals, it was essential that hens spend some time outside to eat bugs, dig in the dirt, and get some sunshine. As with pigs, changes in feed made it possible to keep the hens inside. When putting more hens in a cage led to fighting, beak-trimming was turned to as an answer (despite the numerous nerves in the beak). Male chicks were sorted out and killed. Since the 1940s, these "improvements" helped make the caged system the norm and the White Leghorn the best egg producer (114). Forced molting improved production even more, as hens increase their egg production after they molt (lose their old feathers and grow new ones). Withholding food and water was the standard way to bring on a molt, but this is no longer prevalent, as studies have found it is cheaper to kill and replace birds instead (117–19).

These changes moved production from 153 eggs per hen per year in the 1930s to 250 today (Animal Welfare Approved requires not more than 220 eggs per hen). The price of an egg dropped dramatically as a consequence. These cheap eggs come from barns housing one hundred thousand to one million hens in stacks of cages that are serviced by conveyor belts that bring in feed, remove manure, and carry out the eggs. Even in the barns where the manure is regularly removed, high levels of ammonia accumulate. While Norwood and Lusk state that this is not really a problem for the birds as they still "perform well" (116), the hens do develop eye and lung problems. Each bird has sixty-seven square inches, has had its beak trimmed, and cannot fully extend its wings. Unable to exercise, the hens have brittle bones that break easily; the fact that most of their calcium goes into shell production exacerbates the problems with their bones. They are kept in conditions that provide artificial light to help keep egg production high. Since most of their energy goes into egg production they don't gain weight. When their egg production rates begin to diminish around two years of age they are killed and their depleted carcasses are often used in pet food (116–17).

As consumers came to be more aware of how laying hens are kept they objected. Norwood and Lusk note that the farmer is blamed for the conditions in which the bird lives, but they lay the blame with the consumer: "Farmers with cage systems are vilified. However, consumers had previously communi-cated to farmers through their purchases that they preferred the advantages of the cage system." Norwood and Lusk think consumers must communicate their willingness to pay: "Farmers will produce chicken meat and eggs in any way that appears to meet the consumer's preferences" (47). Because many find the standard or conventional practices objectionable, other systems have been developed. Cage-free is just that—the hens are not in cages, so they can move around. There are perches, nests (usually made of rubber), and sawdust for dust bathing. Some barns have flooring that allows manure to fall below and be removed, while others add sawdust on top of the manure and clean the barn when the hens are replaced at the end of two years (119). These hens are crowded into barns in flocks of thirty thousand or more, much like the broiler chickens, so fighting can be a problem. Norwood and Lusk note that "feral hens tend to roost in flocks of six to thirty birds, suggesting a much smaller natural flock size than is present in cage-free systems. Sometimes the spats are minor and the submissive birds run or fly away, but other times the increased prevalence of fighting results in feather pecking, injuries, cannibal-ism, and higher mortality rates" (120). Beak-trimming would lower the mor-tality rates, but this goes against the welfare goals that usually accompany cage-free production. These hens do average two hundred square inches per bird as opposed to the sixty-seven square inches in the cages. Some cage-free systems add multiple tiers inside the barn to make it more like an aviary, and this allows the hens to use the vertical space to get away from each other (119). Another alternative is the enriched cage system. The goal of this method is to keep the cage in order to prevent the fighting found in large flocks but pro-vide some opportunity for the hens to engage in natural behaviors such as dust-bathing, perching, and laying eggs in a private nest. Fewer birds are kept in each cage, but competition among the birds results in manure in the bath-ing box and eggs laid outside the nest (Norwood and Lusk 123).

All these systems should be seen as important experiments in alternative methods of housing chickens, but they all assume the large scale of industrial egg production. Norwood and Lusk report that egg producers who use both caged and cage-free systems prefer the cages and think the hens are better off when protected in the cages. They say the cages also help keep sick birds from spreading illness throughout the flock and prevent the selling of eggs produced by sick chickens. There are also concerns (not established by any study) about increased salmonella—between 2 and 10 percent of the eggs in the cage-free system are laid on the ground (along with feces) rather than in a nest. A bigger concern from the perspective of the economists is that the cage-free birds are more expensive per bird. This is because the hens most commonly used in cage-free egg production "are less efficient" (121–22). That means they don't lay as many eggs. This, combined with a higher mortality rate, makes the cage-free system more expensive, without the welfare of the hens being much improved. Some argue that from a welfare perspective, cage-free production may be worse than caged systems due to the fighting it allows for.

However, the problems reported with the cage-free production are related to the size of the flock. Most consumers do not picture thirty thousand hens crowded into a barn when they are buying cage-free eggs. The pictures on the cartons certainly do not depict this kind of life either. Norwood and Lusk rightly point to the power of the consumer to communicate their preferences by what they buy, but when a system regularly masks and hides what is actually going on, it is easy for the consumer to be misinformed and misled. Norwood and Lusk suggest that cage-free systems are less preferable than cage systems, but they never question the way the birds are kept or the number of birds kept together. Industrialized egg production is simply taken as a given.

Free-range systems of egg production are another example of misleading the consumer. In the United States, all the term "free-range" means is that the hens are not in cages and that they have access to the outdoors (this is true of organic eggs as well). There are no size requirements for the outdoor area and no requirements for shelter, grass, or protection from predators. There is little difference among free-range, organic (the feed is organic), and cage-free egg production in the United States (123). Smaller farms who sell directly to consumers through CSAs, farmers' markets, and off the farm do often have systems that are more truly free-range. Several farms already discussed, and some discussed later in this chapter, fit this description. The flocks on these farms host a few hundred hens or fewer, and they are housed in ways that provide access to sun and shelter, allow them to move around the pasture to forage in fresh grass, and contain the birds only enough to provide protection from predators. Some are locked in at night for further protection. These hens lead lives that allow them to participate in a number of natural behaviors. With proper management of predators and parasites, these small-scale farms provide the best alternative in terms of chicken welfare. The eggs produced in such a system, however, are more expensive. Norwood and Lusk suggest six dollars per dozen to break even (124–25). Since people want inexpensive eggs, conventional and large-scale caged, cage-free, and free-range eggs still dominate the market. Caged egg production makes up over 90 percent of what consumers buy ("General US Stats").

"Egg Farm" (pseudonym) is a fourth-generation family farm in Washington. When we took a tour of the farm, our guide said, "We are in egg production, not chicken production. We raise eggs." Their fifteen-hundred-acre farm was originally all forested. As the family cleared it, they tried to grow things, but the soil was not productive, so they switched to livestock. Originally they raised chickens, pigs, and dairy cows, but they got rid of the dairy because of runoff into lakes and streams (there was no further mention of the pigs). They went from 500 birds in 1920 to 5,000 at the start of World War II to 40,000 by the 1960s. Today they process 65,000 dozen-count cartons per day—that is, 780,000 eggs per day. They said it takes a quarter-cup of grain per chicken per day to produce one egg, and they use sixty-four tons of grain a day. The feeding, collecting, cleaning, and boxing of the eggs is all automated. As the eggs are sorted, some are deemed not good enough to sell in the shell, so there is one building devoted to making liquid eggs (150,000 pounds per week) and another to hard-boiled egg production (thousands a day). The rest are sorted for different carton sizes with different labels. Not only are there the conventional and the organic packaging, but "Egg Farm" also sell their eggs under a variety of names. That is, they grow for other companies who sell the eggs under their own label. This makes it difficult for consumers to know the source of the eggs they buy. Costco is their main customer. They also sell to Walmart, Albertsons, and a local natural food store.

On one of our tours of the farm we were with a group of elementary school children. One of the kids asked when they would "see the baby chicks." The guide answered, "We make eggs, not baby chicks." One child asked, "Why do you take the eggs from the chickens?" The answer was, "Because we need them to make everything we eat—ice cream, cookies, deviled eggs." When it was asked whether the chickens have toys, the answer was simply "no." When it was asked why there were no boy chickens, our guide simply moved on with the tour. This farm buys chicks at one day old from a hatchery. They are all hens, as the hatchery sorts out and disposes of males. At sixteen weeks of age they move from the brooder barn to the production barn. It takes two more weeks before the hens begin to "produce" eggs. They said they get one and a half years of production (eighty-two to eighty-five weeks) out of each hen. There are thirteen conventional barns—twelve of these house thirty-five to sixty thousand hens, and one has one hundred thousand hens. This makes them a mid-range producer. The smaller barns hold slanted layers that are only cleaned at the end of a cycle. That means they are cleaned after a year and a half. The big barn has belts between the layers of cages that move the manure out. All the barns have automated systems to remove the eggs. When asked about the cages in the conventional barns, the tour guide said that since those birds were more aggressive, "we are doing them a favor by putting them in cages so they don't tear each other apart." There are eight organic barns with twenty to thirty thousand hens each. These barns include access to an outdoor yard. Interestingly, when asked about the difference between the organic and conventional production, our guide said the only difference was the feed and did not mention the outdoor access even though we were looking at chickens who were out in the "yard." The chickens in the organic barns can dust bathe outside and have sand inside. As one drives to the farm, signs on the side of the road proudly proclaim that their chickens roam free. In reality, only a reported 70 percent of their chickens have access to the outside.

We were told that in the conventional barns they use low light all day and have it set to mimic the longest day of year. It is dark at night. This maximizes egg output. When they tried the same lighting in the organic cage-free barns, the hens didn't roost—so they started to emulate a more natural sunrise-to-sunset cycle, and the hens started to roost. The lighting, along with a system of nest boxes, helps the hens to "lay an egg a day." When asked whether the lighting and constant egg production negatively affect the health of the hens, the tour guide stated, "No! They love it!" But this kind of laying, though not actually one egg a day, does affect the strength of their bones, their weight, and their general health. Depleted by egg-laying, the chickens can't fight parasites or disease.

The farm is certified Humane only for their organic cage-free eggs. These eggs are Food Alliance–certified, and this farm got a three-egg rating on the Conucopia Institute's website: "Brands with a three-egg rating are very good choices. Eggs from brands in this category either come from family-scale farms that provide outdoor runs for their chickens, or from larger-scale farms where meaningful outdoor space is either currently granted or under construction. All producers in this category appear committed to meeting organic standards for minimum outdoor space for laying hens" ("Organic Egg Scorecard"). This standard doesn't guarantee much for the consumer, and nothing here informs the consumer that the same farm produces conventional eggs as well. This makes it difficult to make meaningful purchasing choices. The same confusion exists when buying chicken meat.

As some farmers specialized in egg production during the middle of the last century, others turned to specialize in the production of chicken meat. While meat chickens have often been housed inside in close quarters to be "finished" on grain for their last few weeks, the life of today's "broilers" is nothing but this kind of confinement. This resulted in a doubling of the yield of meat that required no additional feed. As Norwood and Lusk explain, "despite the fact that today's birds are almost three pounds larger than their 1925 counterparts they reach this larger weight in 64 fewer days" (128). Because of their breeding these chickens have more white meat, have a consistent taste and texture, and are standardized in size to allow for mechanized slaughter. Economies of scale were also achieved as the mid-range broiler producer increased in size from 300,000 birds in 1987 to 681,000 in 2007 (O'Donoghue et al. 47). All of this combines to make chicken meat much less expensive than it used to be (Norwood and Lusk 128).

But this cheap meat does cost the chickens. These birds grow so fast and get so big that they develop severe leg problems. Studies have shown these birds to actively seek food laced with pain relievers. While they do suffer, the life of the broiler chicken is short—less than two months. They are housed in large flocks (no cages), getting increasingly crowded as they grow, so they are *very* crowded right before the time of slaughter. There is generally no beak-trimming, since the birds are too young to be aggressive. The breeding of these birds also tends to produce less aggressive birds, but many have heart problems. The housing conditions result in polluted air and lung problems for the birds. They are kept in artificial light to keep them eating, and this frustrates their roosting and sleeping patterns. There is nothing to do but eat, so life isn't very interesting, but again it is a short life (Norwood and Lusk 128–31). Because of the short lifespan, Norwood and Lusk conclude that "broiler farms do not cause large-scale suffering" (131).

There are more concerns about those birds used in the breeding of these meat-producing "broilers." Because they live longer and can become aggressive, they often have their beaks trimmed. They also have their combs trimmed—without anesthetic (129). The breeders live one or two years and—because they would otherwise gain the same weight and develop the same leg problems as those chickens used directly in meat production—they receive less than a third of the food they would like to consume. While many people find this very problematic from a welfare perspective, others, like Norwood and Lusk, say that the birds adjust to the reduced feed and that it is better than the alternative of heavy, lethargic birds who can't walk and who develop immune disorders. They even say, "The same problems seen in human obesity is [*sic*] observed in these birds, and the feed restrictions prohibit this from occurring" (128). They don't seem to consider that the desire for such meat-producing machines might be problematic in the first place. Instead they say that given the total numbers of chickens produced for meat (who they don't think really suffer) compared to the number used for breeding (who do suffer), there really isn't a welfare issue in the industry. For the 8,867 million broilers produced in 2007, they say *only* 61.56 million birds were involved in breeding: "Of all the birds involved in broiler production, 0.69 percent are raised in breeding facilities. While the welfare of breeder broilers is likely low due to the feed restrictions . . . their low welfare should be discounted appropriately" (129). This seems more than a little disingenuous.

Free-range and organic labels are as misleading for broilers as for eggs. Smaller farms that provide real time on the pasture produce "pastured poultry," which may or may not be organic depending on the feed and pasture available. The cost of these to the consumer is often four times the cost of "conventional" broilers, and there can be limited availability by season, as weather impacts this kind of production. Predation problems can also raise the costs of production for these farmers. Industrial producers and economists seem to define predation as wasted death that is to be avoided at close to any cost. In our interviews with farmers, though, most found some amount a predation a natural event. They see the benefits of the time outdoors substantially outweighing this risk. One such farmer is Carrie Little.

Situated in the Orting Valley of western Washington, Little Eorthe Farm sits on land that was once a dairy and is now part of the PCC Farmland Trust (which works to protect farmland). The mission statement on the farm's website reads, "Our mission is, quite literally, to help save the earth. Locally grown organic produce is a responsible way of producing food. Our produce is raised without pesticides, herbicides, hormones or antibiotics, and less fuel is used to get the food to our customers. We tread lightly on the earth so you can do the same." Little Eorthe is an organic farm with a wide variety of produce, broiler chickens, and eggs. Soon they hope to use the milk from their sheep to make cheese.

This is the second farm Little has transitioned from conventional use to organic certification with WSDA. She says it costs $750 for organic certification and is a great deal of work. She thinks the inspections are of questionable value, as the inspectors don't know enough to ask the right questions or look for the right things. She also complained that the conventional farms don't have to go through such a process or pay money. "The system seems designed to discourage the small and the organic agriculture system," she said. This was a common complaint among the farmers we talked with, and many of them had opted out of certification. Little thinks being clearly labeled organic is important, though. She is also committed to social equality and developing a sense of community. Little got into farming when she started Guadalupe Gardens in Tacoma. This community garden served the poor and homeless. She wanted to extend the supply of organic produce available to the poor, so she started Mother Earth Farm, also in the Orting Valley. She worked there for many years, getting the land certified organic and supplying food for the Pierce County Emergency Food Network. She also built relationships with the women who came to work on the farm as part of a work program with the Purdy Correctional Facility. It is important to Little to build relationships with people in need as she works to save the land, heritage varieties of seeds, and heritage breeds of livestock. Being organic is just one piece of her larger mission, but the organic certification does help with the marketing of their products at local farmer's markets. They also run a small CSA.

There are milking sheep and Dexter cattle at Little Eorthe, but it is the poultry that keep them in business. The "happy hens at Little Eorthe" have been featured on regional television shows. Little works to preserve various breeds of chickens and turkeys in addition to using heritage seeds for the produce. We visited just after the broiler chickens had been harvested. Little harvests about one thousand chickens for meat. This is an important and relatively reliable source of income. They arrive as chicks and are housed in a completely enclosed structure that is moved between flocks. They are fed organic grain and some of the produce from the farm. She slaughters them when they are between ten and twelve weeks old, using the mobile slaughter truck rather than shipping the animals. While Little names some of the animals on the farm, she stopped naming the animals she is going to slaughter. She said, "It's too hard to name them and then kill them." Eggs are easier. The farm has a reliable market with PCC Natural Markets (the Puget Sound Consumer's Cooperative) for the eggs. The PCC standard for eggs says, "PCC sells only eggs from hens that are raised cage-free on local, family-owned farms. The use of antibiotics is prohibited, and the hens are fed only 100 percent vegetarian feed. Certified-organic eggs come from hens raised on certified-organic feed" ("Our Product Standards"). The cage-free eggs average four dollars a dozen, while the organic eggs average five dollars a dozen. The eggs from Little Eorthe Farm come from pastured organic chickens and so average seven dollars a dozen.

When we visited in 2014, Little housed her laying chickens with her turkeys, but she was getting ready to separate the two species as they do have different needs and sometimes have conflicts over the use of space. The birds were housed in a large wire enclosure that gets moved around the pasture, and there are various forms of shelter and spaces to lay eggs spread throughout the enclosure. She has a smaller area sectioned off for the younger birds. This allows them to sort out their own social hierarchy and to become acquainted with the older birds in a nonthreatening way. This reduces aggression. She gets an average of 150 eggs per chicken per year—far below the industry standard and well below the AWA standard. She said she gets about 250 eggs a day from her 700 chickens. The laying hens are generally used for three years (not eighteen to twenty-four months) and then Little keeps an eye on their productivity. She knows her chickens individually and can tell whose egg is whose based on their different sizes and shapes. The hens aren't killed as soon as their productivity declines but instead are kept in the flock to help keep order and socialize the young hens. Since there is a market for duck eggs, Little hopes to add ducks to the farm soon.

Little did try raising pigs a few years ago. They had thirty-one piglets! She said people kept asking for organic pork, but in the end there were not enough customers willing to pay. The last year they raised pigs they had just three sows and still didn't break even. She likes being pig-free given the work and the added potential of becoming attached to the individuals. In a 2016 email she told me they no longer raise broiler chickens, but she didn't say why. Perhaps some of these same concerns were a factor.

Little is interested in saving the land. She tries to minimize tractor work by rotating the grazing animals to keep the grass cut and the soil fertilized. She said by "following the animals, I follow the manure." This also helps Little reduce her use of petroleum products and, with the use of solar panels, the farm is mainly off the grid. She also talked about the different ecosystems on the farm. The land supports humans, but it is also there to support the surrounding wildlife. Little and her husband invested in an eight-foot elk fence, but they also planted trees to improve the elks' habitat. She said, "We're a part of their system too and must collaborate with them." In an interview Little said, "We planted 1,100 trees in the riparian zone and the animals now have a corridor in the trees. It's all about balance: they were here way before we were; we are borrowing the space. We try to live with those we share it with. We love our swallows, bats, owls, and other predator birds. So, we have to be mindful of how we care for our chickens. I wouldn't trade any of the relationships we have or give up the space we share with them" (Cramer). Their five dogs bark to scare away predators—hawks and coyotes.

It is not uncommon for people interested in organic food and improved animal welfare to also be committed to broader issues of social justice. What is unusual is to see these commitments as seamlessly interwoven as they are in the life and work of Carrie Little. From starting the community garden at Guadalupe House to running her own organic CSA, she cares about human beings, other animal beings, and the land as parts of an integrated whole. Rather than pit groups against each other she works to show and foster the interconnections among them. In this she shares many of the commitments found in a variety of strains of ecofeminist philosophy. I've mentioned the work of Carol Adams in previous chapters and will expand on that discussion here. In her work Adams argues that the "logic of domination" operates in racism, classism, sexism, colonialism, speciesism, and more—and that you can't fight one kind of oppression without fighting all the others. She holds that if you try to isolate one form of oppression from the others—as happens when people say they are feminists but don't care about speciesism—you fail to get at the root causes of the oppression. And she argues that if you exploit one group in order to draw attention to another—as happens with PETA ads that use sexual images of women to make a case for not harming animals— then you perpetuate the logic of domination. Worse yet, she says, if you try to pit one group against another—as happens when women or minorities defend their status as human persons by denigrating other animal beings—you yourself participate in the logic of domination. Instead ecofeminism calls for understanding the intersecting nature of oppression in order to address the logic of domination, and theorists such as Breeze Harper ask people to examine the connections rather than further the divides. As mentioned in chapter 5, she says, "Many of us black female vegans realize that much of how non-human animals are treated in the USA, frighteningly parallels the way black females were treated during chattel slavery" ("Revisiting Racialized Consciousness").

Building on the work of ecofeminist philosophers such as Karen Warren, Adams understands the logic of domination as a framework for most traditions of Western thinking and action. First, in Western thought, humans tend to divide the world into binaries such as male/female, culture/nature, human/animal, reason/emotion, light/dark, and rich/poor. She argues that such exclusionary extremes oversimplify lived experience. Further, she says, people tend to take such dichotomies and add value judgments to them, finding one side of the dualism to be superior to the other. She explains that such value dualisms are then used in the logic of domination to justify the more valued group oppressing the less valued group. On this logic, great power and privilege comes with being a rational, culture-producing, heterosexual, human male who is light-skinned and has money—and being on the other side of any of these value dualisms makes one vulnerable. But, she argues, dismantling one of the value hierarchies does little to undo the larger logic of domination. For instance, Mary Wollstonecraft (1759–97) is famous for defending the rights of women (trying to dismantle the male/female value dualism) by arguing that women are fully human. To do this, though, she reinforced the human/animal dualism (and the rich/poor dualism, as her arguments focus on women of means). Some suffrage activists in the United States argued for granting white women the vote by claiming they were more rational and civilized than black men. Adams rejects such approaches and argues that all forms of oppression are interconnected and must be addressed as a whole. In holding various forms of oppression to be interconnected, Adams agrees with many feminists. But when ecofeminists add the oppression of nature, the oppression of other animal beings, or the oppression of both, many feminists fail to follow. Most continue to insist on some kind of human exceptionalism even as they argue to greatly expand who gets to count as "human." Adams thinks feminists should not make this mistake since women and nature, and women and animals, have long been connected by language, in metaphors, and in how they are treated.

Carolyn Merchant made these connections evident in books such as *The Death of Nature: Women, Ecology, and the Scientific Revolution*. She noted that human women are often portrayed as more connected to nature and animals (as witches are, for example) and that women of color are regularly animal-ized (often depicted wearing animal print or crawling). Adams further noted that the females of other animal species are exploited in many of the same ways human women are. In the United States, for example, there is a particu-lar focus on human women's breasts. The actual function of female breasts is to feed human offspring, but this function is not honored by U.S. society, even as one can find exposed female breasts almost everywhere. The "breasts" of other mammals are turned from the original purpose of nursing their young to feeding humans. Interestingly in ads, dairy cows are often portrayed stand-ing up on their back legs with an hourglass figure—sexualized as human fe-males. Sometimes the commercials play up cows' maternal nature, but in these ads the focus of their maternal attention is often human children rather than their own, paralleling the way black women in the United States were expected to raise the children of white families they worked for at the expense of their own family (and as Asian and South American women do now when employed as nannies). When the ads do portray them caring for their own offspring, these are misleading, as dairy cows don't nurse their own young. Adams describes milk as feminized protein since it comes only from female mammals. She also holds eggs to be feminized protein, as they too are some-thing females produce as part of their own reproductive cycle that is then coopted and used by humans. And the breeding females in all the livestock species are valued primarily for their reproductive capacity, which they no longer control.

Adams draws on the work of feminist philosopher Sarah Lucia Hoagland to explain the human hijacking of other animals' bodily integrity. Hoagland illustrates the linguistic evolution of the logic of oppression with the example "Mary was beaten by John," in which John is an agent of violence, to "Mary was beaten" to "battered woman." In "battered woman" the violence has become something about the nature of the woman and the identity and action of the batterer disappears. Adams argues that, similarly, we move from "An animal was killed by a human so that its meat can be consumed," where the human is an agent of death, to "animals are killed for meat" to "meat animal." Now the nature of the animal is narrowed to this one purpose that already internalizes and necessitates the animal's death. This can be seen in the term "broiler." (Similarly, use value is prioritized with terms like "layer" and "breeder.") So it is seen as in the nature of the animal to die (to be killed) so that humans can consume the meat. They are ontologized as edible (Adams, *Neither Man nor Beast* 101–02). Adams calls on feminists to become vegans as a way of protest and as a way to work to undo the logic of domination and oppression she sees operating in the treatment of women and other animal beings. While some-one like Carrie Little shares many of these commitments with Adams, she does not make the move to end consumption of other animal beings. Instead (like Plumwood) she enters more deeply into relationships with them and works to make those relationships respectful and fulfilling. This is probably most fully done with her laying hens, who are valued for things beyond their egg-laying capacity—for instance their intelligence and social relationships. Since many of the small farmers emerging in the United States are women, and many share an array of these feminist concerns, I worry that Adams's call for veganism creates an unnecessary and unproductive wedge among mostly like-minded people. This is I why I think a pragmatist perspective supports something closer to Plumwood's position (discussed in chapter 7) than to Adams's. That does not mean changes in consumption are not called for, nor that meaningful and critical conversations aren't needed.

Even with Little's approach to egg production she is still tied to the practices of commercial egg production, as most male chicks are disposed of, and only female chicks are sold to supply farms like Little Eorthe. Similarly, the lives and deaths of the broiler chickens really differ only in scale and diet from those of birds in industrial production. While Little's customers think and care about these issues, most people hardly give a thought to the lives behind the eggs they buy, or the chicken they eat. They don't want to pay for better lives for the chickens. At the same time, though, many of these same people object to the idea of cockfighting. The sport is described as cruel and barbaric. But, as Herzog points out, the life of the average rooster involved in cockfighting entails much less suffering than the life of the average "broiler" chicken or "layer" hen. To be clear, this is not meant as an endorsement of cockfighting. Rather, Herzog is pointing out one of the many ways human thinking about animals, and behavior related to the use and consumption of animals, is inconsistent and problematic.

To make the comparison with the lives of the "broilers" and the "layers," Herzog describes the life of the fighting roosters: "Your average east Tennessee gamecock chick will be pampered during its two-year life. For the first six months, it will run free. Then it will have a lawn to loll about and a private bedroom to sleep in. The rooster will get plenty of exercise, eat better than some people, and have a chance to chase the hens around. The downside is that one Saturday night, he will feel the sharp pain of the Mexican short knife slicing his pectoral muscles, or perhaps get a long heel gaff in the throat; he will die in the dirt after a fight that lasts anywhere from a few seconds to over an hour" (169). Herzog asserts that the life of the fighting rooster is better from a welfare perspective than the life of the Cobb 500 chicken. There is nothing illegal about the treatment of chickens in the egg- and meat-producing industries, while cockfighting is illegal in all fifty states and the HSUS is working to make it a felony crime. There is, in fact, limited moral concern for the billions of chickens living on industrial farms compared to the energy and outrage focused on cockfighting.

Here power, race, gender, and money are at play. While the chicken egg and meat industry's National Chicken Council lobbies and gains protections for practices such as debeaking, cockfighting becomes an easy target for moral outrage. It is easier to effect change when one's opponents are largely from working-class, poor, and minority populations than when they are large corporations. Herzog says the "war on cockfighting is about cruelty, but the subtext is social class. The eighteenth-century movement against blood sports was directed toward activities that appealed to the proletariat, such as bull-baiting and cockfighting, rather than the cruel leisure pursuits of the landed gentry such as fox-hunting" (171). Today animal welfare and animal rights groups also target fox-hunting, but the point stands. Dogfighting is more of a focus than dog-racing, and cockfighting is banned while horrific conditions are legally protected in the chicken meat and egg industries.

Cockfighting has a long and varied history. The jungle fowl who were first domesticated were known for their fighting, so it is thought that humans probably fought their roosters as soon as they started keeping them enclosed. Today, in the Philippines, it is estimated that two million people make their living from cockfighting—from the fighting rings themselves to hotels to shipping companies (Lawler 96). The practice probably spread from Asia to the Middle East and then to Greece and Rome. Popular in Spain, France, and Britain, it came to the Americas with the colonists. As with any animal being used in a sport, various techniques are used to improve fighting cocks' performance. Roosters are fed specialized diets, given vitamin supplements, and enhanced with hormones and drugs. To get the roosters in fighting shape many exercise protocols have been developed (Herzog 156).

In an effort to improve fighting ability humans bred for specific traits, and specific strains of chickens were developed: Arkansas travelers, Allen roundheads, blue-faced hatches, Kelsos, Madigan grays, Clarets, and butchers. Herzog says they are breeding for three traits: cutting ability, power, and gameness (155). It is the trait of gameness, or grit, that gets the most attention and praise from those involved in the sport. Words from this sport carry over into everyday life when people speak of "the battle royale, show pluck, remain cocky or cocksure, and sometimes have a set to" (Lawler 108). This desire to beat the opponent is taken as a sign of courage and is seen as a virtue for humans (especially men) to emulate. Many theorists have come to see cockfighting as a way for men to vicariously establish their own dominance. A rooster who refuses to fight, or who turns tail and runs, humiliates his owner. Character is important for both the bird and the handler, and cockfighting is a sport with many rules. As with other sports, the higher-end events are more regulated, with paid referees and enforced rest periods. Less formal events are where more abuse of birds and violence between people are likely to occur. As a blood sport, cockfighting involves less blood than is usually imagined, but the injuries are painful and death is inevitable (Herzog 156–60).

In *Pets, People, and Pragmatism* I argued that using horses, dogs, and cats in shows and other sporting events is not inherently wrong or cruel. Rather, I argue, it is the abuses that occur in these settings that are problematic; often the activity itself is something the various animals want to do. It may even improve their mental, physical, and social well-being to participate in things like racing, herding, and agility. I argued that this did not apply to dogfighting, though, as dogs rarely fight to kill. They have to be taught and baited into killing. The defenders of cockfighting, however, say it is in the nature of the birds to fight to the death. Herzog reports,

> Johnny laid it out for me: "What we do is an act of nature in a controlled situa-
> tion. That rooster's going to fight if we are there or not. We make things as even
> as possible for them to perform an act of nature. We don't make these roosters
> fight. That's what they were put here for. It is their purpose." (This, by the way
> is also the reason most cockfighters I met did not approve of dog fighting. As
> Eddy's wife told me, "Cockfighting is not like dogfighting. They have to make
> the dogs mean. But these chickens are born to fight. They do it regardless of
> whether you are there or not.") (162–63)

It is the case that these birds have some natural tendencies to fight, and these have been augmented by centuries of breeding. However, in natural conditions there is more room to maneuver and the choice to flee. There are also plenty of counterexamples in barnyards around the world where more than one rooster resides. I visited the Agua Branca Park in Sao Paulo, Brazil, where peacocks, ducks, and lots of chickens roam freely under the government's protection. There are hens with their chicks, solo roosters, and bands of roosters roaming everywhere. I visited repeatedly and saw no fighting. While I'm sure there are some altercations over territory and mates, this park shows that fighting is not a necessary part of chickens' version of "a good life."

However, as Herzog points out, the harm from fighting may well be less than the harm from farming and hunting birds. I've already described the life of suffering faced by many birds on various farms. Herzog points out that wild birds suffer as well: "As many as 30% of the 120 million wild birds shot by hunters each year in the United States will fall from the sky wounded and fully conscious. While the lucky ones will be found and killed quickly, millions of others will die lingering deaths" (162). (This might give one pause when considering Leopold's defense of hunting and Myers's relationship with Ducks Unlimited—see chapter 3.) Some involved in cockfighting point to the use of various cutting blades as a way to reduce the pain that would otherwise occur from repeated blows. Some, however, deny the suffering of birds altogether, reasoning that chickens' brains are not very developed, so they are not smart and they do not feel pain. Current research on the intelligence of birds generally, and of chickens in particular, tells a different story. Birds have long been ignored in studies of animal intelligence and communication. The derogatory idea of the "bird brain" is still strong. But according to Andrew Lawler in his book *Why Did the Chicken Cross the World?* this term did not come into use until 1936. At least since Aesop, chickens have had a reputation as intelligent. But as birds left the barnyard, people had less experience with them, and their reputation went downhill. During World War II, terms like "chicken out" and "chickenshit" came into use (239–40). As scientist began to study corvids and parrots, though, our thinking about birds, including chickens, began to change.

According to Lawler, research shows that chickens can add, subtract, "understand geometry, recognize faces, retain memories, and make logical deductions." They can also "practice self-control, alter their message to fit the receiver, and . . . can feel empathy. Some of these cognitive abilities equal or surpass those of assorted primates and it is possible that the chicken possesses a primitive self-consciousness." They have a well-developed memory and have been found to have thirty calls that correlate with specific behaviors, indicating they have a complex system of communication (240–42). None of this complexity is taken into account, much less honored, in the living conditions of industrially farmed birds. While there is more respect shown for birds on some of the farms we visited, the question remains whether farm life can provide for the needs of mammals and social birds whose neuronal organization promotes bonding, distress when separated, and nurturing behaviors directed at others, even others beyond kin (Johnson 59). Such interactive and empathetic social creatures find value in things that help with cooperation, cohesion, and harmony.

Growing Things Farm, run by Michaele Blakely, does try to honor the complex capacities of chickens and turkeys. This farm in Carnation, Washington, sits on thirty acres, seven of which are in production while the rest are pasture. When she started twenty years ago, Blakely operated one of the first CSAs in Washington. It was originally an organic CSA, but as the government regulations got more and more complicated she switched to Certified Naturally Grown (CNG), a set of standards for livestock focused on feed and medication. For CNG, all the feed must be free of synthetic fertilizers, pesticides, herbicides, fungicides, and GMO seeds. In addition, the requirements go beyond the USDA Organic requirement that the animals have *access* to the outdoors: CNG requires that the animals do actually go outside for most of the time. The animals must have access to fresh air, sunlight, outdoor areas with shade, and shelter that is appropriate "to the species, its stage of life, the climate, and the environment" ("Livestock Standards"). The standards note regional differences based on weather and seasons as well.

The pigs at Growing Things clear the pasture, and all the animals supply manure for fertilizer. Blakely said the weeds (properly managed) are good as they attract beneficial microorganisms and bugs. She said that the fungus in the soil is good plant food, and that if you bombard the soil with chemical fertilizers, herbicides, and pesticides you lose these "partners." Farming requires the manipulation of nature, she said, but it's best to "try to stay within what nature would like. It's all part of a whole system." She pointed to conventional fields next door and commented that nothing was growing there. No plants volunteered in the barren soil, but morning glory had recently arrived on her property with the last flooding event.

Blakely's farm floods regularly. That's part of what makes the soil good for growing things. When it floods, she and the birds stay up on the hill. At the time of our visit in 2010 she had three hundred laying chickens in the greenhouse, who were starting to lay eggs, and six hundred more out on the pasture. She uses a commercial breed, but since they are outdoors in natural light, they don't lay as many eggs as those in industrial production. She leaves the grass tall in the poultry pastures. The blooms attract insects for the birds to eat, and the height of the grass gives them a place to hide. She also puts strings across the top to keep eagles out. Blakely noted that her meat turkeys and chickens are standard breeds—"nothing special, but they do just fine in pasture." The chickens are the standard Cornish cross, and the turkeys are Standard Bronze and Broad Breasted White turkeys (discussed in the previous chapter). She said, "The turkeys are smart and have a lot of personality which makes it hard to slaughter them." (The pigs, who are friendly and love belly rubs, are also hard for her to slaughter.) Nonetheless, these animals are all presold and slaughtered on-site. Because it is already hard to slaughter them, Blakely does not name them. Only the dogs and cats have names, but she considers them associates, not pets—they all have jobs and all work together. Her family did farm, so she had some experience, but she wanted to do things differently. She said her family thinks she's crazy: "They're proud of me, but still see what I do as strange." Part of what is strange to many is the acknowledgment that the animals she raises are intelligent, have personalities, and experience complex social bonds. That she describes the pigs this way may not surprise many people, but her inclusion of turkeys in such a description might.

While most of the domesticated animals discussed in this book were brought to the Americas from Europe, turkeys were first domesticated in

PHOTO 13. Turkey at Growing Things Farm.
Photo by Michaele Blakely.

the Americas, exported to Europe, and then reintroduced by European colonists. Turkey remains have been found at sites of human habitation as early
as 3700 BCE. In New Mexico they have been found in the Mogollon culture
area dating to 300 BCE and near Anasazi settlements dated around 400 CE. By
400–700 CE the concentration of young birds indicates that they were domesticated. Turkeys are thought to have been first domesticated in the region of
present-day Mexico between 200 BCE and 700 CE. The Aztecs used them for
food and as religious offerings. Coronado saw wild and domesticated turkeys
in the areas of present-day Kansas, Oklahoma, Texas, and New Mexico in the
mid-1500s. They were valued for their feathers among a number of American
Indian tribes, and some of these tribes ate their meat and eggs. Other tribes
eschewed the bird and thought of turkeys as cowardly (A. Smith 8–11). The exported turkeys started to take hold in Europe in the 1500s. They were popular
animals to take on ships, and so their presence spread quickly. Since turkeys
were known to eat crops, early turkey keepers kept them in pens so narrow the
turkeys couldn't move. Some were force-fed—fattened in these pens and then
driven to market. They had one wing cut to prevent their escape on the trip to
market, and drives of three hundred to one thousand birds are described (24,

33, 84). Having become a common part of the European diet, turkeys returned to the Americas with migrating European settlers.

Colonists in the present-day United States hunted and ate wild turkey and also raised domesticated birds, using the feathers for dusters, quills, whips, pillows, mattresses, hats, and corsets. The wild and domesticated birds regularly interbred and created new breeds, such as the Blue Virginian (54–55). John James Audubon wrote about wild turkeys in the early 1800s, noting that males foraged in groups of ten to one hundred birds and remained separate from the females and their young. Great flocks gathered in October and moved from Ohio to Mississippi. Mating began in mid-February, and by mid-April the hens separated to lay their eggs. Some females were observed to lay eggs in a shared nest and then cooperate to sit on the eggs, help the chicks out of the eggs, and feed the young. The turkeys roosted in trees to stay safe from predators such as foxes, cougars, owls, eagles, skunks, wolves, and opossums. But this made them easy targets for human hunters, who shot them out of the trees while they slept (45–47). As settlement destroyed their habitat and hunters took their toll, the wild turkeys began to disappear. Their disappearance from Connecticut in 1813 was followed by their disappearing from Vermont, New York, Massachusetts, Kansas, South Dakota, Ohio, Nebraska, Wisconsin, Illinois, Indiana, and finally Iowa in 1907 (50–51). By 1930 it is thought that were only about a hundred thousand wild turkeys in the United States. Around that time there was an effort to reintroduce wild turkeys. As the Depression resulted in abandoned farmland, habitat became available for reintroduction, and by the late 1950s turkeys had rebounded to five hundred thousand and by 1973 to 1.5 million. In 1973 the National Wild Turkey Federation was formed to focus on these efforts. In 2005 there were an estimated seven million wild turkeys, and they are now in all states except Alaska. Turkey-hunting has again become a popular pastime—and (as with wild pigs) a profitable one for those who outfit the hunters, netting almost two billion dollars in 2003 (A. Smith 131–32). One reason the reintroduction of wild turkeys was possible was because people could turn to the domesticated bird for food.

While people ate turkey eggs, turkeys were not used for egg production, as they lay only about one hundred eggs a year and the chicks take longer to mature and begin laying (60). They were, and are, raised primarily as a meat bird. The tradition of having a turkey for Christmas carried over from England, and later the tradition of turkey at Thanksgiving was established in the United States. Thanksgiving became an official holiday in 1863, and by the late 1880s the holiday was already being called Turkey Day (76–78). With money to be made, by the mid-1850s farmers began paying more attention to the breeding of these birds, and poultry books, exhibitions, and competitions emerged. The American Poultry Association was founded in 1873. Shows such as the North-

west Turkey Show in Oregon and the All-American Turkey Show in South Dakota encouraged innovations in breeding, and the International Turkey Association was formed in 1927 to do the same. The main breeds were the Bronze,
Narragansett, Black, Buff, Slate, and White. These birds had different characteristics, and all were popular for different reasons in different regions. But
by the 1920s two breeds dominated commercial production: the large bronze
Holland and the medium white Holland (86, 89). Then Jesse Throssel of British Columbia began focusing on increased meat yield, improved hatchability,
and early maturity. He got birds to forty pounds in nine months. Their large
breasts and short legs made it hard for them to mate, so the USDA turned to
artificial insemination:

> First, semen is collected by picking up a tom by its legs and one wing and lock-
> ing it to a bench with rubber clamps, rear facing upward. The copulatory organs
> are stimulated by stroking the tail feathers and back; the vent is squeezed; and
> semen is collected with an aspirator.... A syringe is filled, taken to the hen-
> house, and inserted in the artificial insemination machine. A worker grabs a
> hen's legs, crosses them, and holds the hen with one hand. With the other hand
> the worker wipes the hen's backside and pushes up her tail. Pressure is applied
> to her abdomen, which causes the cloaca to evert and the oviduct to protrude.
> A tube is inserted into the vent, and the semen is injected. (97)

The eggs produced from this unpleasant experience are put in an incubator
that hatches ten thousand chicks at a time. This was a bird for industrial operations, not backyard breeders. The broad breasted bronze dominated the
market by the 1950s. Scientists at Cornell University crossed these birds with
the Holland white, and the resulting broad breasted white became the industry standard by the 1960s. The birds were bred not for flavor but instead for
docility, early maturity, and maximum growth (90–91). They were inexpensive,
and turkey meat became increasingly popular.

As it became possible to freeze and ship meat, the big producers could hold
their stock for times when they could demand higher prices. Bigger operations
could negotiate for lower feed prices and start hatcheries of their own. Small
farmers began to disappear in the 1920s as new feeds added vitamin D to the
mix and made it possible to raise the birds inside without access to sunlight.
By the 1940s many of the birds were raised in cages, and their bodies became
more disproportionate, as described above (95–96). They are routinely de-
beaked, desnooded, and detoed and have their spurs trimmed between three
and five days of age. They stay in a brooder for four weeks—"warm, safe, and
free from predators" (98)—then go to a barn with 7,000–10,000 other chicks
to live in twenty-four-hour light in order to reach their slaughter weight by
twelve to fourteen weeks of age. In 1929, the United States produced 18 million

turkeys, but by the 1940s, 32 million birds were being produced. By the 1960s that number was 107 million, and today U.S. production hovers around 250 million birds. While the natural seasonal production of the birds fit well with the increased demand in the fall for Thanksgiving and Christmas dinners, year-round turkey production required creating year-round demand for the meat. This was done with processed lunch meats, sausages, burgers, meatballs, and frozen dinners (99–102).

As commercial production became industrialized it moved from New England to the Midwest and the South. In 1890 the largest producing states were in the Midwest and the South, but by the 1920s production had moved further west, to California and the Northwest. With the increasing use of vertical integration, a few companies came to dominate the industry—Butterball Turkey Company, Carolina Turkeys, Cargill Turkey Products, and Jennie-O Turkey Store (104–05). This concentration of birds in life and death resulted in inexpensive, but not always safe, meat. Since 2001, the CDC estimates, at least 13 percent of turkeys are contaminated with salmonella. Listeria contamination has resulted in several recalls, and turkeys are blamed for causing dysentery due to shigellosis bacteria (108–09). In addition to health concerns, many have become concerned for the birds themselves. United Poultry Concerns seeks to promote respectful use of birds in labs and on farms (127). Their website provides information on the various domestic fowl—their histories, their intelligence, their complex lives, and their current suffering. They point out that these various birds are intelligent and sensitive and make great companions: "Turkeys have a zest for living and enjoying the day. Treated with respect, they become very friendly. . . . Up close one sees their large, dark almond-shaped eyes and sensitive fine-boned faces. In nature, turkeys spend up to 5 months close to their mothers. Turkeys raised for food never know the comfort of the mother bird's wings or the joy of exploring the woods and fields with her" ("Turkeys").

The state of Minnesota is the largest producer of commercially raised turkeys with an estimated forty-six million. In 2015 an outbreak of bird flu on several Minnesota turkey farms spread to South Dakota, Arkansas, Missouri, and several western states (Hughlett and Walsh). With more than nine million birds dying in Minnesota alone, consumers were warned that their Thanksgiving turkey would cost more. The blame for such outbreaks is usually placed on free-living migratory birds, though in this case (and in others) none of the wild birds tested positive for the flu strain. This is another example of the tension between how humans value and deal with farmed animals and how they value and deal with "wild" animal beings. The free-living birds are seen as threat from which the farmed birds need protection. This is one of the justifications given for confining commercial poultry. However, despite confinement and elaborate biosecurity measures, birds raised in large confined flocks continue to get sick. Confinement and overcrowding suppress turkeys' immune systems and so create the very problem confinement is supposed to solve.

Clearly several of the farms we visited are doing things differently than are the big commercial producers. Smaller flock sizes, time outdoors, and semi-stable social relations all contribute to more respectful relationships that recognize individual personalities and desires. Several of the farmers also focus on heritage breeds. Smaller and more local is not the answer to everything, though. As discussed in chapter 8, with all the interest in eating locally, many people with no farming experience have ventured into animal agriculture. Sometimes they lack knowledge about the varied nutritional and housing needs of the species and breeds they are raising. As important, they often lack the knowledge and skills for handling the various kinds of livestock. In her book *Livestock/Deadstock*, Rhoda M. Wilkie examines the changing demographic of those working in the livestock industry in the United Kingdom. She saw many small-scale hobby farms run by people who had no farming background. She saw that while these farmers meant well, they did not always have the requisite knowledge and skills to provide good care for the animals. The Farm Animal Welfare Council presents their take on the "three essentials of stockmanship": *Knowledge of animal husbandry*. Sound knowledge of the biology and husbandry of farm animals, including how their needs may be best provided for in all circumstances. *Skills in animal husbandry*. Demonstrable skills in observation, handling, care and treatment of animals, and problem detection and resolution. *Personal qualities*. Affinity and empathy with animals, dedication and patience" (39). While one can study and learn information about nutrition and disease, it is often harder to acquire the skills of "reading stock." Because of their inexperience, some farmers make the mistake of overly anthropomorphizing the animals in their care. This same "mistake," however, may be what helps them excel at empathy, dedication, and patience.

Such farmers are generally less likely to think of these animal beings as primarily being commodities. Wilkie refers to livestock as "sentient commodities" to draw attention to their paradoxical status (along the lines of Plumwood's combining of use and respect). Wilkie writes, "Livestock animals are atypical market commodities that have an ambiguous product status. Producers may, to all intents and purposes, routinely regard them as articles of trade, but they also, to varying degrees, have to feed them, clean them out, attend to their health and welfare, and learn how best to handle them." Because of the intimacy involved in good care, though, the animals become more than things. She writes, "Those who come face-to-face with these animals are acutely aware of the biotic and temperamental attributes and sometimes 'get to know' the animals as more than just things" (123). Wilkie observes that in addition to reminding us that these animals are commodities (the origin of "stock" that now normally takes a paper form), the term *livestock* also reminds us that these are live animals. Where Wilkie is primarily interested in how people handle their role in perpetuating this paradox, I am interested in what it means for the animal beings themselves.

Wilkie suggests that people who have more long-term relationships with their stock because they deal primarily with breeding stock or dairy stock are more likely to form bonds than those who "finish" stock. She says, "Finishers have been likened to businessmen, rather than farmers, because . . . that part of the process requires much less investment than the breeding end" (137). It is important to note that her critique is offered of "finishers" who are finishing animals out in the field. In the United States the problem is exacerbated, as most animals are "finished" in highly confined conditions on a CAFO. Fifty percent of the meat animals today come from CAFOs, which have become the main method of production in the United States (4). The move to more mechanized and larger-scale production is generally accompanied by an attitude that turns the animal into a machine, a commodity, or both, depriving animals of their status as sentient beings. Wilkie is hopeful that Europe's recent declaration that farm animals *are* sentient beings will help stop them from being seen merely as "agricultural goods" (177). She thinks viewing farm animals as sentient beings goes hand in hand with the attitude of many of the farmers in her study who have particular relationships with particular animals and often want nothing to do with the killing end of the business. This ability of farmers to connect with their animals, combined with consumer concerns, may help animal agriculture make a shift. She argues that seeing animal agriculture as synonymous with factory farming, though, is not helpful, and her book attempts to show the diversity of views among those involved in animal agriculture in the United Kingdom.

I agree that when factory farming is presented as the only way of raising animals for meat, milk, or eggs, there is little to defend. This encourages animal rights groups to call for the abolition of all farming of animals. This in turn sets up a hostile relationship between the various animal groups and a whole range of people involved in raising farmed animals. This shuts down discourse and often increases ignorance on all sides. Caricatures of animal advocates as seeing all animals as human children abound; farm workers are all painted as abusive and uncaring. Most people, however, are found somewhere in the middle. It is in this messy middle that I am trying to work, as I suggest that it is not ethically necessary (nor even desirable) to end all farming of animals. Nor, however, can we continue with most of the practices

PHOTO 14. Ducks at "Soft Farm." Photo by Danielle Palmer.

found in large-scale industrial agriculture. This requires changes from everyone, though. Consumer desire helps shape the fate of these animal beings. To end this chapter I turn to two bird species whose lives are being changed due in large part to consumer demand: ducks and geese.

Although (according to USDA estimates) people in the United States consume only about one-third of a pound of duck each year and their consumption of goose is even less, there is a growing market for both duck meat and duck eggs. The United States doesn't make the list of the leading duck- and goose-producing countries, but in 2007 there were more than thirty million ducks raised in the United States, and more than twenty-five million of these were processed in federally inspected facilities. In the same year an estimated 339,000 geese were raised ("Ducks and Geese"). And they are raised for more than just meat and eggs, as duck and geese feathers are used in down bedding and clothing. The main use for ducks and geese is liver pâté. The production practices of this industry are controversial, though, and many states seek to end its production while giving no thought to how other (more numerous) birds are raised. Many chefs sing the praises of duck and goose eggs for baking, and duck meat is seen as a "wild" meat and touted as healthier for humans, dogs, and cats. However, the reality is that while there are some small farms that produce duck meat and eggs locally, most meat and eggs come from commercial farms that resemble commercial chicken and turkey farms. For meat ducks, operations range from 6,000 to 100,000 birds (B. Stein). While the stocking density is lower for ducks than it is for chickens, most everything about this industry is modeled on the commercial chicken industry. Ducks are raised in semi- and total-confinement systems with wire mesh flooring. These buildings require extensive ventilation. One management guide says, "When properly designed and managed, modern duck housing provides ducks a high degree of protection from the detrimental effects of extremes in weather and entry of duck diseases." As with chickens and turkeys, the high level of confinement is justified by the perceived danger of introducing diseases from wild birds. However, the main "advantage" of such confinement seems to be that it allows for continuous production of meat and eggs. As an article on duck housing and management notes, "In addition to allowing year-round production and marketing at an earlier age," the benefits of confinement include "improved feed conversion and more predictable, and usually better weight gain." Semi-confinement duck housing is similar to the above in many respects with the exception that ducks over two to three weeks of age are allowed outdoors during the day (Dean and Sandhu).

This is a far cry from the image of ducks on a pond, or ducks flying, that many people have in their minds, if they aren't picturing Donald Duck. It is thought that Donald Duck is modeled on the Pekin duck—which is the primary breed for the meat industry, though some hybrids are emerging. While these ducks would have a natural lifespan of about ten years, most are slaughtered much earlier. Even those kept for eggs rarely live past three or four years because they are slaughtered after their productivity drops. Many of these ducks have lost their nest-building instinct and broodiness in the process of domestication, so chicks are hatched in an incubator or sometimes under a broody chicken. Ducks and geese have been domesticated for about four thousand years and have developed into a number of different breeds with distinct characteristics and personalities. Because they have been "under-utilized" in agricultural production, though, most breeds of duck still share many behaviors in common with their wild cousins. Most of these behaviors are frustrated by how the birds are kept on farms. They like to swim, fly, forage on land and in water, preen, and sleep. They are also very social, with complex communication systems (Kalita).

The most confined and unnatural confinement and feeding is found in the production of foie gras. This high-end "gourmet" food is made from the fatty liver of geese and ducks who are force-fed in order to enlarge their livers. The force-feeding of these birds makes foie gras the moral equivalent of veal for many people and has prompted campaigns seeking to end its production and ban its sale. While I agree that this is a morally problematic production system, with an extra degree of suffering for the animals involved, I disagree that it should be singled out. The problem with the veal and foie gras campaigns is that they get people to focus on a single "product" and become outraged about the treatment of those particular animals. But they generally don't place this in the larger context of industrial agriculture as a whole. It is not veal per se that is the issue but rather the way veal is raised within this larger system. There is pastured veal, as we saw on Neunzig's farm. While it is not as "white" as stall-raised veal, many people find it quite good. It still requires the death of the calf at a young age, but those calves have good physical and social lives up until that point and may be spared the stress of weaning. The same can be done with foie gras from migratory geese. Geese add fat in preparation for migrating and can be harvested more humanely and sustainably as long as consumers contain their demand and pay a higher price for what they do consume.

Consumers need to adjust their expectations for both what they eat and the amount they eat in order to make the lives of the various livestock animals good lives. Consumers also need to work to stay informed about what is involved in the lives and deaths of these animals. The lives of the many different animals commonly considered livestock in the United States are intertwined in many complex ways. Ducks and geese provide just one more example. On a small scale, some ducks and geese are raised (for at least part of their life) by ponds where tilapia are raised. The duck manure provides food for the fish. While more commonly manure from poultry kills fish when it leaks from the lagoons on industrial farms, this alternative model shows another way the lives of birds and fish can work together. But when it comes to fish farms, the intersection is more likely the feeding of industrial poultry by-products to farmed salmon, while fish meal is fed to poultry in an industrial system that fails to respect any of the beings involved—human, fish, or poultry. And this brings me back to where I started—on a boat headed toward a vortex, on my way to a salmon farm.

In the last few hundred years, humans have approached food in much the same way as those who blew up the rock that was in the way of the ships approached the problem posed by the rock. The way they solved the problem of the rock created the problem of the vortex. The way the problems of predation, disease, and parasites were solved improved the lives of livestock animals until the feed and drugs allowed for the ability to completely confine the animals and raise them in large numbers. At that point, the very practices that had originally been meant to improve the animals' lives were turned around to create an almost total disregard for the animals themselves and a focus on profit and cheap food. Humans removed the vulnerabilities of the livestock that limited the numbers the humans could raise, but that move created a whole host of new problems—the vortex of industrial agriculture. Up until this point I have tried to use various philosophical perspectives to examine the current conditions for animals in industrial agriculture and to propose and examine alternatives. I have argued that important but often missing perspectives—pragmatism and ecofeminism—provide insights that help explicate the root of the problems with the current approach to animal agriculture and provide ways of thinking about alternatives that don't fall prey to absolutist thinking. The works of John Dewey and Val Plumwood are particularly important for developing a pragmatist ecofeminism that can help create room for dialogue, understanding, and amelioration between humans and livestock. I will now conclude by returning to the difficult problems of objectification and death (of human and other animal beings) and point to some possible ways forward that might help humans and livestock avoid the vortex of exploitative and disrespectful relationships and find a way forward to a future based on mutual enrichment, cooperation, and friendship.

CHAPTER TEN

Better Options Moving Forward

EXAMINING SLAUGHTER AND
LIMITING CONSUMPTION

The killing of animals has long been a part of human existence, and that is unlikely to change. For many, the most troubling part of raising animals for food is that they must die. Even those animals involved in dairy and egg production are eventually killed (not to mention the "surplus" animals produced by those industries, who are killed at a very young age). While death is a loss of a kind, it is an inevitable one. If done well, the killing of livestock animals can involve little pain and suffering. To make this possible, though, on-site slaughter involving fewer animals would need to be the norm, and social groups would need to be slaughtered at the same time to minimize social stress. Currently, however, the animal slaughter and processing industry in the United States suffers from many of the same problems of centralization and scale that plague industrialized farming. If consumer demand went down and consumers paid more for what they ate and used, the quality of the animals' life and death could change dramatically, improving the lives of the humans who farm and kill the animals as well.

The slaughter and processing industry occupies a place in "animal production" where the treatment of the animal beings has clear parallels to the treatment of human beings. In this setting both the human and livestock animals are treated as pieces of a machine and there is little to no regard for their physical, social, and emotional well-being. In his book *Every Twelve Seconds*, Timothy Pachirat shows how the lives and deaths of the cattle in an Omaha slaughterhouse mirror the lives of the human employees who do the work of turning cattle into beef for a consuming public that is kept in the dark and at a distance. Working in the chutes to send the cattle to the "knocker," in the cooler hanging livers, and in a quality control position for the slaughterhouse, Pachirat describes how the business of killing is kept out of the minds even of the employees working there, not to mention the distanced consumer. Most people working in the slaughterhouse do not think of themselves as involved in the killing of cattle even though they work on the "kill floor." The "knocker" is seen as the one who kills. When Pachirat expresses interest in learning to be a knocker he is discouraged:

> "Man, that will mess you up. Knockers have to see a psychologist or psychiatrist or whatever they're called every three months."
> "Really? Why?"
> "Because, man, that's killing," he says, "that shit will fuck you up for real."
> (160)

The other employees put the moral weight of slaughter in the hands of the knocker because he (it was always men) puts the gun to the head of a live creature and pulls the trigger. That this only renders the cattle unconscious and it is the sticker who deals the deathblow does not matter to them, since the cattle are no longer (or hopefully no longer) conscious when the sticker severs the carotid arteries and jugular veins (56). While hanging livers reveals the immense scale of the operation it is still "psychologically and morally seg-regated." Pachirat notes, "I prefer to isolate and concentrate the work of kill-ing in the person of the knocker, to participate in an implicit moral exchange in which the knocker alone performs the work of killing, while the work I do is morally unrelated to that killing. It is a fiction, but a convincing one" (159–60). The segmentation of the work into the dirty side (when the cattle have hides) and the clean side (after the hides have been removed) is just one of many ways that "the killing is neutralized" (84). No worker on the kill floor takes in the whole process. When Pachirat moves to quality control he is involved in the whole process but finds that the focus of that work is on audits. He said this focus transforms "the killing of live creatures into a technical process with precise measurements of when the procedure counts as humane and when it does not" (229). While he knows and sees the whole process it "fails to produce an attendant experiential understanding of the overall work of kill-ing, demonstrating that surveillance remains compatible with compartmen-talization and fragmentation. . . . The QC looks at workers but sees failure to sanitize knives. The QC looks and listens to cattle, but sees statistics on slips, falls, and vocalizations—quantifiable data points within a technical proce-dure designed to facilitate rather than confront the work of killing" (232). The reality of killing (and suffering) is masked.

In one of the most graphic instances of reality hiding behind an abstraction Pachirat discusses his reluctance to use electric prods on the cattle in the chute. He could move them with plastic paddles, but not at the speed the managers desired. He writes, "Once the abstract goal of keeping the line tight takes precedence over the individuality of the animals, it really does make sense to apply the electric shock regularly. Rather than electrocuting an individual animal, the prod keeps a steady stream of raw material entering the plant, satisfies co-workers and supervisor, and saves me from having to expend the energy it takes to move the animals with plastic paddles" (149). The same mentality applies to the workers in the plant. From the point of view of management, workers have no individuality and are seen as either productive or problematic labor. Spreadsheets "calculate total labor costs, pounds of meat produced per man hour, and the labor cost to kill, eviscerate, and split each cow. These spreadsheets, in turn, are summarized by week in yearly aggregates, an exacting metric, in dollars and cents, of whether the kill floor managers are maximizing the amount of meat produced for each hour of labor" (211).

The turnover in the industry is over 100 percent each year, and most working in it are immigrant men and former convicts (86). To obtain a job the men must come each morning to see whether there is an opening. All labor is "at will," and so workers can quit or be fired without notice. This means that to be hired and stay employed, the workers must please and obey. Pachirat says that "application" passes into "supplication" (94). This situation has changed little since the 1906 publication of Upton Sinclair's *The Jungle*. Describing the management's view of the men who were repeatedly disappointed when they assembled at the stockyard gates looking for work, Sinclair wrote, "While there are so many who are anxious to work as you wish, there is no occasion for incommoding yourself with those who must work otherwise" (22). This still holds true today, as do the basic jobs on the line and the pressure for speed.

Once hired, workers are pressured to do whatever it takes to keep the line moving. The segmenting of the tasks not only hides the truth but means that no one actually feels responsible for the quality of the product. They know that reporting a problem will get them in trouble, so they hope someone else will see and address things like fecal contamination. There is no attempt to enforce the Humane Methods of Slaughter Act (1958) that requires that animals be insensitive to pain before being killed. In Pachirat's experience this was as true for the supervisory and quality control positions as it was for those working on the line. The only thing they all had in common was a mandate to keep the inspectors from issuing reports. Speaking of a particular inspector, the other quality control person said, "This guy is not on our side, and it's not our job to help him" (183). While many workers said they took pride in the work of producing clean and healthy meat, they also said, "We have to try to pass the product no matter what, and to beat the inspectors to the punch whenever there is a problem" (194).

What makes the work so hard, and health and safety impossible, is the speed of the line. This is something known to the workers, supervisors, management, and inspectors. But it does not change, except to go faster. In his book *The Chain: Farm, Factory, and the Fate of Our Food*, Ted Genoways says this speed had consequences "up and down the supply chain—from the confinement facilities where high-density hog farming increasingly threatens environmental quality and animal welfare to the packing houses where workers face some of the most dangerous working conditions in the country and hostility from the communities where they live to the butcher counter at the supermarket, where the safety and wholesomeness of the food supply have been jeopardized." He says his book "is a portrait of American industry pushed to its breaking point by the drive for increased output, but also a cracked mirror in which to see our own complicity every time we choose low-cost and convenience over quality. It is, in short, an attempt to calculate the true price of cheap meat" (xiii–xiv).

While Pachirat and Genoways are writing in 2011 and 2014, respectively, what they document is nothing new. From Sinclair's work in 1906 to Gail Eisnitz's 1997 book *Slaughterhouse*, greed is blamed for the speed of the line, endangering both human and other animals. Eisnitz's investigation began when she received a report of a plant "skinning cattle alive." If the "knocker" doesn't get the shot right, the cattle can regain consciousness while shackled and hanging in the air. Their panic causes them to start kicking and thrashing, which makes it both difficult and dangerous for the "sticker" to deliver the deadly cut. This means the cattle can proceed to the "skinner" still alive and conscious. Sometimes the skinner can cut the spinal cord to cause paralysis and make the work safer, but the animal remains alive and conscious. These animals can break free and fall from the line, creating yet another hazard for humans and an excruciating experience for the cattle (28–29).

Complaints by employees are rare, due to their vulnerability and to retaliation against whistleblowers. Eisnitz did interview the "knocker" at the plant in question, who said "'They [USDA inspectors] used to watch the animals stand up after I knocked them. They'd complain but they never did anything about it,' he said. 'Never. The USDA vet . . . would stand there to see how many live ones were going in. . . . She'd yell at me but she'd never stop the line. They don't slow that line down for nothing or nobody'" (44). Problems that result from the speed of the line exist in all segments of the slaughter industry. Poultry and pigs are no exception.

Rather than being stunned mechanically with a gun, the pigs Eisnitz saw were stunned by electrodes applied to the head. Too much current results in "bloodsplash" from burst capillaries and lowers the value of the meat. She writes, "Plant managers didn't want to slow down the line, ease up on the prodding, or train the stunners to do their jobs correctly. They preferred to simply lower the current to the stunning equipment. The weaker jolt prevented bloodsplash but often stunned the hogs only momentarily, if at all" (66). Eisnitz tells the story of a "sticker" named Vladak who was repeatedly injured trying to "stick live hogs." In addition to the danger to the employees, Vladak noted, this also meant that once stuck the pig's muscles contracted around the cut and they didn't bleed out before they got to the scalding tank, where 140-degree water removed the hair from their skin (71). While Pachirat's account of the beef plant focused on the psychic toll experienced by the "knocker," in this case the person stunning the pigs doesn't look them in the face. If they are not properly stunned, though, the sticker does. Vladak says, "There was one night I'll never forget as long as I live. . . . A little female hog was coming through the chutes. She got away and the supervisor said 'Stick that bitch!' I grabbed her and flipped her over. She looked up at me. It was like she was saying, 'Yeah, I know it's your job, do it.' That was the first time I ever looked into a live hog's eyes. And I stuck her" (74). He goes on to say that the job took a toll on his family as he was unhappy and abusive. He said that the job made him emotionally dead and sadistic. Other stickers support this view, saying that the emotional toll is worse than the physical danger: "If you work in the stick pit for any period of time, you develop an attitude that lets you kill things but doesn't let you care. Pigs down on the kill floor have come up and nuzzled me like a puppy. Two minutes later I had to kill them—beat them to death with a pipe. I can't care" (87). Again, Sinclair noted the same issue over one hundred years ago when he wrote that "men who have to crack the heads of animals all day seem to get into the habit, and to practice on their friends, and even on their families. . . . This makes it a cause for congratulations that by modern methods a very few men can do the painfully necessary work of head-cracking for the whole of the cultured world" (21). Once he quit "sticking" Vladak got back together with his wife and said he'd never do that kind of work again.

He also realized he was of no value to the company. His complaints went unaddressed; his job was threatened. When a live hog kicked his arm and caused the knife in his hand to slash his own face, some at the company told him he was lucky. Vladak said, "That was the last straw. I decided my life was a little more important than somebody's damn hogs" (74). He also noted that from the company's point of view "nobody's irreplaceable. The minute I left they just hired somebody else. And the minute he gets hurt bad, they'll put somebody else down there. And the chain will just keep going" (76). As another sticker put it, "why protect workers when you can replace them?"

(86). What Vladak misses is that the logic that discounts the lives of the hogs would also imply that human individuals don't matter either. Sinclair presented this connection in *The Jungle*. After describing the horrible conditions he witnessed during a tour of the slaughter plant, the main character, Jurgis, says "I'm glad I'm not a hog!" The irony, of course, is that his life unfolds in much the same way as do those of the hogs. It is quite easy in the following passage to substitute "immigrant" for "hog" and the United States for the plant:

> It was all so very businesslike that one watched it fascinated. It was pork-making by machinery, pork-making by applied mathematics. And yet somehow the most matter-of-fact person could not help thinking of the hogs; they were so innocent, they came so very trustingly; and they were so very human in their protests—and so perfectly within their rights! They had done nothing to deserve it, and it was adding insult to injury, as the thing was done here, swinging them up in this cold-blooded impersonal way, without a pretense at apology, without the homage of a tear. (36)

As the story unfolds, Jurgis is subjected to the same math counting him as being as replaceable and disposable as the hogs. Few see and shed a tear for the cattle and pigs, and few acknowledge the injury, death, and poverty faced by those who work in these plants.

While the focus of this book is on the well-being of the various animal beings killed for meat and used for eggs and dairy products, it is important to note that the human beings in this industry are ontologized in much the same way—they are seen not as individual beings but as commodified units of production. Many ecofeminists have argued that the logic of domination operates in all kinds of oppression and will continue to operate among humans as long as it operates within our relations to nature and other animal beings. They argue that this logic extends to how the industry views the consumer as well. While consumer welfare is not my main focus here, it is still worth noting that feedlot production, the speed of the slaughter line, and all the infractions that result from that speed result in unsafe meat and animal by-products. As discussed previously, mad cow, E. coli 0157H7, salmonella, listeria, and campylobacter bacteria are just the most publicized examples of such concerns. Eisnitz says that while the USDA's official reports indicate that 20 percent of chickens are contaminated with salmonella, reports of five particular plants in 1992 showed that number to be 58 percent before the birds were dipped in the chill tank and 72 percent after the cross-contamination enabled by that process. Even after chlorine was added to the chill tank (a health hazard of its own), contamination rates remained around 48 percent. Contamination rates are much higher for campylobacter bacteria—regularly

90 to 100 percent (Eisnitz 175–77). It is worth noting that in January 2015 the USDA announced its intention to lower the acceptable percentage of chicken parts with salmonella after an outbreak traced to Foster Farms. However, Eisnitz says, by 1985 there were 450 fewer USDA inspectors examining a billion and half more birds than in 1975. With inspectors having one and a half seconds to inspect each bird and no authority to stop production over contamination and given the fact that they can sample less than one-tenth of one percent of the birds at the end of the line, there is little reason to be confident in the safety of the meat that is packed and shipped to consumers.

In all of this, the workers and owners of the slaughterhouses are usually the ones who become the focus of any discussion of the morality of killing animals in industrialized plants. Pachirat asks whether it is the workers or those who eat the meat who have the larger share of the moral responsibility for the killing. While one of his friends argued that it is those who take the physical actions that cause the deaths who are more responsible, Pachirat disagrees. He says, "Those who benefited at a distance, delegating this terrible work to others while disclaiming responsibility for it, bore more moral responsibility, particularly in contexts like the slaughterhouse, where those with the fewest opportunities in society performed the dirty work" (160). Consumers evade responsibility by evading any experience killing and processing. Pachirat suggests that if consumers had to participate in some way in the killing of animals, in the execution of the death penalty, in the violence of war, or in the actual disposal of trash, such work would be radically altered or even eliminated—and that these continue in the violent and wasteful ways they do only because the majority of people do not directly experience the reality. At the same time, however, Pachirat notes, the segmentation of things like war and slaughter hide the reality even from most of those who do participate directly. It was not a reality hidden from the farmers we talked with who walked their cattle and sheep into the mobile slaughter truck and stood with them while they died, or from those who slaughtered and processed their own chickens. In many cases, though, the reality is still hidden from their customers.

In the treatment of the animals while they are alive as well as in the slaughter process, those carrying it out need to be attentive to the different needs of each species. Big slaughterhouses tend to specialize in poultry, pigs, or cattle—and with that kind of specialization it can be possible to improve the experience. Temple Grandin is famous for her work trying to see the process from the animal's point of view and eliminating things that cause stress and injury. She points out that cattle don't like yelling, sudden movement, or humans "looming" above them. She designed a curved chute with a roof to help keep the cattle settled. But, she writes, "there is no technological substitute for understanding and working with an animal's behavior. The equipment I design is all behaviorally based; it will work only if you're handling the cattle properly" (Grandin, *Animals Make Us Human* 169). She laments that many plants install only parts of her system since they fail to understand cattle. Grandin says that plants need to teach and enforce good handling practices; they need good "stockpersons" who can read the animals. When writing about the slaughter of pigs, she acknowledges that despite training, many workers revert to rough handling unless the management takes it seriously. One important thing to do, she says, is to "get the electric prod out of workers' hands" (192). People get gentler and kinder without the weapon in their hands. But enforcement of humane handling at the plants remains a problem. One of her solutions requires working with the animals throughout their lives and deaths. She suggests training the pigs to walk single file to get to food at the farm. This would then transfer to them walking calmly through the chutes at the meat plant, lessening the need for humans to do anything to "push" them.

None of this addresses the problems of transporting animals to such facilities or holding them there. Eisnitz reports that hogs frequently arrive frozen in the trucks and are sent off to the rendering area to be used in feed, fertilizer, cosmetics, plastics, and other products. Some are still alive when found in the rendering area and may be ground up alive (102). Cattle travel twelve to fifteen hundred miles, collapse from heat exhaustion in the summer, and stand in frozen urine in the winter (not to mention the wind chill) (211). Cattle who are hurt in transport are called "haulers" and are sometimes dragged from the truck to the "knocker" (130). Pigs raised in confinement will often collapse on the walk from the truck and have "drivers [jab] meat hooks in their mouths or anuses and [drag] them through the chutes alive" (132). Sick or injured horses are dragged by a chain, pulled by the tail, shocked, or stuck "in the rectum till they bleed to make them get up" (137–38).

With cattle, for those who own and operate feedlots, there may be a slaughter plant adjacent to the feedlot. Smaller feeding operations, though, have to ship the cattle some distance, as centralization, and the increased size of these plants, has resulted in fewer being in operation. In 1997 Eisnitz reported that between 1984 and 1994 one-third of these plants (about two thousand) went out of business as the large slaughterhouses consolidated, reduced the workforce, and sped up slaughter lines. She notes that according to the USDA, in 1980, it took 103 plants (owned by fifty different companies) to slaughter two-thirds of the cattle killed in the United States. By 1996, 11 plants killed 40 percent of the cattle, and 10 plants killed 40 percent of the hogs (62).

Grass-fed growers have trouble finding plants willing to take their smaller lots (as discussed in chapter 3). This is why many sell animals "on the hoof" or use a USDA-approved mobile slaughter truck. The expense of these trucks makes it difficult for one farmer to own one, but cooperatives that share such a truck are increasingly common. Regulations do allow small farms to process a certain amount of poultry on the farm if they follow specific safety and record-keeping rules (the Humane Methods of Slaughter Act does not apply to birds). Since poultry generally travel the furthest, and in the most cramped conditions, on-site slaughter can greatly reduce the suffering (for human and bird) involved in poultry production if it is done well.

Horse slaughter has received the most public attention in recent years, resulting in the closing of the last three plants that processed horses in 2014. There is a long history to the concerns over the slaughter of horses that is tied to the plight of wild horses as well as the fate of many race, show, and pet horses. In the past, most horsemeat ended up in pet food (returning to some of the concerns with which this book started), but more recently it has been shipped to Europe and Asia for human consumption. Eisnitz reported that the USDA estimates between one and three hundred thousand domesticated horses are slaughtered each year (109). As I discussed in *Pets, People, and Pragmatism*, many people would rather be paid to "dispose of their horse" than pay to have a horse put down and taken away. When prices are high enough, horses are also stolen to be slaughtered. They suffer in the same ways that some cattle do—being dragged, prodded, improperly stunned, and skinned while still alive. The slaughter of "wild" horses, which is directly related to the presence of livestock on the western ranges, is also of concern.

While the whole history of wild horses in the United States is beyond the scope of this book, it is important to note that horses were indigenous to the territory. Early species of Equus were here twelve million years ago, with the "true horse" emerging about one and a half million years ago. This species is genetically linked to the horses who returned to the continent by way of Cortés. Many think that changing climate pushed the species to migrate but that their arrival by way of human transportation was a return, not an invasion of a nonnative species (Stillman 40–42). This history is important today because wild horses are under threat. These horses are the descendants of the domesticated horses brought from Europe who became feral, and those who classify these horses as a "nonnative" species find them necessary to remove. While environmental damage is often cited as a reason to remove herds (or reduce their numbers) the root problem is competition for the rangeland that comes from livestock interests (as discussed in chapter 4). In her book *Mustang*, Deanne Stillman notes that "stockmen considered them mostly expendable animals that shouldn't have been on the range in the first place, recent arrivals to the ecosystem who were stealing food from cows. This view created a new alliance among old enemies, cattlemen and sheep men, who found a common foe in the mustang even as they continued their own war" (Stillman

238). Grasslands and water sources had been damaged by overstocking the range with livestock, but the mustang was a convenient and profitable target.

Given this attitude, an unofficial policy of removal was in force. As discussed in chapter 4, it took over twenty years, but the Wild Free-Roaming Horses and Burros Act was passed in 1971, offering protections for the horses and calling for the horses to be managed in ways that maintain a thriving ecosystem. Enforcement of the 1971 legislation has always been spotty at best, and the official multiple-use management assigned to the BLM led quickly to the reintroduction of mechanized roundups of horses and adoption programs. Many of these animals are not adopted, though, and remain in crowded conditions in captivity. Many of the adopted animals end up at the slaughterhouse (276). Stillman reports that this became profitable enough that "agency employees had allegedly been siphoning mustangs out of government pipelines, fattening them up in corrals, and then selling them to killer buyers—that is, brokers from the rendering plants who purchased horses by the pound.... Investigators estimated that as many as thirty thousand mustangs had disappeared from the pipeline" (279–80). Simultaneously individuals also took it upon themselves to kill horses on the range—using them as target practice. Some were used as bait for trapping and killing coyotes (also at the behest of the ranchers).

Attempts to save the horses from such abuse, and from possible extinction, have been ongoing. Several sanctuaries now exist for their protection. One motive behind the efforts to close the slaughterhouses that processed horses was to remove the profit motive that resulted in the roundup and killing of wild horses. This often includes an argument that horses should not be killed and processed in the ways other livestock are—they are seen as special. This argument is problematic for a number of reasons. It artificially divides horses from cattle, sheep, pigs, chickens, and fish. It reinforces the idea that the current conditions of transport and slaughter are fine for some animals. While I realize it would be a political nonstarter to call for the closing of all slaughterhouses, the call to end the slaughter of horses could have been used to limit and improve the slaughter of other animals, but this was not done. In fact, horse advocates went out of their way to reassure the livestock industry that this move would *not* endanger their livelihood. Nancy Perry of the Humane Society said, "There is a slippery-slope argument suggesting that ending the slaughter of animals not bred for meat and not consumed in America will lead to a ban on slaughtering all animals for meat.... Such fear mongering simply aids the interests of foreign corporations operating on US soil who buy our stolen and auctioned horses" (quoted in Malkin 20). This kind of activism pits species against each other and fails to address the larger logic of domination and exploitation.

Interestingly, it seems that any animal intentionally bred for consumption is considered fair game for the slaughter industry. Animals such as elk and bison who are bred for meat are processed with little to no complaint from the public. Alternative livestock such as bison present specific challenges when it comes to slaughter. Their size does not fit the increasingly standardized operations, and their strength and demeanor make them "less cooperative" than cattle. As a brochure from Bison Bluff Farms in Illinois notes, "their most obvious weapon is their horns. But their head, with its massive skull, can be used as a battering ram.... Their legs can also be used to kill or maim with devastating effect." While their bison are grass-fed, "feedlot trials have shown that in the summer bison make better weight gains than cattle do on low-to medium-quality forages." But this adaptation coincides with low weight gain in the winter, even on high-quality forage. This is true for elk and deer as well (Holechek et al. 393). These nondomesticated animals retain the feeding rhythms of their free lives and so do not "benefit" from feedlot production in the same way domesticated species do.

The rise of alternative livestock such as bison, elk, ostrich, and insects is an interesting and somewhat disturbing development. It seems that the logic of domination is being extended to "wild" animals in a new way. Long applied to justify the hunting and fishing of free-living animals, the view of these animals as a "resource" to be managed for human sport and food now justifies the practice of raising them in confinement and slaughtering them on a large scale. Bison are a particularly interesting case. While bison were seen as pests and removed from the plains to make way for the railroad and to "help" with the elimination of American Indians (see chapter 3), in 2016 the bison was declared the national mammal. But this status does not mean they cannot be culled, hunted, ranched, or eaten. If it is wrong to eat a horse, why does this not apply to the national mammal? Something further complicating this issue is that part of the allure of bison farming is the idea of recovering the bison and all it symbolized. This entails having bison out on grass in herds. Moves to commercialize bison farming into an industry resembling those for the main livestock animals run into an image problem. If bison are commercially bred, fed, and contained, they are no longer the animal they once were, since one allure of bison is their "wildness." While bison ranching is often described as restoring the number of bison in existence (rather than reintroducing them "in the wild"), there is still a concern that the animals be "authentic." Commercially raised bison found in a feedlot eating grain are not what the public has in mind. This kind of life transforms rather than restores the animal. The National Bison Association (NBA) stresses the importance of the romance of the bison and the need for "mystique marketing": "On the one hand, the NBA and bison producers must continue to promote the romance surrounding the

American bison.... On the other hand, we need to de-mystify bison so that consumers quit associating bison with the meat that is only eaten on special occasions" (Carter, quoted in Wilkie 98). To promote the romance, some bison operations "slaughter" by having people come "hunt and shoot" the bison. The Buffalo Ranch in Colorado provides such an experience, and not only does their website instruct their customers on how to shoot the animal but they also have the animal butchered and the meat packaged for the customer. They provide taxidermy services so that the customer can mount the head, take home the hide, or both. These "trophies" seem to be as important as the meat.

Wildlife conservation in the United States (as discussed earlier with Leopold) has often involved managing ecosystems to encourage higher populations of game animals that can sustain regulated hunting. Farming of these game animals is also increasingly common. While the husbandry of game animals is more common in Africa, it is beginning to take hold in the United States as well. The idea is that native wildlife species are better adapted to a specific area than introduced livestock, so they are ranched and slaughtered or hunted for their meat. Farming deer and elk is seen as environmentally friendly and profitable, as the farmer can make money from hunting and tourism as well as by selling the meat. Such farms often include a stocked trout pond or some system of aquaculture. The Agricultural Marketing Resource Center notes that "deer farming in the United States started in the early 1970s, when people began to look for alternative land uses. Today, it is a viable alternative livestock business. The farmed breeds exhibit strong herding instincts, are efficient converters of forage and adapt well to the farm environment. Also, the species used in farmed venison tend to be disease resistant and handle close association well. Some industry advocates consider deer as a livestock alternative that has the potential to boost a sagging agricultural economy without the use of subsidies or government incentives" (Burden). Deer and elk provide many "marketable products" such as velvet, antlers, musk, milk, meat, skins, tails, glands, livers, tongues, and other organs in addition to the "thrill" of trophy hunting.

Other animals, such as ostrich, emu, and rabbits, are also farmed for meat. While ostrich and emu numbers are declining, rabbit production is increasing. Almost a million rabbits are sold for meat, and many are raised for personal consumption—"rabbits have become the urban chickens of the 2010s" (Isaacs). Rabbits are not classified as livestock, so they are not governed by the USDA, but they are protected under the Animal Welfare Act. There are not many plants that slaughter and process rabbits, so most are slaughtered directly by producers or in mobile slaughter trucks. Notably, all the animals discussed here are listed as products and commodities by the Agricultural Marketing Resource Center, not as animals. Rabbits pose a particular problem in this regard, as the public is more likely to identify them as pets rather than as livestock and be less willing to eat them or wear their fur. The center suggests using language that distances the consumer from the live animal to help with marketing—making Carol Adams's point about mass terms and absent referents for her!

A little less cuddly, however, is the emerging market for insects. In many parts of the world insects are a regular part of the diet, and insect farming can be a good business. Insects are a source of protein and they require far fewer resources such as land, water, and oil to produce. They emit few greenhouse gases and can be produced in an "urban farming" environment. This appeals to people looking to eat in environmentally sustainable ways. In the United States there is resistance to eating "bugs," especially if they are cooked whole. However, as with many other animals, if they are processed (hiding the individuals by grinding them into flour or mixing them into a cooked dish) more people are willing to try them. Many who object to eating the meat of pigs and cattle find insects preferable, as they seem less morally considerable. While bees and silkworms have been farmed for quite some time, the call to expand the eating of insects would expand such practices exponentially. Since insects are not mammals, humans can feel more distance from them (as they do with fish). However, many insects are highly social and seemingly intelligent. It is quite likely that they suffer in a number of ways when farmed and slaughtered. Some insects (as with some shellfish) are eaten, boiled, fried, or frozen while alive. Still others are sold to be eaten alive by reptiles and birds—as pet food. Insects seek out certain conditions and try to avoid others. Large-scale farming frustrates this ability and can rely on keeping the insects in conditions they would prefer to avoid. Temperature, humidity, and stocking density all have to be managed with particular species and individuals in mind. This is hard to do when raising such animals on a large scale. Given that most insect production seeks to find a way to "industrialize" the process to "scale up" and compete with other livestock farming, it is also clear that turning to insects as food does nothing to combat the logic of domination and the commodification of life. One still has to feed insects something (plant or animal) and then eat the insect. Given the large number of insects required to feed humans it may still be more environmentally friendly to bypass the "middle man" of the insect. This pushes others to try to find a way to have meat without any animal at all.

Interest in lab-grown meat is growing. While it is currently energy-intensive and relies on harvesting stem cells, those concerned primarily with issues of animal suffering find hope in this as a possible future alternative to factory farms. For my purposes here, what is interesting about this alternative is the near-total removal of the animal. It seems that rather than reduce meat consumption to sustainable levels there is a desire to produce meat without animals and without death. An assessment of the drive to produce lab meat might be made that is similar to Plumwood's take on the call for veganism: that it is born of a desire to get out of the material cycles that govern animal bodies—to get away from bodies, excrement, birth, and death. From an ecofeminist and pragmatist perspective I find this troubling. While neither perspective is inherently anti-technology, and neither believes situations remain static, both schools of thought call for understanding the human in terms of relationships with the rest of nature—not for escaping nature. Shared dependencies and vulnerabilities help shape our being. Calls to master and control nature deny these dependencies and vulnerabilities and often result in many of the unintended consequences Dewey warns about.

These various alternatives for feeding human and other animals deserve some careful thought, but I worry that they all share a common assumption that humans should consume as much meat as they want. Despite some concerns about the soil, water, wildlife, climate change, or animal suffering, the general view is that these can be addressed in ways that make the eating of meat raised in industrial farms or labs a morally acceptable choice. There is some acknowledgment of the moral tension when people turn to animal sanctuaries as a way to assuage their feelings of guilt, remorse, or discomfort with the current relationships between humans and most livestock animals. There is a big show of the president pardoning two turkeys at Thanksgiving. When animals escape a truck bound for the slaughterhouse there is usually a public cry to save those individuals and send them to a sanctuary as well. When animals meant to be meat gain status as individuals, many people find it hard to follow through with killing and eating them. But rather than think through what this might mean for decisions about what to consume, there is instead a tendency to change the animals in some way, or to get meat without live animals, so that meat will pose no ethical or existential questions or concerns. This kind of thinking pushes us toward ideas like breeding blind chickens who won't fight in the crowded conditions on factory farms, breeding lean pigs who turn out to be more prone to fighting, and genetically modifying salmon who grow year-round. Such scenarios fail to fully respect the needs and desires of the creatures involved. Instead they promote the human-centered view of the world that expects the rest of life to adapt to our needs and desires.

As I hope I've shown, a pragmatist ecofeminist approach provides a strong critique of this kind of human-centeredness. I have used this perspective to argue that much of animal agriculture in the United States is problematic for a number of reasons. The vast majority of livestock animals are in industrial production systems that fail to respect their needs and desires, require large inputs of resources (grain, water, oil, and land), exploit human laborers, and pollute land, water, and air. This system has concentrated the breeding, feeding, and slaughtering of these animals in a handful of vertically integrated corporations that exploit the animals, the farmers, other laborers, and consumers. Most of these corporations show little regard for the communities in which they operate, seeking exemptions from taxes and environmental standards. This system has made it possible to produce vast quantities of meat on a predictable schedule and so supply the large grocery chains, restaurants, and fast food franchises on which so many in the United States rely. Because these corporations are not required to pay for externalities such as the pollution their production systems cause, and because they benefit from programs such as subsidized grain production, they are able to make a substantial profit while keeping the price of meat, dairy, and eggs low. This has allowed more people to eat more meat on a more regular basis. For some this is a cause for celebration, as access to food should not be a privilege of the rich. However, from the start, this system's scale and centralization have presented numerous health and safety challenges. The quality and safety of animal products is very much in question, and recalls have become a regular occurrence in the United States. While Upton Sinclair wrote about this array of issues in *The Jungle* over one hundred years ago, today writers such as Michael Pollan, Eric Schlosser, Gail Eisnitz, Jonathan Foer, and many others try to raise awareness. Books about, and mainstream media coverage of, the various problems with the current food system abound. But the convenience to the consumer seems to override the array of moral, political, economic, aesthetic, health, and safety concerns. Most people continue to buy animal products from the industrialized system, and those products that are produced in other ways are presented as a niche market for "elite foodies" who have the time and money to seek out alternatives. But I don't think this needs to be the case.

In the previous chapters I have sketched the history and development of the industrial system. While it arose as a response to a variety of problems, it itself is now a problem that we must approach with intelligent foresight. There are alternative approaches. I believe any viable future of farming must entail a critical examination of current consumption patterns in the United States (and elsewhere). I see no healthful and sustainable way to support the contemporary fast food and meat-focused diet of most of the U.S. population. We live in a culture of fads and excess. When this combines to focus on meat—like the recent bacon craze—it is dangerous on many fronts. Overconsumption of eggs and dairy products can also be problematic. Human health suffers, land is depleted, air and water are polluted, and livestock suffer. At the same time, I don't see a future without the production and consumption of animal products, nor do I see a near future without the human use of animal fiber for things like leather and wool, and the use of various animals' organs to repair the human body—often repairing damage done by eating too many of these very same animals. Many argue for the abolition of animal agriculture, but this is unlikely. Further, it may be a problematic goal.

While there are certain resemblances between the call to abolish human slavery and the call to end what is seen as animal slavery, I think there are differences that are important to take into account (as noted by Kimberly Smith—see chapter 5). The animal beings in question—cattle, sheep, goats, pigs, chickens, turkeys, and fish—are not capable of "autonomous" citizenship on a human model. While, in the past, arguments were made that some humans (e.g., women and non-Europeans) are "natural slaves" because they lack intelligence or certain capacities of reason, evolutionary history and lived experience tell a different story, and laws and practices have changed over time. However, while "human rights" have been formally extended, it is still clear that different lives are valued and protected differently within various societies. It has often been the case that formal rights were extended without a corresponding extension of genuine respect for those receiving the rights, with the result that the newly granted rights mean little in the lives of those who have gained them—and so sexism and racism persist. I would argue the same predicament would emerge if some animals gained formal rights without there being a more thoroughgoing change in attitudes about those animals. Livestock animal beings are not human beings, though, and it seems that even on a rights approach, a non-speciesist case can be made that any "rights" they might be due do not include a right to never be used (many of the farmers we interviewed make such a case). This is true for humans as well, but humans can insist on fair and compensated use. This does not mean, however, that humans can do as they please with the animals they use for food and fiber.

One problem with a rights approach (noted in chapter 5) is that it is rooted in classical liberal theory that presupposes a model of the individual that is rational, atomistic, and autonomous. Pragmatism and ecofeminism both reject this model of the individual and embrace the notion of a social self. Such a critique of the liberal self can go even further when considering how humans and other animal beings constitute each other. In her book *Interspecies Ethics*, Cynthia Willett draws on research that shows that "shared ecosystems or intimate symbiosis allow for mutual flourishing through 'social behaviors' found all the way down to bacteria, which communicate with each other and their hosts, most likely from their home in the gut, through chemical signaling" (71). This kind of cohabitation and co-constitution means that no individual exists on its own but rather only in complex communities of beings that include microbes, fungi, plants, and animals. Willett writes, "Organisms do not have clear and distinct boundaries that separate them from other living things. They survive cooperatively and symbiotically or in struggle, but not alone" (64). This presents an important challenge to the liberal notion of the autonomous individual, which means it also presents a challenge to the rights approach.

I have argued that we need relationships of respect rather than rights (this may be true for relationships among humans as well). Rights tend to focus on negative liberties—what you shouldn't do to me and what you will be punished for doing. For instance, you shouldn't kill me or take my property. With other animal beings there has been a similar tendency to focus on not killing them and not causing them to suffer. This minimalist approach of not harming, though, does not necessarily constitute a good life for the animal beings in question. Nor does complete separation from human use and relationships. Humans can help provide rich and varied lives for a variety of domesticated animal beings. Since many livestock animals enjoy social contact with humans (and vice versa), these can be mutually beneficial relationships. There is the possible added benefit of the animals improving the quality of the ecosystems in which they live; this helps a variety of "wild" animals flourish as well.

Further, even with something like the abolitionist movement, change does not occur all at once. The goal to end legalized slavery did not occur in one fell swoop, nor did the legal end of slavery bestow equality upon former slaves (or their descendants today). Such changes are always the result of more gradual processes (unjust and frustrating as that may be). While it is important to identify and argue against moral wrongs and injustices, habits must change along with laws; ways of thinking must make room for previously rejected or unconsidered possibilities. This kind of gradualist approach is rarely satisfying for those who have come to see the many problems with the current way of doing things. It is deeply unfair and tragic for those suffering the moral wrongs and injustices themselves. But untenable and extreme positions (the zealotry Fesmire critiques) create new moral wrongs and injustices. Rarely do we face all-or-nothing propositions, though.

I have shown a variety of responses to the current state of livestock production in the United States. Some try to opt out altogether. As discussed, though, vegans and vegetarians are still tied to the lives and deaths of livestock in a number of ways. Others seek major shifts in our understanding of, and relationships with, livestock. They work to make this shift operative in methods of raising, using, and killing these animals. Still others just tinker at the edges of the system with changes in labeling that may or may not reflect real changes in the lives of livestock. And, of course, there are those who like things just as they are. From a pragmatist ecofeminist perspective I reject the extreme of leaving the status quo as is, and I reject the extreme of calling for abolition. There are a number of possibilities (returning to pragmatism's commitment to pluralism) in between.

One middle option that some ecofeminists support is contextual moral veganism or vegetarianism. Their argument is that one should be vegan or vegetarian unless one's context (e.g., location, income, health) makes that not a realistic possibility. This position is not a universal or absolute call for being vegan or vegetarian but does maintain that a vegan or vegetarian diet is the moral default. At the same time, many of these theorists reject abolitionist views that call for the end of all relationships among human and other animal beings. As Lori Gruen writes, "not only are we in a shared community that would be destroyed if some of us were to be forced out of existence, but others (human and non) co-constitute who we are and how we configure our identities and agency, our thoughts and desires. We can't make sense of living without others, and that includes other animals." Since animal beings co-constitute each other and have coevolved, trying to end such relationships is a denial of who human being are and a form of moral evasion. Gruen continues, "We are entangled in complex relationships and rather than trying to accomplish the impossible by pretending we can disentangle, we would do better to think about how to be more perceptive and more responsive to the deeply entangled relationships we are in. Since we are already, inevitably in relationships, rather than ending them we might try to figure out how to make them better, more meaningful, and more mutually satisfying" (131). Like Val Plumwood, Gruen acknowledges that such relationships can entail a use component but argues that they must not permit exploitation. Understanding the dependencies and vulnerabilities that humans share with other animal beings (and the rest of the environment) exposes the lie that promotes the exploitative instrumentalization of these others while still acknowledging that "we can't live and avoid killing. . . . Vegan diets are less harmful than those that include animal products, to be sure, but the harms and deaths occur nonetheless" (132–33).

Gruen argues that human relationships with pets often result in a moral obligation to assist with their deaths (euthanasia in the face of disease or when warehoused in shelters) but that raising animals to kill and eat is always a system "that violently instrumentalizes individuals in deeply troubling ways, obliterates their personalities and interests, and turns them into both real and metaphorical fodder." For Gruen this applies equally to industrialized farms and the "so-called sustainable or pasture-based farms." Her reason is the "painfully short lives and violent deaths of the animals used for food" (130). However, a good short life is not necessarily an evil, and not all killing is violent (or even stressful). While I agree with Gruen's goal to minimize harm and killing, vegan and vegetarian diets (as already discussed) can inadvertently harm more animals (and the environment) than diets that include some meat and dairy from pasture-raised animals. Even if one chooses not to directly consume such meat and dairy, it is important to acknowledge that having some pasture-based animal agriculture is beneficial for growing the plant-based crops on which vegans and vegetarians depend.

In *Meat: A Benign Extravagance*, Simon Fairlie argues that veganism and vegetarianism are not the only ethically and environmentally responsible dietary options. In fact, he argues, in some circumstances they can be a less sound choice than diets that contain some meat and dairy. In the foreword to Fairlie's book Gene Logsdon writes, "The no-meat versus pro-meat camps might ponder the lesson of Prohibition days. No doubt trying to make old demon alcohol disappear was a noble idea, but we learned the hard way that it just isn't going to happen. And so it is with eating meat. As Fairlie argues, allowing for moderation works better for overall food security than trying to make farm animals disappear, and just might make it easier for vegetarians to follow their diet preferences, too" (viii). Fairlie agrees that with the current production model meat is an extravagance that only a few can sustainably indulge in (as are coffee, tea, wine, and chocolate) (12). While Fairlie sees no justification for the intensive animal agriculture that dominates the market, he does think that there is room for what he terms "default livestock." Growing food to feed animals for people to eat does not make sense to him. However, some livestock can thrive on land not readily used for growing food for human consumption (cattle, sheep, and goats), and some animals can survive on various waste products produced by humans (pigs and chickens). So ruminants who can convert grass into an energy source humans can consume, and scavengers who can convert waste into consumable energy, are the livestock animals who should be raised; these are "default livestock." These animals have the added benefit of providing nutrients that can be used to enrich the soil so that there is less need to rely on the petrochemical industry in order to grow food. The manure may also be a source of fuel. For some, such animals provide increased mobility and important companionship (24). Their death also supplies a number of "by-products," such as pet food, leather, and feathers. The uses are numerous, and most of the alternatives humans have developed rely on petrochemicals and water in their production and add to the noncompostable waste stream that is overwhelming the planet. For instance, using hides for leather shoes can make good sense as they last a long time, can be repeatedly repaired, and are biodegradable. One example that demonstrates the complexity of one's food choices is the growing use of palm oil as a substitute for animal fats in vegan foods (22). The animal suffering and

environmental harm caused by palm plantations is quite significant—defor-
estation and the growing endangerment of orangutans is just the beginning.

Most economists and politicians seem to take the "demand" for livestock
as a given and look for ways to increase the available and affordable supply.
While the Food and Agriculture Organization of the United Nations (FAO)
recommends an increased reliance on industrial animal agriculture, despite
the harms to the environment and small farmers, Fairlie suggests a reduction
in consumption and a move to "default livestock":

> A vegan diet is one without animal products; the industrial meat diet advanced
> by the FAO is one that allows for anything that the consumer can afford and
> the producer can supply. In the muddy spectrum between, there are not many
> secure footholds, but the default livestock diet can be reasonably clearly defined
> as one that provides meat, dairy and other animal products which arise as the
> integral co-product of an agricultural system dedicated to the provision of sus-
> tainable vegetable nourishment. . . . As such it provides, not orthodoxy to which
> we should aspire, but a benchmark by which we can assess the sustainability
> and the environmental justice of what we eat. (42)

He wants to support small farmers "in their struggle against agribusiness"
and he believes "the world would be much the poorer without domestic livestock" (3). In this view grass-fed ruminants and pigs and poultry fed on waste
and by-products, when killed humanely in small abattoirs, are an important
and sustainable component of feeding the world (67). Not surprisingly this is
a view that supports much of what my students and I heard from the farmers with whom we talked, and it fits with the Deweyan approach to ethics
sketched earlier in this book.

Animal welfare is not Fairlie's concern in his book, though he is clear that
a clean kill at the end of a good life seems far preferable to life (and death)
on a factory farm or in a laboratory. He is not opposed to those who choose
a vegetarian or vegan diet (though I find his caricature of them a bit unfair)
and credits them with teaching the world that meat is not a necessity for
human life. However, as with any all-or-nothing solution, he finds the call
to stop eating meat too simplistic, given the complexity of food issues. He
worries that without more careful thought, those interested in following a vegetarian or vegan diet may find themselves increasingly reliant on
petrochemical-driven agribusiness and the technology of lab-grown meat—
options that he argues are not in line with views that seek sustainability and
connectedness to nature (9, 212–31). I think this is why Kimberly Smith also
rejects the idea of a future with lab-grown meat in favor of one with small
farms that include livestock. Further, any attempt to rely solely on plant
products would require that more land be put into use growing edible crops,

that the use of petrochemical fertilizers, herbicides, pesticides, and genetically modified seeds increase, or that both occur (84). (This is also noted by
Nicolette Niman.) Both these options have problematic consequences for
the rest of nature.

Fairlie's concerns go deeper, though, and have some points in common
with the views of Val Plumwood. He cautions the reader about the "vegan
agenda," which may result in a world without nature. He writes,

> We are what we eat, and by eating animals we help to ensure that we ourselves
> remain animals, participants in the food chain that momentarily we head be-
> fore we too become flesh for worms. By declining to eat meat we abandon our
> status as predator, ostensibly to take on the more humble role of middle rank
> herbivore, but increasingly to assume the roles of manager and absentee land-
> lord. As we detach ourselves from the natural world, it fades to a spectral im-
> age, . . . a world we can no longer be part of because we are too squeamish to
> partake of it. As a species we are slowly resigning from nature, and for those
> of us who lament this tragedy, there is at least one consolation: That for some
> time to come there will be poachers lurking in the woods for the vegans and the
> wildlife managers will never catch them all. (231)

While I think this view paints an extreme (and disturbing) view of the beliefs of most vegans, it does raise a concern I share. When humans try to pull
themselves out of any complicity in the death and consumption of other animal beings some strange things happen.

First, the idea that it is even possible to succeed in doing so is an illusion.
Living requires eating, and all eating requires death. Even if one discounts the
death of plants (which is becoming increasingly difficult to do), it is not possible to consume plants without killing (and often consuming) insects, rodents,
and a variety of other small mammals and birds. The production of plants for
human (and livestock) consumption harms "wildlife" by destroying their habitat. The felling of trees, the plowing of soil, the diversion of streams, and various forms of pollution just start the list. When such production takes place on
a large scale, the use of monocultures and the reliance on pesticides and herbicides that this entails do an incredible amount of damage and result in air
and water contamination. While "wild" animals such as wolves, coyotes, and
sea lions (and many more) are hunted and killed to protect "meat animals,"
animals such as deer, elk, pigs, and elephants (and many more) are hunted
and killed to protect cropland. Even those people who grow their own plants
for food kill and displace a whole host of other beings. The mere presence of a
garden can disrupt an ecosystem as it attracts certain plants and animals to
an area to the detriment of others. All animal beings affect the world in which
they live, and their actions, including what they do and don't eat, have an im-

pact on others. Humans are no different, though the scale of human impact can be quite large and far-reaching.

Second, the attempt to pull out of human complicity in death seems to rest on our forgetting that we are food for others. Fairlie briefly alludes to this when he points out that we will become food for the worms. But we are seen as prey by most of the carnivores of the world too. Val Plumwood's book *The Eye of the Crocodile* is helpful on this score as she reflects on surviving a crocodile's attempt to kill and eat her. She said she had the sense of being watched before the "attack" and is quite clear that, while she fought back and did escape, she was the intruder in the crocodile's space. She argued against those who wanted to find and kill the "offending animal" as she placed no blame on the individual and noted that many other crocodiles did not attack her as she lay waiting for help. But, historically, humans have had no such humility and have decimated animals such as crocodiles, big cats, wolves, bears, and others who might make humans their prey (as recently shown by the killing of alligators at Disney World after one drowned a toddler). I share Plumwood's and Fairlie's concern that there is often something in the impulse to be vegan or vegetarian that involves a desire to hide from our own nature as predator of other animals. It is not only the desire to not participate in the death of other animal beings, though, but also a desire to hide from the fact that our flesh can serve (and often has served) to sustain the life of others—that we are prey.

For most humans there is a deep discomfort with the thought of being eaten but little discomfort with the practice of eating others. Ralph Acampora argues that if one isn't willing to eat other humans, one is being speciesist eating other animals. He sees contextual moral vegetarianism as a cop-out for allowing exceptions. Acampora thinks it's difficult to see flesh-eating as respectful since "eating is literally a case of consumption, of using up somebody—such that there is no remainder whom one could any longer respect or care for/about." Plumwood allows for some limited consumption, given that the eater will one day reciprocate and that this demonstrates the interdependency of all life (and death). Acampora is doubtful that many would actually reciprocate (at least not willingly), and so argues against making allowances for "so-called humane farming practices" (150, 152). He says the logic of domination is at work on all farms and farming remains "despotic and prone to oppressive backsliding as it perpetuates speciesist hierarchy in a crypto-sexist vein" (153). The argument is that since keeping, killing, and using farm animals in any manner can be potentially abusive, all such use should be avoided. With the added assumption of death being bad (especially "premature" death at the hands of humans), there remains no acceptable model of animal agriculture. Some contextual vegetarians argue that no farming will be morally permissible once in vitro meat is available and farming can be eliminated.

But, for me, relying on lab-grown meat just deepens the illusion that humans are not part of nature with shared dependencies and vulnerabilities. Humans are both predator and prey. To look for ways to live and eat that deny such interdependencies is to reinscribe the mastery-of-nature narrative that ecofeminists critique.

The pragmatist ecofeminist perspective presented here does not deny the complex role of humans as both predator and prey, does not think all death is unacceptable, and does not find all farming practices to be despotic. Further, given the complex interactions among livestock and various "wild" animals, this view acknowledges it would be harmful to some ecosystems to eliminate all livestock production. However, the overall number of livestock animals must decrease if these relationships are to be ethical, sustainable, and mutually beneficial. Consumption of meat, dairy, and eggs must decrease. One way to help make that happen is to eliminate the subsidies that keep meat prices down and so artificially elevate rates of consumption. In *Meatonomics*, David Robinson Simon notes that money to promote consumption of animal products is provided by the very groups (the USDA) who caution against consuming too many animal products (7, 10). Further, he thinks that if more consumers were aware of the realities of livestock production, and the industry were no longer protected against criticism and exposure by "ag gag" rules and the labeling of those who try to expose the realities as terrorists, then things would change. For instance, if people understood that Customary Farming Exemptions (CFEs) undercut any real enforcement of anti-cruelty laws they would either lobby for changing such rules or change their habits of consumption (Simon 24, 36–39). Simon says, "Consider the case of Daniel Clark, a pig farmer who, in the winter of 2009, abandoned 832 pigs to die in an unheated barn in Pennsylvania. . . . Clark was charged with 832 counts of animal cruelty, but he pled guilty to only ten counts and was fined $2,500. The remaining 822 counts were dismissed, and he received no jail time" (40). Even with laws about animal welfare and humane slaughter, livestock animals really aren't protected (not to mention that most rules don't apply to poultry at all). But it's hard to inform people and work for changes when the industry is protected by the Animal Enterprise Terrorism Act and the FBI labels "eco-terrorism" and the "animal rights movement" as the main domestic terror threats (Genoways 125–26).

Some of the most common welfare concerns can be ameliorated by eliminating the need for some of the practices commonly known to cause livestock animals pain and stress. Since dehorning is painful and stressful, farmers could either adjust housing and handling practices to accommodate horns or breed naturally polled animals. Since branding is painful and stressful, farmers could adjust range management so that such a permanent form of identification would not be necessary or they could use paint markings, ear tags, or electronic chips. Money is lost on the hides of branded animals, so there may be an economic incentive to push people in this direction. Since weaning (especially early weaning) is painful and stressful, farmers could allow offspring to stay with their mothers longer (ideally until natural weaning occurs), employ low-stress weaning techniques such as fence-line weaning instead of abrupt and complete separation, or use some combination of both. In *Animals in Translation*, Grandin stresses the need to understand that while humans and other animals share many characteristics there are also important differences. Good handlers try to understand the experiences from the animals' point of view. She argues that while we need to breed responsibly so as not to create aggressive roosters or lame pigs, humans and other animals need each other and can read each other (176). She writes, "People and animals are supposed to be together. We spent a long time evolving together, and we used to be partners. Now people are cut off from animals unless they have a dog or a cat" (5). Reconnecting with livestock and reinstituting respectful partnerships will improve the lives of both livestock and human animals. All of these improvements would be more possible if the scale of livestock farms were smaller.

To help make that a more realistic possibility, Simon suggests a three-part solution: tax animal foods to increase prices and lower consumption, restructure the USDA so that it does not simultaneously police and promote animal products, and adjust subsidies so that they do not inadvertently promote animal suffering and environmental degradation. He argues that a tax on meat would be fair in order to help pay for the externalities in industrialized meat production. (It might be worth considering exempting pasture-based systems that meet certain requirements for animal welfare and environmental sustainability from such a tax.) He notes that this was effective with cigarettes (166–70) and it is increasingly being tried with products like soda. These are just some examples of possible ways to move forward in a way that might bring consumption in line with the scope of ethical and sustainable farming. This needs to happen in order to allow for the possibility of a future that promotes the flourishing of all life.

For those who care about animals such as horses, dogs, and cats, I have shown that those caring relationships and concern for well-being should transfer to the livestock animals on whom those pet animals (and humans) depend. Cats not only eat the meat and milk of other animals, but they are also often an integral part of farm life as they hunt rodents in the barns and fields. Dogs not only eat the meat, hooves, and hides of other animals but they too are also an integral part of farm life as they herd sheep and cattle, guard flocks, and sometimes form friendships with individual animals under their care. Horses find themselves in both the pet and livestock categories. They may be the animal cared for as a pet, the animal working other livestock, or a meat animal themselves. Some horses fit the "wild" animal category as well, as do some feral dogs and cats.

By now it should also be clear that relationships with pets and livestock implicate one in many complex beneficial and destructive relationships with "wild" animals. One example in this book is the complicated relationship between "wild" horses and grazing livestock such as cattle and sheep. Why does it make moral sense to hunt and "remove" (but not eat) horses in order to make room to graze animals who will be killed to serve as food? Similarly, as I have argued elsewhere, it is morally problematic to argue against the eating of chimpanzees and gorillas in the bushmeat trade while eating meat from factory-farmed pigs and cows. It is hypocritical to criticize the Makah whaling practices while eating farmed salmon or fast food. It is counterproductive to contribute to organizations trying to save orangutans while eating vegan and vegetarian foods laced with palm oil. It should be clear that there is no one universally morally preferred diet; who and what we eat is a complex issue that involves humans in a variety of intimate and complicated relationships with a variety of other animal (including human) beings. We need to think carefully about how our choices impact these relationships and make changes to improve the possibilities of these relationships going forward.

To do this, it helps to recall some aspects of the arguments put forward by pragmatist philosophers that were discussed in chapter 1. Peirce focuses on the idea of human ontological continuity with the rest of nature (the common presence of mind) and the consequent possibility of understanding and communicating with the rest of nature. Domesticated animals in particular are in reciprocal relationships with humans, but all animal beings have personalities for Peirce, and we need to be attentive to these and take them into account in our relationships with them. James calls for an approach that also entails respecting others' differences. Continuity does not mean sameness, and much can be learned from stretching oneself, encountering other perspectives, and being changed by them. Dewey emphasizes that life is always changing and generally seeks growth and "improvement." Such growth, if it is to be successful, engages any particular aspect of life or situation as being in a web of relationships with other life. No one and no thing stands alone. Individual and species development depends on transactive (mutually transformative) relationships with the rest of the environment (living and nonliving). His theory commits him to seeing a continuum of traits such as intelligence, emotions, and consciousness in all animal beings and calls out respect for their individuality. This, in turn, supports Gilman's and Addams's call to ameliorate situations in which humans fail to respect socially rooted individuality in other beings and so to make real friendship a possibility. The combination of these views is summed up nicely by Plumwood when she suggests that humans need to acknowledge the presence of mind in the rest of nature, be open to mutual transformation, seek active dialogue with earth others, and aim for relationships of mutual enrichment, cooperation, and friendship (*Feminism* 131–39). This is a good model for improving human relationships with wild animals, pets, and livestock—and with each other.

BIBLIOGRAPHY

"About Jacob Sheep." *Jacob Sheep Breeders Association*. Jacob Sheep Breeder Association, 2009. Web. 24 June 2016.

"About Us." *Taylor Shellfish Farms*. Taylor Shellfish Farms, 2016. Web. 13 March 2016.

Acampora, Ralph. "Caring Cannibals and Human(e) Farming: Testing Contextual Edibility for Speciesism." *Ecofeminism: Feminist Intersections with Other Animals and the Earth*. Ed. Carol J. Adams and Lori Gruen. New York, Bloomsbury, 2014. Print.

Achilli, Alessandro, et al. "The Multifaceted Origin of Taurine Cattle Reflected by the Mitochondrial Genome." *PLOS One*, vol. 4, no. 6, 2009. Web. 17 March 2016.

Adams, Carol J. *Neither Man nor Beast: Feminism and the Defense of Animals*. New York, Continuum, 1994. Print.

———. "Sexual Politics of Meat." *Carol J. Adams Website*. Web. 6 June 2016.

Anderson, Virginia DeJohn. *Creatures of Empire: How Domestic Animals Transformed Early America*. Oxford, Oxford UP, 2004. Print.

Animal and Plant Health Inspection Service. "The Goat Industry: Structure, Concentration, Demand and Growth." Web. 6 June 2016.

Balcombe, Jonathan. *What a Fish Knows: The Inner Lives of Our Underwater Cousins*. New York, Farrar, Straus, & Giroux, 2016. Print.

Berry, Wendell. *The Unsettling of America: Culture and Agriculture*. San Francisco, Sierra Club Books, 1977. Print.

Bidwell, Percy W., and John I. Falconer. *History of Agriculture in the Northern United States, 1620–1860*. New York, P. Smith, 1941. Print.

Bradford, Alina. "Facts about Goats." *LiveScience*. 21 October 2015. Web. 24 June 2016.

Braithwaite, Victoria. *Do Fish Feel Pain?* New York, Oxford UP, 2010. Print.

"Breeds of Livestock—Hereford Cattle." *Department of Animal Science*. Oklahoma State University, 27 January 2000. Web. 6 March 2016.

"Breeds of Livestock—Katahdin Sheep." *Department of Animal Science*. Oklahoma State University, 22 February 1995. Web. 6 March 2016.

"Breeds of Livestock—Tamworth Swine." *Department of Animal Science*. Oklahoma State University, 25 February 2002. Web. 6 March 2016.

Bulliet, Richard W. *Hunters, Herders, and Hamburgers: The Past and Future of Human-Animal Relationships*. New York, Columbia UP, 2005. Print.

Burden, Dan. "Deer (Venison) Ranching Profile." *Ag Marketing Resource Center*. Ag Marketing Resource Center, November 2013. Web. 19 June 2016.

Caesar, Julius. "Gallic War (English)." *Latin Texts & Translations*. University of Chicago. Web. 24 June 2016.

Callicott, J. Baird. *Beyond the Land Ethic: More Essays in Environmental Philosophy*. Albany, SUNY Press, 1999. Print.

Cheesman, Shannon L. "Oregon Rodeo Cancels Wild Horse Race after Tragedy." *KBOI Online*, 13 March 2013. Web. 8 May 2017.

Clutton-Brock, Juliet. *A Natural History of Domesticated Mammals*. Cambridge, Cambridge UP, 1989. Print.

"The Country Natural Beef Story." *Country Natural Beef*. Country Natural Beef. Web. 17 March 2016.

Cramer, Jacqueline. "Little Eorthe Farm." *Tilth Producers*. Tilth Producers of Washington, September 2013. Web. 15 March 2016.

"Dairy Goats." *Ag Marketing Resource Center*. Ag Marketing Resource Center, 2016. Web. 23 June 2016.

Dale, Edward E. *The Range Cattle Industry*. Norman, University of Oklahoma Press, 1930. Print.

Dean, William F., and Tirath S. Sandhu. "Duck Housing and Management." *Animal Health Diagnostic Center*. Cornell University, 2008. Web. 13 March 2016.

DeMello, Margo. *Animals and Society: An Introduction to Human-Animal Studies*. New York, Columbia UP, 2012. Print.

De Steiguer, Edward. *Wild Horses of the West: History and Politics of America's Mustangs*. Tucson, University of Arizona Press, 2011. Print.

Devall, Bill, and George Sessions. *Deep Ecology: Living as if Nature Mattered*. Salt Lake City, G.M. Smith, 1985. Print.

Dewey, John. *The Collected Works of John Dewey, 1882–1953*. Ed. Jo Ann Boydston. Carbondale, Southern Illinois University Press, 1967–1990. Print.

Dewey, John, and Arthur F. Bentley. *John Dewey and Arthur F. Bentley: A Philosophical Correspondence, 1932–1951*. Ed. Sidney Ratner and Jules Altman. New Brunswick, Rutgers UP, 1964. Print.

Donovan, Colleen. "Organic Raw Milk and Agri-Tourism." *Tilth Producers*. Tilth Producers, 15 June 2012. Web. 6 June 2016.

"Ducks and Geese." *Ag Marketing Resource Center*. Ag Marketing Resource Center, 2016. Web. 23 June 2016.

Dunham, Delicia. "On Being Black and Vegan." *Sistah Vegan*. Ed. A. Breeze Harper. New York, Lantern Books, 2010, 42–46. Print.

Eisnitz, Gail A. *Slaughterhouse: The Shocking Story of Greed, Neglect, and Inhumane Treatment Inside the U.S. Meat Industry*. Amherst, Prometheus Books, 1997. Print.

"Emerging Issues." *Animal and Plant Health Inspection Service*. United States Department of Agriculture. Web. 15 March. 2016.

Eriksson, Jonas, et al. "Identification of the Yellow Skin Gene Reveals a Hybrid Origin of the Domestic Chicken." *PLOS Genetics*, vol. 4, no. 2, 2008. Web.

Essig, Mark. *Lesser Beasts: A Snout-to-Tail History of the Humble Pig*. New York, Basic Books, 2015. Print.

Estabrook, Barry. *Pig Tales: An Omnivore's Quest for Sustainable Meat.* New York, W. W. Norton, 2015. Print.

Fairlie, Simon. *Meat: A Benign Extravagance.* White River Junction, Chelsea Green Publishing, 2010. Print.

Ferdman, Roberto A. "Americans Once Ate Nearly Twice as Many Eggs as They Do Today." *Quartz,* 2 April 2014. Web. 8 May 2017.

Fesmire, Steven. *Dewey.* London, Routledge, 2015. Print.

"Freedom Ranger Chickens." *Freedom Ranger Hatchery.* Freedom Ranger Hatchery. Web. 20 March 2016.

Fulton, Linda K., et al. "The Goat as a Model for Biomedical Research and Teaching." *Institute for Laboratory Animal Research Journal,* vol. 36, no. 2, 1994, 21–29. Web. 6 March 2016.

"General US Stats." *United Egg Producers.* U.S. Poultry & Egg Association, May 2016. Web. 23 June 2016.

Genoways, Ted. *The Chain: Farm, Factory, and the Fate of Our Food.* New York, Harper, 2014. Print.

Gilman, Charlotte Perkins. *Women and Economics: A Study of the Economic Relation between Men and Women.* New York, Harper Torchbooks, 1966. Print.

Glaser, Chrinte, et al. "Costs and Consequences: The Real Price of Livestock Grazing on America's Public Lands." *Center for Biological Diversity.* Center for Biological Diversity, January 2015. Web. 24 June 2016.

"Goat Farmers, Producers Handle Increased American Demand for Unusual Dairy." *Fox News,* 24 February 2015. Web. 23 June 2016.

"Goats." *Ag Marketing Resource Center.* Ag Marketing Resource Center, 2016. Web. 23 June 2016.

Gorey, Tom. "Fact Sheet on the BLM's Management of Livestock Grazing." *U.S. Department of the Interior Bureau of Land Management.* Bureau of Land Management, 17 June 2016. Web. 24 June 2016.

Grandin, Temple. *Animals in Translation: Using the Mysteries of Autism to Decode Animal Behavior.* Orlando, Harcourt, 2005. Print.

———. *Animals Make Us Human: Creating the Best Life for Animals.* New York, Houghton-Mifflin Harcourt, 2009. Print.

———. *Humane Livestock Handling: Understanding Livestock Behavior and Building Facilities for Healthier Animals.* North Adams, Mass., Storey Publishing, 2008. Print.

"Grass Fed Beef—J. Hutton." *Animal Welfare Approved.* The Animal Welfare Institute, 7 July 2009. Web. 15 March 2016.

Gray, L. C., and Esther Katherine Thompson. *History of Agriculture in the Southern United States to 1860.* Washington, Carnegie Institution of Washington, 1933. Print.

Gregoire, Carolyn. "Cows Are Way More Intelligent Than You Probably Thought." *Huffington Post,* 28 July 2015. Web. 8 May 2017.

Gruen, Lori. "Facing Death and Practicing Grief." *Ecofeminism: Feminist Intersections with Other Animals and the Earth.* Ed. Carol J. Adams and Lori Gruen. New York, Bloomsbury, 2014. Print.

"A Guide to All Things Sheep." *Premier1*, 2016. Web. 15 March 2016.

Harper, A. Breeze. "Revisiting Racialized Consciousness and Black Female Vegan Experiences: An Interview." *The Sistah Vegan Project: A Critical Race Feminist's Journey through the "Post-Racial" Ethical Foodscape . . . and Beyond*. 6 December 2009. Web. 23 June 2016.

———. "Social Justice Beliefs and Addiction to Uncompassionate Food for Thought." *Sistah Vegan*. Ed. A. Breeze Harper. New York, Lantern Books, 2010, 20–41. Print.

Harper, A. Breeze, ed. *Sistah Vegan: Black Female Vegans Speak on Food, Identity, Health, and Society*. New York, Lantern Books, 2010. Print.

Hayes, Denis, and Gail Boyer Hayes. *Cowed: The Hidden Impact of 93 Million Cows on America's Health, Economy, Politics, Culture, and Environment*. New York, W. W. Norton, 2015. Print.

Herzog, Hal. *Some We Love, Some We Hate, Some We Eat*. New York, Harper Collins, 2010. Print.

Holechek, Jerry L., et al. *Range Management: Principles and Practices*. Upper Saddle River, N.J., Prentice Hall, 1998. Print.

Howlett, Doug. "Hog Hunting U.S.A." *American Hunter*, 11 February 2013. Web. 8 May 2017.

Huddleston, John. *The Earth Is But One Country*. London, Baha'i Publishing Trust, 1976. Print.

Hughlett, Mike, and Paul Walsh. "Bird Flu Strikes Another Commercial Turkey Facility in Minnesota." *Minneapolis Star Tribune Weekly*, 2 April 2015. Web. 8 May 2017.

"Industry Overview." *American Egg Board*. American Egg Board, 2016. Web. 23 June 2016.

"Integrated Multi-Trophic Aquaculture." *Canadian Aquaculture Industry Alliance*. Canadian Aquaculture Industry Alliance (NFP), 2016. Web. 6 June 2016.

Isaacs, J. S. "Rabbits Profile." *Ag Marketing Resource Center*. Ag Marketing Resource Center, November 2013. Web. Accessed 19 June 2016.

James, William. *Pragmatism and Other Writings*. Ed. Giles B. Gunn. New York, Penguin, 2000. Print.

Johnson, Mark. *Morality for Humans: Ethical Understanding from the Perspective of Cognitive Science*. Chicago, University of Chicago Press, 2014. Print.

Kalita, Kula Prasad. "Behavioural Characteristics of Domestic Ducks." *Academia.edu*. Web. 6 March 2016.

Kingsolver, Barbara. *Animal, Vegetable, Miracle: A Year of Food*. New York, Harper Collins, 2007. Print.

Korten, David. *Agenda for a New Economy*. San Francisco, Berret-Koehler Publishers, 2010. Print.

———. "New Economy 2.0." *Living Economies Forum*. Web. 13 March 2016.

"Larkhaven Farmstead Meats." *Larkhaven Farm*. Larkhaven Farm. Web. 13 March 2016.

Larson, G., et al. "Patterns of East Asian Pig Domestication, Migration, and Turnover Revealed by Modern and Ancient DNA." *Proceedings of the National Academy of Science*, vol. 107, no. 17, 2010. Web. 23 June 2016.

Lawler, Andrew. *Why Did the Chicken Cross the World? The Epic Saga of the Bird That Powers Civilization*. New York, Atria Books, 2014. Print.

Leopold, Aldo. *A Sand County Almanac (Outdoor Essays & Reflections)*. New York, Oxford UP, 1949. Print.

Leopold, Aldo, and Charles Walsh Schwartz. *For the Health of the Land: Previously Unpublished Essays and Other Writings*. Washington, D.C., Island Press, 1999. Print.

Lichatowich, Jim. *Salmon without Rivers: A History of the Pacific Salmon Crisis*. Washington, D.C., Island Press, 1999. Print.

"Livestock Standards." *Certified Naturally Grown*. Certified Naturally Grown, 2015. Web. 6 June 2016.

"Llama History." *BuckHorn Llama Company, Inc.* Buckhorn Llama Company. Web. 23 June 2016.

Malkin, Nina. "American Tragedy: The Horrors of Horse Slaughter and the Fight to Protect Our National Treasure." *All Animals: Humane Society of the United States Magazine*, Summer 2007, 19–20. Web.

Mann, Charles C. *1491: New Revelations of the Americas before Columbus*. New York, Vintage Books, 2006. Print.

Marshall, Fiona, and Elisabeth Hildebrand. "Cattle before Crops: The Beginnings of Food Production in Africa." *Journal of World Prehistory*, vol. 16, no. 2, June 2002, pp. 99–143. Web.

Masson, Jeffrey Moussaieff. *The Face on Your Plate: The Truth about Food*. New York, W. W. Norton, 2009. Print.

——. *The Pig Who Sang to the Moon: The Emotional World of Farm Animals*. New York, Ballantine Books, 2003. Print.

McBride, William D., and Nigel Key. "US Hog Production from 1992 to 2009: Technology, Restructuring, and Productivity Growth." *United States Department of Agriculture Economic Research Service*. USDA, 12 January 2015. Web. 23 June 2016.

McKenna, Erin. *Pets, People, and Pragmatism*. New York, Fordham UP, 2014. Print.

——. "Pragmatism and the Production of Livestock." *Animal Pragmatism: Rethinking Human-Nonhuman Relationships*. Ed. Erin McKenna and Andrew Light. Bloomington, Indiana UP, 2004. Print.

——. *The Task of Utopia: A Pragmatist and Feminist Perspective*. Lanham, Rowman & Littlefield, 2001. Print.

McKenna, Erin, with Sarah Curtis and Jon Stout. "Philosophical Farming." *Pragmatism and Environmentalism*. Ed. Hugh P. McDonald. Amsterdam, Rodopi, 2012. Print.

McMahan, Jeff. "The Moral Problem of Predation." *Philosophy Comes to Dinner: Arguments About the Ethics of Eating*. Ed. Andrew Cuneo and Matthew C. Halteman. New York, Routledge, 2016. Print.

Mellor, David J. "Updating Animal Welfare Thinking: Moving beyond the 'Five Freedoms' towards 'A Life Worth Living.'" *Animals*, vol. 6, no. 3, 2016, p. 21. Web. 9 January 2017.

Midgley, Mary. *Animals and Why They Matter*. Athens, University of Georgia Press, 1983. Print.

Montgomery, David. *Dirt: The Erosion of Civilizations*. Berkeley, University of California Press 2007. Print.

Moss, Michael. "Lawmakers Aim to Protect Farm Animals in Research." *New York Times*, 5 February 2015. Web.

———. "U.S. Research Lab Lets Livestock Suffer in Quest for Profit." *New York Times*, 19 January 2015. Web.

National Agricultural Statistics Service. *2005 Dairy Goat and Sheep Survey*. Web. 17 March 2016.

———. *Minnesota Ag News—Goats*. 29 January 2016. Web. 23 June 2016.

———. *Sheep and Goats*. 29 January 2016. Web. 23 June 2016.

"National Animal Health Monitoring System (NAHMS)." *Animal and Plant Health Inspection Service*. United States Department of Agriculture. 3 June 2016. Web. 23 June 2016.

Natterson-Horowitz, Barbara, and Kathryn Bowers. *Zoobiquity: The Astonishing Connections between Human and Animal Health*. New York, Vintage, 2013. Print.

Nienhiser, Jill C. "About the Foundation." *The Weston A. Price Foundation Website for Wise Traditions in Food, Farming, and the Healing Arts*. The Weston A. Price Foundation, 1 January 2000. Web. 6 June 2016.

Niman, Nicolette Hahn. *Defending Beef: The Case for Sustainable Meat Production*. White River Junction, Chelsea Green Publishing, 2014. Print.

———. *Righteous Porkchop: Finding a Life and Good Food beyond Factory Farming*. New York, Collins Living, 2009. Print.

"Ninety Farms." *Ninety Farms*. Ninety Farms. Web. 3 March 2016.

Norwood, F. Bailey, and Jayson L. Lusk. *Compassion by the Pound: The Economics of Farm Animal Welfare*. Oxford, Oxford UP, 2011. Print.

O'Donoghue, Erik, et al. "The Changing Organization of U.S. Farming." *Economic Information Bulletin*, vol. 88, 2011, 1–83.

Ogle, Maureen. *In Meat We Trust: An Unexpected History of Carnivore America*. Boston, Houghton Mifflin Harcourt, 2013. Print.

O'Neill, Christopher J., et al. "Evolutionary Process of *Bos Taurus* Cattle in Favourable versus Unfavourable Environments and Its Implications for Genetic Selection." *Evolutionary Applications*, vol. 3, no. 5–6, 2010, 422–33. Web.

"Organic Egg Scorecard." *Cornucopia Institute*. 2 June 2016. Web. 22 June 2016.

"Our Heroes: The Newhalls and Joneses of Windy N Ranch." *EcoCentric: A Blog about Food, Water and Energy*. GRACE, 24 July 2014. Web. 23 June 2013.

"Our Product Standards." *PCC Natural Markets*. Puget Consumers Co-Op, 2000–2016. Web. 15 March 2016.

Pachirat, Timothy. *Every Twelve Seconds: Industrialized Slaughter and the Politics of Sight*. New Haven, Yale UP, 2011. Print.

Pappas, Gregory Fernando. *John Dewey's Ethics: Democracy as Experience*. Bloomington, Indiana UP, 2008. Print.

"The Pasture Grass." *Pride & Joy Dairy*. Web. 6 June 2016.

Peirce, Charles Sanders. *Collected Papers of Charles Sanders Peirce*. New York, Thoemmes Continuum, 1998. Print.

Plumwood, Val. *Environmental Culture: The Ecological Crisis of Reason.* London, Routledge, 2002. Print.

———. *Feminism and the Mastery of Nature.* London, Routledge, 1993. Print.

"Profiling Food Consumption in America." *Agriculture Fact Book.* United States Department of Agriculture, 23 June 2016. Web. 23 June 2016.

"Raise Well." *Country Natural Beef.* Country Natural Beef. Web. 17 March 2016.

Rifkin, Jeremy. *Beyond Beef: The Rise and Fall of the Cattle Culture.* New York, Dutton, 1992. Print.

Robson, Peter A. *Salmon Farming: The Whole Story.* Victoria, Heritage House, 2006. Print.

Russell, Nerissa, et al. "Cattle Domestication at Çatalhöyük Revisited." *Current Anthropology,* vol. 46, no. S5, 2005, S101–08.

Salatin, Joel. *Everything I Want to Do Is Illegal: War Stories from the Local Food Front.* Swoope, Polyface, 2007. Print.

Schoenian, Susan. "Dairy Sheep Basics." *Sheep 201: A Beginner's Guide to Raising Sheep.* The Baalands, 28 May 2016. Web. 15 June 2016.

———. "Got Milk?" *Sheep 101.* The Baalands, 21 September 2015. Web. 23 June 2016.

———. "Meat, Milk, or Wool?" *Sheep 201: A Beginner's Guide to Raising Sheep.* The Baalands, 28 May 2016. Web. 15 June 2016.

———. "Sheep in History." *Sheep 101.* The Baalands, 21 September 2015. Web. 23 June 2016.

Scully, Matthew. *Dominion: The Power of Man, the Suffering of Animals, and the Call to Mercy.* New York, St. Martin's, 2002. Print.

Shewchuck, Julia. "21 Things You Should Know about Goats before You Start a Goat Farm." *Mother Earth News: The Original Guide to Living Wisely,* 2 February 2014. Web. 13 March 2016.

"Shorthorn Cattle." *A Site about Cows . . . and Stuff.* Third Row Productions. Web. 15 March 2016.

Shubin, Neil. *Your Inner Fish: A Journey into the 3.5-Billion-Year History of the Human Body.* New York, Pantheon, 2008. Print.

Simon, David Robinson. *Meatonomics: How the Rigged Economics of Meat and Dairy Make You Consume Too Much—and How to Eat Better, Live Longer, and Spend Smarter.* San Francisco, Conari Press, 2013. Print.

Sinclair, Upton. *The Jungle.* New York, Doubleday, Page, 1906. Print.

Smith, Andrew F. *The Turkey: An American Tale.* Chicago, University of Illinois Press, 2006. Print.

Smith, Kimberly K. *Governing Animals: Animal Welfare and the Liberal State.* New York, Oxford UP, 2012. Print.

"Standard Bronze." *The Livestock Conservancy.* American Livestock Breeds Conservancy. Web. 23 June 2016.

"Standards." *Animal Welfare Approved.* The Animal Welfare Institute. Web. 15 March 2016.

Stein, Byron. "Introduction to Commercial Duck Farming." *Department of Primary Industries.* NSW Department of Industry, June 2012. Web. 13 March 2016.

Stein, Gil. "Herding Strategies at Neolithic Gritille." *Expedition Magazine*, vol. 28, no. 2, 1986. Web. 13 March 2016.

Stillman, Deanne. *Mustang*. Boston, Mariner Books, 2009. Print.

"Summary of Meat Processing Issues in Washington State." *Washington State Department of Agriculture*. Access Washington. Web. 6 June 2016.

"Tamworth Pig." *The Livestock Conservancy*. American Livestock Breeds Conservancy. Web. 23 June 2016.

Thomas, David L. "Overview of the Dairy Sheep Sector in Canada and the United States." *Proceedings of the 10th Annual Great Lakes Dairy Sheep Symposium (Nov. 4–6, 2004)*. Dairy Sheep Association of North America. Web. 16 June 2016.

Thompson, Paul B. *From Field to Fork: Food Ethics for Everyone*. New York, Oxford UP, 2015. Print.

"Thundering Hooves Postmortem." *Meat: Raising Animals for Food in Western Washington*. 30 April 2011. Web. 6 June 2016.

"Turkeys." *United Poultry Concerns*. United Poultry Concerns. Web. 23 June 2016.

United States Department of Agriculture. "Animal Health." Web. 23 June 2016.

Van Saun, Robert J., et al. "Dairy Goat Production." *Penn State Extension*. Penn State College of Agricultural Sciences, 2008. Web. 23 June 2016.

"Wagyu Beef." *Sweet Grass Farm*. Sweet Grass Farm. Web. 24 June 2016.

"Who We Are and What We Stand For." *Akyla Farms*. Akyla Farms. Web. 6 March 2016.

Wilkie, Rhoda M. *Livestock/Deadstock: Working with Farm Animals from Birth to Slaughter*. Philadelphia, Temple UP, 2010. Print.

Willett, Cynthia. *Interspecies Ethics*. New York, Columbia UP, 2014. Print.

Wright, Thompson. "Unridable." *ESPN: The Magazine*, 9 July 2013. Web.

Wu, Gui-Shen, et al. "Population Phylogenomic Analysis of Mitochondrial DNA in Wild Boars and Domestic Pigs Revealed Multiple Domestication Events in East Asia." *Genome Biology*, vol. 8, no. 11, 2007. Web. 6 March 2016.

INDEX

Conservation Reserve Program (CRP), 72

consumers: and demand, 3, 7, 45, 58, 163, 181, 183–84, 205, 207, 209, 223, 228; ethical concerns of, 3, 45, 66, 70, 79, 114, 183, 204; impact of on farming industry, 29, 79, 163, 205, 233; hypocrisy of, 5, 78, 85, 89–90, 223; misconceptions by, 3, 8, 185–86, 187, 188–89, 220, 221, 231; moral evasion of, 131, 210, 215, 221; responsibility of, 79, 179, 184, 207, 209, 215, 222; welfare of, 50, 110, 214–15, 223

corn, 29, 45; corn belt system, 56, 57, 121, 172

corn-fed cattle, 58, 59, 68–69, 77

corn-finishing; 56, 57, 66; environmental impacts of, 76, 96, 91; and health problems, 50, 59

cowboys: and advertising, 46; culture of, 99–101; myth of, 46, 55, 99, 112; Professional Rodeo Cowboy Association (PRCA), 99

cows, 101; Ayshire, 47, 150; dairy, 138, 142, 147–48, 150; Holstein, 142, 150; Jersey, 150, 164, 168; Normandy, 150; sexualization of, 183; Swedish Red, 150; tail-docking of, 53, 148, 151. See also cattle; dairy; domestication; weaning

Customary Farming Exceptions (CFEs), 231

dairy: cheese, 16, 61, 79, 124, 135–36, 137–40, 142–43, 144, 149, 189; and meat production, 143, 148–49, 150; milk, 16, 22, 23, 78, 101, 120, 121–22, 125, 130, 136, 137–38, 140–49, 154, 155, 189, 193; milking practices, 10, 21, 148; pasteurization, 137, 142. See also cows: dairy; goats: dairy; lactose intolerance

Dale, Edward E., 56–57

death: and eating, 2, 8, 77, 87, 108, 128, 148–49, 229; euthanasia, 5, 6, 53, 99, 226; evasion of responsibility for, 108, 125, 128, 215, 222, 229–30; mortality rates, 19, 26, 80, 81, 151, 172, 184, 185; objectification of, 10, 36, 55, 99, 127, 134, 189, 193, 196, 208, 209–14, 226; as part of life, 71, 77, 87, 104, 106, 125, 127, 131–32, 134, 154, 209, 222, 225, 229–31; quality of, 40, 53, 88, 106, 110, 116, 145, 154, 169, 209, 216, 228; relationship to, 13, 62, 71, 77, 155, 222, 225, 227, 230. See also slaughter

debeaking: of chickens, 87, 183, 184, 188, 195; of turkeys, 201

deep ecology, 14, 69, 82–84, 97, 113; and biocentrism, 81–82; and Naess, Arne, 82, 83

dehorning and debudding, 231; of cattle and cows, 53, 64, 148; of goats, 141, 145

de Steiguer, Edward, 92–93

Deval, Bill, 82

developmentalism. See under pragmatism

Dewey, John, 20, 22–24, 41, 51, 84, 103, 105, 169, 208, 222, 233; and ethics, 40, 43, 110, 111–13, 171, 179, 228; and moral deliberation, 43; and transactive relationships, 15, 24, 39, 51, 233

disease, 132, 139, 157, 159–60, 206, and confinement, as contributing to, 10, 19, 31–32, 37, 67, 98, 141–42, 148, 172, 184; in food, 22, 137, 214–15; resistance to, 3, 16, 154; spread from animals to humans, 55, 59–60, 121–22. See also antibiotics; bacteria

dogs, 2, 4, 5, 8, 18–19, 60, 122, 141, 145, 154, 172, 232; dogfighting, 196; and herding, 2, 19, 117, 123–25, 127, 130, 232; and livestock, as protectors of, 53, 87, 97, 117, 123–34, 128, 139, 140, 143, 191, 232; as predators, 139, 177

domestication, 4, 5, 9, 15–19, 21–22, 102–3, 104–7, 110, 138, 206; of alpacas, 117; of cattle, 101–2; of chickens, 181, 195; of dogs, 9, 18, 117; of ducks, 206; ethics of, 17; of geese, 206; of goats, 117–18; of llamas, 117; of pigs, 10, 159, 195; of sheep, 117–18; of turkeys, 198–200

dualisms, 18, 192; human/animal, 192; male/female, 192; nature/culture, 17; private/public, 152; use/respect, 153. See also logic of domination; metaphysics

ducks, 8, 72, 86, 87, 89, 181, 190, 196, 205–7; egg production, 190, 205–6; Pekin, 206

Ducks Unlimited, 70, 71–72, 74, 196

Dunham, Delicia, 104

Dust Bowl drought, 50, 71

early weaning. See under weaning

ecofeminism, 8, 13–18, 44, 98, 135, 174, 214, 224–27, 231; and Adams, Carol, 4, 21, 151–52, 191–94; and Merchant, Carolyn, 192; and Plumwood, Val, 8, 21, 152–53, 194, 208, 222, 226, 230, 234. See also feminism; Harper, A. Breeze